The Players

University of Nevada Press / Reno, Las Vegas

The Players

The Men Who Made Las Vegas

EDITED BY Jack Sheehan

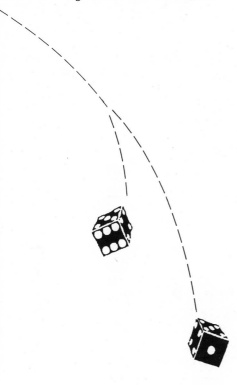

University of Nevada Press, Reno, Nevada 89557 USA

Copyright © 1997 by University of Nevada Press

Manufactured in the United States of America

Book design by Carrie Nelson House

Library of Congress Cataloging-in-Publication Data

The players : the men who made Las Vegas / edited by

Jack Sheehan.

p.   cm.

Includes bibliographical references (p.   ) and index.

ISBN 0-87417-306-X (paperback : alk. paper)

1. Gambling—Nevada—Las Vegas.   2. Gamblers—

Nevada—Las Vegas—Biography.   I. Sheehan, Jack,

1949–   .

HV6721.L3P58   1997   97-24443   CIP

The paper used in this book meets the requirements

of American National Standard for Information Sci-

ences—Permanence of Paper for Printed Library Ma-

terials, ANSI z39.48-1984. Binding materials were

selected for strength and durability.

First Printing

06 05 04 03 02 01 00 99 98 97   5 4 3 2 1

The players

In memory of Sam Boyd and Dr. Norman Sheehan:
two good, honest, hard-working men and exceptional fathers.
Their inspiration guided us through this work.

Contents

Illustrations

Preface

Because Las Vegas has such a brief history, nearly all the men who shaped it were alive at the same time.

Except for Bugsy Siegel, who was unceremoniously dismissed by a hidden gunman's bullet in 1947 as he peacefully sat reading the *Los Angeles Times* in Virginia Hill's Beverly Hills mansion, all of the "players" in this book could conceivably have toasted one another at a grand cocktail party sometime in the 1970s. Oh, it might have been tough to get Howard Hughes out of bed; and Steve Wynn might have been deemed too green behind the ears to attend, but he probably would have finagled an invitation anyway and charmed the socks off his predecessors by the end of the evening.

What a gathering it would have been. With Moe Dalitz, Benny Binion, Parry Thomas, Kirk Kerkorian, Bill Bennett, Sam Boyd, Jay Sarno, and the others spinning yarns and tales of gaming lore, it would have recalled the energy of the founding fathers of our country sitting around discussing the elements of the U.S. Constitution, albeit with a lot more salt and pepper.

Dalitz might have chuckled over the intrigue of selling the Desert Inn to Hughes after an eviction notice to the billionaire went unheeded; Binion would have dispensed some of his countrified gambling wisdom, making perfect sense despite murdering the king's English; Sarno could have waxed eloquent over the delicate decisions that were made in designing cocktail-waitress uniforms at Caesars Palace; and Boyd would have enjoyed sharing how his enormous birthday cakes packed them in at the downtown Mint. Kerkorian might have stayed to himself, acting somehow unworthy to be in the presence of such entrepreneurial genius, but quietly confident in the knowledge that his bank account was deeper than any of theirs. Whatever the texture of the dialogue, it certainly would have been worth eavesdropping on.

It was with that guiding spirit, to endeavor to collect many of these gaming and hotel entrepreneurs' pertinent stories in the same volume, that Bill Boyd contacted me not long after the death of his father, Sam, to see if it would be possible to gather much of this information before any more time, and Las Vegas legends, passed on.

You see, every time a Moe Dalitz or a Sam Boyd or a Benny Binion dies, a large chunk of Las Vegas civic history goes with him. And while the lore of our city—frequently exploited by Hollywood without much regard to the facts (*Bugsy*, *Casino*, and *Melvin and Howard* come instantly to mind)—has been largely ignored by the literary world, it is of great interest to the rest of the country these days as one municipality after another embraces legalized gambling as a panacea for economic woes. Every region that adopts gambling wants to know how it was done in Nevada.

I concurred that Bill had a splendid idea and suggested that a team-writing approach would be most effective, in terms of time and economy. All of the men whose stories we discussed, after all, are worthy of their own biographies, and several of them already have had complete volumes written about them. We decided, therefore, to choose professional writers and journalists who had some familiarity with their assigned subjects, a criterion being that the author had previously written about his subject or at the very least brought a head-start of information and background to the assignment. A. D. Hopkins, for instance, had known Benny Binion personally for more than twenty years, had been privy to many of Binion's confidences, and had excellent access to surviving family and friends who knew the Cowboy well. John L. Smith understood the importance of Moe Dalitz in the chronology of Las Vegas and had penned many newspaper columns on the diminutive man who led two distinctly different lives, the one before and the one after he arrived in Las Vegas. Gaming industry reporter Sergio Lalli knew Cliff Jones's background as a businessman and politician well and had been a longtime Howard Hughes aficionado. Dallas author Mark Seal had profiled Steve Wynn for a national magazine and brought a good feel to the task of writing about the flamboyant king of modern-day Las Vegas.

Chapters on the evolution of the Gaming Control Board, on sports betting, and on the way in which popular literature has treated Las Vegas were included to provide a context from which to view the activities of the players.

Whenever possible, we interviewed the subject himself, but this was not without its glitches. Parry Thomas, for instance, agreed to an interview, but with the condition that he would proof his chapter upon its completion. Although his quotations were supported by a tape recording of the interview, he insisted on revisions in the chapter that we were not comfortable making. And so, while Thomas is certainly a towering figure in the history of the gambling industry in Las Vegas and was paid verbal homage to by nearly everyone we interviewed, we elected to omit his chapter and allow others to comment on the role of the handsome banker who became legalized gambling's best friend.

Out of his friendship and respect for Sam and Bill Boyd, Kirk Kerkorian agreed to a rare interview, but when Dave Palermo and I arrived for the session, he would not allow a tape recorder to be used. Kerkorian also dodged nearly every question pertinent to the building of his three expansive hotels, the International (now the Las Vegas Hilton), the original MGM Grand (now Bally's), and the recent MGM Grand Hotel and Theme Park. But he was open and generous when discussing his friend and rival Hughes, Elvis Presley, and his lifelong passion for flying.

Considering that Kerkorian had not sat for anything resembling a formal interview in more than a decade, we were happy to get what he was willing to give us.

Our writers did their best to cross-check facts and references, but it is a necessary concession to history to have to rely, at times, on the memories of interview subjects. Where embellishment or overstatement is found within these pages, it is presented as part of a quotation. We hope the reader will condone the occasional lapse of memory or hyperbole as being in the best tradition of Las Vegas itself, a city that has never understated anything.

While one might think at first that these giants of the gaming world hardly ever ventured beyond the seclusion of their executive offices or casinos, we learned a different truth. Nearly all of these men were intricately involved in the community growing up around the Strip. One would be hard-pressed to find a civic organization or prominent charity that one of the players did not head up at one time or another. They understood that politics and business are not mutually exclusive passions, and that those who sought to make their fortunes from the gambling and tourism industries had to work closely with decision makers in city and state government. This made for some interesting and colorful clashes through the years.

The men who built Las Vegas into what it is today were working, we must remember, without a script. There has never been a city remotely like this one ever before, where gambling is glorified and nightlife and entertainment are the *raisons d'être*.

Essayist Michael Ventura wrote recently in the *Los Angeles Times* that "Las Vegas is the last great, mythic city that Western civilization will ever create." He argues that a city can reach mythic status only when its very name becomes symbolic of a culture or aura that is unmatched in the world. He lists ancient Babylon, ancient Rome, Cairo, Paris, London, and New York as cities having that mythic aura about them. And while legalized gambling can be found nearly any-where in the world these days, no place defines the images and symbols of gambling and gaudy nightlife like Las Vegas. This is verified by all the attention paid to the city in recent years by front-rank media outlets:

· *Time* put Las Vegas on the cover a few years back, and declared it the new all-American city.
· The *New York Times*, in a recent op-ed piece, pounced on the irony of New York and Las Vegas trying to emulate each other during New Year's Eve celebrations.
· The television magazine show *20/20* declared Las Vegas the boomingest city in the country and the settlement of choice for people looking for a second chance at the gold ring.
· *National Geographic* devoted twenty-three pages in a recent issue to the new Las Vegas, with its dazzling theme parks, expanding re-tirement communities, sprawling airport, inviting atmosphere for high-tech companies, and eclectic religious community.

Did the players we profile in these pages envision this degree of success and attention for Las Vegas when they brought their dreams to the desert? One could argue that they did, because if a consistent note runs through their individual stories, it is that all of these pio-neers were urged by their friends and associates *not* to move to Las Vegas, that godforsaken inferno in the middle of nowhere. And yet all of them had the vision and foresight to ignore the bad advice and come anyway.

We're glad they did.

JACK SHEEHAN

The Players

A Peculiar Institution

Sergio Lalli

On May 2, 1957, as Frank Costello returned to his apartment in the Majestic on Central Park West, a gunman in the foyer lunged at him from behind and shot New York's most prominent mobster in the head. The gunman retreated from the fashionable apartment house before making sure he had finished the job. The bleeding Costello had received only a grazing wound. While doctors examined Costello at a hospital, police searched through Costello's clothes and found, in one of his pockets, a slip of paper that listed the gross receipts, the table game income, the slot revenue, and the markers outstanding from an unnamed casino.

With the help of Nevada gaming authorities, the FBI discovered that the casino wins listed on the scrap of paper perfectly matched the actual totals recorded for the first three weeks of operation at the recently opened Tropicana resort on the Las Vegas Strip.

The note in Costello's possession bore the signature of Louis Lederer, a casino supervisor who also owned some partnership shares in the property. Lederer lost his job and was forced to sell his investment share by order of state gaming officials; and one of the Tropicana's major investors, Phil Kastel, was denied a gaming license because of his past associations with Costello. No charges were filed against Costello, who was not a gaming-license holder, because the piece of paper alone did not prove any criminal wrongdoing and was insufficient evidence to link him to a conspiracy to skim money from the casino.

This scenario of organized-crime infiltration, repeated in many ingenious variations over the years, was the greatest bugaboo haunting the state of Nevada as it strove to regulate its gaming industry. The state's gaming control apparatus would struggle with this problem and would define itself by how successful it was in scotching it, or at least keeping it at bay.

Las Vegas was to be where almost all of the sensational skullduggery took place. The presence of undesirable individuals and of their Las Vegas associates would provide the city with its notoriety and its mystique. From the beginning, mobster infiltration in Las Vegas was the most popular subject of press exposés, federal inquisitions, and public outcries. Today, with the evolution of casino gambling into a legitimate industry composed mainly of publicly traded corporations, mob infiltration is considered a bygone problem, but one that requires constant vigilance.

How did it get to be that way? How did Las Vegas change from being a "neon-lit leprosarium" (in the words of journalist Lucius Beebe) to a mobsterless adult Disneyland? This is a double-edged tale of agony and glory. Without the tribulations of Nevada's gaming control experience, the gaming industry as a whole never would have reached its present, wholesome condition. But it was a bumpy journey indeed.

In the early days, casinos were the pariahs of the business world. Casino owners consisted of a motley collection of outcasts, misfits, and business mavericks. Only Nevada granted them sanction to operate. When freshman assemblyman Phil Tobin of Humboldt County introduced the "wide-open" gambling bill in 1931, no other sponsors could be found to put their name on the bill. Although the bill had its backers, no politician wanted to appear to be in favor of a "vice." The measure passed in the waning days of the legislative session, and Governor Fred Balzar signed it into law.

One of the main reasons for passage of the gambling bill was to bring out in the open what already was common practice in the back rooms of saloons throughout the state. During Prohibition, the existence of speakeasies had fostered a culture of political corruption throughout the country as bootleggers bribed public officials to protect their illegal businesses. Nevada wanted to avoid that experience with gambling.

Another reason for the legalization of casinos was to raise a little money. Licensing fees were set up, with 75 percent of the fees going to the county and 25 percent to the state. A county shared fee revenues with cities if a casino was located in an incorporated municipality. The fees were based on the number of slot machines and table games in a casino.

Even so, the prospect of a huge gaming tax windfall was not imagined. As an editorial in the *Las Vegas Review-Journal* commented after passage of the bill: "People should not get overly excited over the effects of the new gambling bill—conditions will be little different than they are at the present time, except that some things will be done openly that have previously been done in secret. The same resorts will do business in the same way, only somewhat more liberally and above-board."

Because of this attitude, relatively scant attention was paid to gaming control itself. The earliest casino operators were mainly local businessmen, well-known in their community. Gaming enforcement was handled by the local county sheriff, and the issuing of gaming licenses was handled by a county board composed of the sheriff, the district attorney, and three county commissioners.

Then something quite unforeseen happened. States throughout the country, often prodded by the federal government, began to crack down on illegal casinos, thereby forcing casino operators to look elsewhere for opportunities. The first outside investors in Nevada's gaming industry came from California. Others later came from Texas, the Midwest, Florida, New York—from wherever illegal gambling had thrived with the tacit approval of local public officials.

As a result of this influx, Nevada's gaming industry grew to the point where the state realized that sizable tax money could be gathered from the casinos. In 1945 the state legislature placed casinos under the authority of the Nevada Tax Commission, which already supervised the collection of taxes from such industries as mining and ranching. The tax commission was granted authority to issue, deny, and revoke state gaming licenses. Thus, county and city licenses were still required on order to operate a casino, but the dominant licensing authority was given to the state.

This shift from local authority to state authority was mainly a revenue-raising measure. The state's interest in gaming was mainly to collect taxes. The state imposed a 1 percent gaming tax (raised to 2 percent in 1947 and to 5.5 percent in 1995, it was 6.25 percent in 1997) on casino gross revenues. Relatively little attention was paid to gaming control. The tax commission was neither an investigatory nor a law enforcement agency. It had not yet developed a body of administrative law—the gaming control rules and regulations—

needed to attack the problem of hidden ownership and undesirable characters. In its early years of casino involvement, the commission was busy enough just trying to figure out how casinos operated so it could properly audit them. Since no handbooks on the subject existed, the state had to learn from experience.

The men who came to Nevada brought not only their investment dollars (at a time when financial institutions avoided casino loans) but also their expertise. Las Vegas in particular needed both of these commodities if it was going to overtake Reno as the premier gaming locale in the state. As long as casino owners did not break the law, the citizens and authorities in Las Vegas were not too fussy about who did business there.

The federal government thought otherwise. Even before the advent of gambling, the federal presence in Nevada was immense, and it remains so to this day. Nevada has been of special interest to the federal government ever since the state was rushed into the union because President Abraham Lincoln needed two extra votes in the Senate during the Civil War and extra votes in the electoral college in time for his reelection effort in 1864. After the war, the federal government was keenly interested in Nevada because of its mineral resources. Later, Nevada became the site of Hoover Dam, the atomic testing grounds, and many military bases. The federal government still owns about 85 percent of the total land in Nevada; at times, it has treated the state more as a federal province than as a sovereign state. This interest and this attitude became magnified with the advent of casino gambling.

Nevada's "live-and-let-live" attitude toward casino owners first came under sharp attack during the celebrated hearings chaired by Senator Estes Kefauver during his traveling road show in 1950 and 1951. The purpose of Kefauver's special committee was to alert Americans to the existence of various crime syndicates that made money from gambling. Kefauver's group highlighted the extent to which gangster associates corrupted the body politic by bribing public officials. Since Kefauver had presidential ambitions, he also exploited the gangster-gambling issue to get national publicity.

When the Kefauver Committee came to Las Vegas, it called forward most of the major casino operators and subjected them to ridicule because many of them had engaged in bootlegging or gambling or tax evasion before coming to Nevada. The committee also drew the testimony of two state officials who happened to be casino owners.

One of the witnesses was William Moore, who owned a piece of the Last Frontier and also was a member of the Nevada Tax Commission. Moore was asked why the tax commission had granted gaming licenses to men with previous criminal records, specifically to William Graham and James McKay of the Bank Club in Reno. Graham and McKay had been convicted in New York for altering and passing government bonds stolen from the Bank of Manhattan. Moore's questioner was Senator Charles Tobey of New Hampshire.

TOBEY: Was this conviction known to the Tax Commission in Nevada when you voted them a license?

MOORE: Yes.

TOBEY: How do you reconcile that?

MOORE: Just because you (the state) get the privilege of controlling the thing (gambling), is that any reason why you should put the man out of business, if he is operating in the state of Nevada?

The other state official called to testify was Cliff Jones, who owned a part of the Thunderbird and was Nevada's lieutenant governor. Jones's exchange was with the committee's counsel, Rudolph Halley.

HALLEY: Wouldn't you say that prior to 1949 a great many undesirable characters with bad police records were engaged in gambling operations in the state of Nevada?

JONES: Well, of course. I would say that as long as they conduct themselves properly that I think probably no harm comes of it. . . . There were some people that you might say had police records and reputations of gambling in other places. But this seems to hold true, that people who came here when the state started to grow, they weren't particularly Sunday school teachers or preachers or anything like that. They were gamblers.

Jones and Moore both expressed the prevailing attitude of their time, and it was a more sophisticated viewpoint than the Kefauver Committee could grasp. Nevadans, as much as anyone else, did not tolerate criminal wrongdoing. That is to say, if a casino owner was found guilty of skimming untaxed revenue from his operation, he would have been brought to justice, just as he would be now. The difference was in approach. Nevadans of that time judged men by the way they had always judged people on the frontier: not on their background but on the way they conducted themselves at present. Kefauver's

Clifford Jones with his former wife, Christie, in 1981. (Courtesy Las Vegas News Bureau)

committee judged men on the basis of a black-or-white morality. Kefauver's stance recognized no middle ground.

Nevada would have to come around to the prevailing national view. Although laws against embezzlement and income-tax evasion already existed, Nevada eventually took greater precautions against mob infiltration. Under federal prodding, the state took measures to brand a certain class of individuals—members of organized crime syndicates and associates who obtained loans from them—as undesirable. No state government in the United States had ever established a state-guided capitalism on the scale that Nevada would be forced to do. The notorious Meyer Lansky, for example, could legally and openly invest in the stock market and place his money in many respectable companies. And he did so, as his tax returns showed. But he would never be able to get a gaming license in Nevada, although he did invest secretly in several casino companies.

The Kefauver hearings spurred Nevada to a stricter stance toward casino investors for a very practical reason: After the committee hearings concluded, Kefauver proposed a 10 percent federal gaming tax, which would have seriously hampered, if not altogether killed, the casino industry in its infancy. Nevada senator Pat McCarran had to use all his considerable clout in Congress to have that bill killed. But the threat of federal intervention in gambling persisted.

Nevada's new attitude toward gaming participants was exemplified in the Thunderbird case, which marked the first time the state tried to revoke the gaming license of a major resort. The case came to the tax commission after a series of stories in the *Las Vegas Sun* charged that Meyer Lansky and his brother Jake had hidden interest in the Thunderbird casino on the Las Vegas Strip. The articles also reported that one of the hotel owners, Lieutenant Governor Jones, was using his political and gambling connections to "buy" the gubernatorial election for Vail Pittman so hoodlum gamblers could have their way with the tax commission.

The newspaper's corruption charges were never proven; but coming as they did just a few weeks before the gubernatorial election, the allegations were political dynamite. In effect, the stories helped turn the tide in favor of incumbent governor Charles Russell, who had been the underdog in his campaign against Pittman. Russell won the election of 1954, and one of his first steps in the legislative session of 1955 was to establish a Gaming Control Board division within the tax commission.

The substantive charges against the Thunderbird proved to be partly correct; but under the law as it was then written, they were misplaced. The "hidden ownership" charges were taken up at hearings held in 1955. Marion Hicks, the principal owner of the Thunderbird, testified that in 1948, when one of his original investors dropped out unexpectedly, he obtained a $160,000 personal loan from gambler George Sadlo so the Thunderbird could be completed. Hicks said he brought this loan to the attention of Robbins Cahill, the tax commission's executive secretary, in 1953, but Cahill did nothing about it.

In 1955 Cahill obtained the federal income tax returns of both Sadlo and Jake Lansky. The tax returns showed that Sadlo and Jake Lansky were listing interest income from the $160,000 loan to Hicks. The Thunderbird owner testified that Sadlo never told him he had obtained half the money for the loan from Jake Lansky, and Sadlo swore in an affidavit that he had indeed never told Hicks of Lansky's participation in the loan.

What bothered the commission was that the loan was made by two men who had links to organized crime, even though there was no proof that the Thunderbird was subjected to any skimming operation. The Thunderbird case shows how far the tax commission had moved from its previous, laissez-faire philosophy and how far it was willing to go to repair Nevada's tainted image. The commission voted to revoke the gaming licenses of both Hicks and his minority partner Cliff Jones.

The Thunderbird obtained an injunction in state district court to continue operating until the matter could be resolved on appeal in the state supreme court. The trouble with the tax commission's ruling was that it held Hicks and Jones to standards that were not in effect in 1948 when the Thunderbird was being financed. Justice Charles Merrill of the Nevada Supreme Court overruled the commission and restored the gaming licenses of Hicks and Jones. But in doing so, Merrill laid down the ground rules of Nevada's new era in gaming control:

> We note that while gambling, duly licensed, is a lawful enterprise in Nevada, it is unlawful elsewhere in the country; that unlawfully followed elsewhere it tends there to create as well as to attract a criminal element; that it is a pursuit which, unlawfully followed, is conducive of corruption; that the criminal and corruptive elements engaged in unlawful gambling tend to organize and thus obtain widespread power and control over corruptive criminal enterprises throughout the country; that the existence of organized crime has long been recognized and has become a serious concern of the federal government as well as the governments of several states.

In his ruling, Merrill also obliquely gave the higher court's blessing to a new state statute that denied a revoked gaming licensee the right to a trial *de novo*—that is, the right try a case all over again in district court after the Gaming Control Board had made its decision. A gaming licensee or gaming applicant could appeal a decision by the control board, but only on procedural grounds, not on the merits of the case.

The judge went on to say that "it is not for the courts to fix the standards by which (licensing) suitability is to be determined. . . . That determination remains for the Tax Commission to make."

Nevada took the judge's advice. The Gaming Control Acts of 1957 and 1959 enabled the Gaming Control Board to establish standards of suitability demanded of licensees and license applicants, licensing qualifications and procedures, methods of operation, accounting rules, provisions for suspension or revocation of licenses, financing rules on transfers and loans, designation of the number of stockholders allowed, and rights of representation in control board hearings. The rules and regulations set forth in this body of administrative law have been amended and refined over the years, but they remain the bedrock of Nevada's gaming control posture.

The Thunderbird case also pointed out the need to insulate, as much as possible anyway, the control board apparatus from politics. In 1959 Governor Grant Sawyer created the five-member Nevada Gaming Commission as a separate supervisory agency in place of the tax commission. He also separated the three-member control board from the tax commission, allowing it to act as the enforcement and investigative arm of the gaming commission. All control board and gaming commission members are appointed by the governor, thus giving him a measure of influence. But the governor no longer sits on these boards, as he once did as an *ex officio* member of the tax commission.

Today, the Gaming Control Board has the power to both prosecute and judge gaming control matters. The board's decision must be either ratified or overturned by the gaming commission. A negative vote by the control board can be overturned only by a unanimous vote of the gaming commission. Gaming jurisdictions outside Nevada have copied the state's gaming control regulations, but they have not copied its organizational structure. Other gaming jurisdictions give their enforcement agencies only a prosecutorial role, not requiring the agencies also to judge the case before them.

Nevada's double-tiered approach to gaming control gives the state ample latitude to act against unsavory and criminal elements, but it also safeguards the state's paramount interest in maintaining its chief industry. In Nevada, unlike any other gaming jurisdiction, gaming is the mainstay of the state's economy. The state, therefore, has approached the industry more as a partner than an adversary.

This position—a middle ground entailing both boosterism and self-criticism—was nicely expressed, although in another context, as early as 1951 by Senator McCarran, who found himself in the same dilemma as other state officials. "It isn't a very laudable position for one to have to defend gambling," McCarran wrote in a letter to Joseph F. McDonald (McCarran Papers, Nevada State Archives). "One doesn't feel very lofty when his feet are resting on the argument that gambling must prevail in the state that he represents. The rest of the world looks upon him with disdain."

The state's dependence on gaming was all the more reason for

Nevada to show it could run a clean house. The state decided to get tough on gangsters. A gaming license applicant must now show that he is a person of "integrity, honesty and good character" whose background will not in any manner result in adverse publicity to Nevada and its gaming industry. He also must be a person who has adequate "business probity, competence and experience" in gaming. The burden of proof is on the license applicant, not on the state.

In 1959 Governor Sawyer specifically directed the Nevada Gaming Commission and the Gaming Control Board to keep out "criminal elements, mobs or syndicates. My feeling, to state it briefly, is this, get tough and stay tough. A gambling license is a privilege—it is not a right. If you err, err on the side of rigidity rather than laxity. Hang tough, and you will be doing a great service."

In addition to enacting its tougher administrative laws, the state devised an innovative technique of excluding certain unsavory characters from entering a casino altogether. In 1960, under Gaming Control Board chairman Ray Abbaticchio, the state compiled a List of Excluded Persons, commonly called the Black Book. Nine of the first eleven men listed in 1960 were suspected mobsters.

Several people on that list have challenged the state's right to subject them to such a ban, claiming that the Black Book violates their Constitutional right of equal protection under the law. Louis Dragna, Marshal Caifano (alias John Marshal), and Tony Spilotro challenged the list in court; and although these plaintiffs won on some procedural matters, the courts have consistently upheld the state's right to keep them out of casinos.

As Judge Walter Pope of the Ninth District Court of Appeals in San Francisco wrote, "The problem of excluding hoodlums from gambling places in the state of Nevada can well be regarded by the state authorities as a matter of life or death. It would be altogether out of place for any court to say that the state of Nevada could not reasonably anticipate serious and adverse consequences to its peculiar institution if the criminal element is permitted to participate in gambling in its casinos."

Caifano's case also is noteworthy because of the extent to which state gaming officials had to go to boot him out of casinos. Caifano was thought to be the enforcer for the Chicago mob in Las Vegas. He was well known by casino owners and managers throughout the city. At first, his inclusion in the Black Book met with noncompliance by casino executives, even though they stood to lose their gaming licenses by allowing Caifano in their casinos. The Gaming Control Board decided to send all its available agents to the Las Vegas Strip, where they engaged in a deliberate harassment campaign to get their point across. Under the pretext of checking on the honesty of the games, the agents entered the casinos that had violated the Black Book ban, and they turned over cards, inspected dice, and looked at the balance springs underneath roulette wheels. Subsequently, when Caifano entered the Desert Inn one night, the casino denied him admittance.

Another famous incident instigated by the Black Book concerned Frank Sinatra, who owned 9 percent of the Sands in Las Vegas and 50 percent of the Cal-Neva Lodge in Lake Tahoe. In 1963 Chicago mob leader Sam Giancana, who was listed in the Black Book, took a vacation at Lake Tahoe. He stayed in a Cal-Neva chalet registered to singer Phyllis McGuire, who was performing at the lodge. During the course of his stay, Giancana received visits from Sinatra, but the singer made no effort to ask Giancana to depart.

Gaming Control Board agents were spying on Giancana, having been alerted to the mobster's presence by the FBI. When Sinatra learned about this, he placed a call to Gaming Control Board chairman Ed Olson. As Olson stated in his complaint, "Sinatra used vile, intemperate, obscene and indecent language in a tone which was menacing in the extreme and constituted a threat to the chairman of the state Gaming Control Board. . . . Frank Sinatra maligned and vilified . . . by the use of foul and repulsive language which was venomous in the extreme."

Sinatra was ordered to explain and defend himself before gaming authorities. But the singer decided to sell his casino interests altogether rather than put up with the Gaming Control Board. In his book *Hang Tough*, Governor Sawyer says that as early as 1961, President John F. Kennedy urged the governor to take it easy on Sinatra, but that he politely told Kennedy to mind his own business. Sinatra continued to sing in Las Vegas casinos, but not as a part owner of any of them.

Despite its efforts, however, Nevada's new gaming control apparatus did not succeed in stopping crooks from skimming money from casinos. Some of the largest and most far-flung skimming operations in Las Vegas history occurred during the 1960s, at the very time that Nevada was implementing its "hang tough" policy. These scams were mainly discovered, not by the state, but by the federal government through the use of wiretaps, hidden listening devices, and covert surveillance under a policy initiated by Attorney General Robert F. Kennedy.

In 1961 one of the FBI's hidden microphones was placed in the office of Ed Levinson, an owner of the Fremont Hotel.

"Meyer wants a breakdown," Ben Sigelbaum says on the tape, as he talked to Levinson. Sigelbaum was a pal of Meyer Lansky and his messenger to Vegas. The secret recordings captured Levinson as he seemingly counted out shares of money. Levinson used to work for Lansky in the Havana Riviera casino, owned by Lansky. After the hotel was closed during Fidel Castro's takeover of Cuba, Levinson came to Vegas. Levinson had owned points in the Sands; then he owned a 27 percent interest in the Horseshoe and a 20 percent interest in the Fremont.

The tapes seem to indicate that skim money was coming into Levinson's office from the Sands, the Fremont, the Flamingo, and the Horseshoe. The Fremont apparently was the central clearing-house, where the money was counted and divided, each share going to different hidden mob partners via courier. At least, that is how the federal government interpreted the goings-on.

Other secret recordings led federal authorities to conclude that separate skimming operations were taking place at the Desert Inn and at the Stardust. None of these tapes was acceptable as evidence in court, so the tapes could not be used to indict anyone. But the intelligence gleaned from them was more than enough to arouse the wrath of Robert Kennedy.

Later that decade, yet another skimming operation was discovered when IRS agents raided the New York office of Morris Lansburgh and Sam Cohen, two Miami hoteliers who had bought the Flamingo hotel-casino from Albert Parvin in 1960. The New York office was used to organize junkets of East Coast gamblers to the Flamingo. When these junket gamblers returned from Las Vegas, they settled their debts (their outstanding markers) directly with Lansburgh, without the money being officially recorded on the books at the Flamingo. The casino would write off the markers as uncollected debt.

Here was another ingenious skimming operation, apparently undertaken on the advice of Meyer Lansky. Lansburgh and some of his partners pleaded guilty to this conspiracy. They admitted to stealing $36 million in untaxed income from the Flamingo between 1960 and 1967. Lansky, who received a finder's fee of $200,000 when

Lansburgh and Cohen bought the Flamingo, was charged but never brought to trial.

The rampant embezzlement in Las Vegas brought Robert Kennedy down on Nevada with a vengeance. He vowed to clean up what he called "the bank of America's organized crime." If Nevada failed to cooperate, Kennedy said, he would press Congress to close down gambling. In 1961 Kennedy asked Nevada's attorney general to deputize sixty-five federal agents in order to raid all the major casinos in Nevada.

The plan was never activated, mainly because of the opposition of Governor Sawyer, who took a state's rights stand against the federal government. Sawyer was particularly incensed by the FBI's secret wiretaps of Nevada citizens—wiretaps that were operating without court approval and therefore illegal. The "hang tough" governor now found himself in the same position as Senator McCarran and Lieutenant Governor Cliff Jones: trying to explain and defend Nevada's peculiar institution to critics who could be so stern and high-minded because they did not depend on the casino industry for their welfare.

The federal government had engaged in illegal wiretaps. It had leaked confidential documents to the national press. It had refused to turn over information to the state. And it continued to conduct investigations without indictments. This curious conduct, which in its own way was just as egregious as that of the tax cheats, amounted to, Sawyer said, "a shocking story of espionage and harassment against the state . . . determined to damage or destroy the major business of this state—without regard to morality or law."

Nevada had learned yet another lesson from this clash with the federal government. The state's new gaming control mechanism, which had adopted such strong measures against licensing mobsters, now had to go after their "front men" as well. These "front men" acted on the mobsters' behalf but might occupy such innocuous casino jobs as entertainment director or company consultant or junketeer.

The federal wiretaps also showed that Nevada needed to keep a closer eye on the casino count rooms. In the 1960s it was still possible for a casino executive to enter the count room and make a withdrawal of funds without too much fuss, simply by having a set of double keys to the table drop boxes. Therefore, the state instituted new accounting procedures to create an audit trail for the count room and the casino cage, and for the transfer of money from the cage to the table games. The state also eventually mandated the use of electronic surveillance in the count rooms, as well as in the casino pits.

In major casinos today, the "soft-count" room, the place where the paper bills from the table games are counted, is the scene of a carefully choreographed show. The middle of the room is occupied by a large table for counting. One wall contains shelves with cash-laden boxes from the table games from a particular shift. Another wall contains empty boxes. Another wall contains a one-way mirror to allow live observation of the count. Mounted on the ceiling, several closed-circuit cameras tape record the proceedings.

Five people might take part in the count. One person counts the money, and a second person checks the count. A third person adds the value of fill slips (documents that record the amount of gaming chips sent out to the gaming tables). A fourth person bundles the counted money. A fifth person, who possesses the keys to unlock the drop boxes from each table game in the casino for that shift, empties the cash from the drop boxes on the main table and shows the empty boxes to the overhead camera.

The count room also contains a signature list of persons authorized to be in the count room. The Gaming Control Board maintains a copy of that list. Each person on the list must be approved by the control board and must be independent in authority from the casino staff itself. After the money is counted and bundled, it is temporarily stored in the casino cage safe, from where it is picked up by armored-truck personnel for delivery to a bank.

Despite these measures, new ways of stealing were found. Before we delve further into the operational refinements of skimming, more has to be said about why skimming continued to be an imperative in some Las Vegas casinos. If mobsters and their henchmen were not allowed to participate in gaming, why did they continue to influence legally licensed casino owners with clean records?

The answer lies in the casino owners' overwhelming need for investment capital—the need for a constant source of loans to build or expand their properties in order to keep up with the intense competition in Las Vegas. Throughout the 1960s and well into the 1970s, most of that investment money came from the Teamsters Central States Pension Fund, which provided the money to make Las Vegas the capital of gaming at a time when most financial institutions still steered clear of casino investments. Las Vegas would not be what it is today without the Teamsters Union. Casinos that received Teamsters pension fund loans or mortgages—investments representing close to $250 million in loans—include the Desert Inn, the Stardust, the Fremont, the Tropicana, Caesars Palace, Circus Circus, and the Dunes.

All the casino loans, however, seemed to come with strings attached. The top leaders of the Teamsters Union—from Jimmy Hoffa to Frank Fitzsimmons to Jackie Presser—were all allegedly beholden to different mob families for their rise to power, as were the union pension fund trustees (leaders of union locals) who voted on the requests for capital investment loans to Las Vegas casinos. Since they influenced the votes of these trustees, the mobsters considered themselves entitled to a hidden stake in the casinos that received the loans. Indeed, the casino loans had to be first endorsed by the mobsters. The casino owners who received these loans knew that Teamsters investment funds meant having to pay a "cash consideration" to the mobsters. The cash came from the skimming operations in the casinos.

This clever, circuitous way of acquiring "hidden ownership" in Las Vegas casinos was, in a sense, the mob's response to the Gaming Control Board's strict licensing qualifications. The prolific Teamsters fund loans created havoc with the control board's anti-mob crusade and also frustrated the FBI.

The control board retaliated by holding suitability hearings. Just about anyone directly or indirectly connected to a casino business can be called in for a hearing on whether he or she is suitable for the job. This applies to a casino owner, casino host, junketeer, entertainment director, or consultant. The control board adopted this tactic in part to drive out certain mob associates who held seemingly innocent jobs in the casino hierarchy but who in fact acted as middlemen for various mob factions by conducting casino skim operations. The state's campaign was aimed at individuals who had not gone through a gaming license investigation and who were not candidates for the Black Book.

In one famous case, the control board trained its sights on one of the cockiest "wise guys" Vegas had ever seen. Frank Rosenthal, a former illegal bookie and sports fixer before coming to Nevada, had been appointed the $250,000-a-year executive corporate consultant of Argent Corporation. This company owned the Stardust in Las Vegas, then the largest hotel-casino in the world; the property also was the beneficiary of a large Teamsters loan. (It was later discovered that in exchange for this loan, mobsters coerced Argent Corporation president Allen Glick to hire Rosenthal, who oversaw a large-scale skimming operation at the Stardust.) Rosenthal was known to have friends within the mob, including his Chicago boyhood chum Tony Spilotro, the mob's enforcer in Las Vegas during the 1970s.

In 1975 the control board ruled that Rosenthal was unsuitable for his job. Rosenthal fought the case in court, and his appeal gave rise to one of the landmark judicial decisions supporting Nevada's gaming control effort. Rosenthal's appeal claimed that he was not notified of the charges against him, was not given sufficient notice to oppose the charges, did not know the claims against him because the charges relied on confidential information, and was not given the opportunity to cross-examine the witnesses at his hearing. Rosenthal charged that he had been denied his "due process of law" rights as stated in the 14th Amendment of the U.S. Constitution.

The Nevada Supreme Court ruled in 1976 that the control board could transcend the "due process" clause because the gaming industry was a special sphere of society with distinctive opportunities for criminal activity. Membership in the gaming industry was not a Constitutional right but rather a special privilege granted by the state of Nevada. The court said that Nevada could take extraordinary measures to protect the gaming industry's integrity and reputation.

After losing his appeal, Rosenthal was named the Stardust's entertainment director. He maintained that he wielded no influence in the casino. The control board again called him in for a suitability hearing and again denied him permission to work for the casino. The case then went to the Nevada Gaming Commission for final disposition. This was Rosenthal's last chance for licensing, his last hope to remain the mob's middleman in Las Vegas.

Rosenthal thought he could bully his way into Nevada's gaming industry, as others had done in the past. But in a quick vote, the commission denied Rosenthal a work permit. Immediately after the unanimous vote, Rosenthal charged to the commissioners' table and vented his outrage, as reported by the *Las Vegas Sun*.

"It's what I should have expected," Rosenthal shouted snidely. "A kangaroo court."

Later, outside the meeting chamber, Rosenthal blustered, "Frontier justice, that's what I call it."

While the control board was chasing Rosenthal out of gaming, it also zeroed in on the Stardust gaming operation. In 1976, the same year that Rosenthal lost in court, control board auditing agents, under the direction of audit division chief Dennis Gomes, raided the Stardust casino after receiving a tip from a slot department employee.

The agents discovered that one of the casino's slot change booths was being used as a secret bank for skimmed funds. This auxiliary booth was not on the casino's record books. The booth contained coins provided by the casino's "hard-count" room, the place where coins from slot machines are counted. In the hard-count room, the contents of the coin buckets are dropped on a weight scale, which converts the weight of the coins into dollar amounts. The Stardust skimmers had miscalibrated the scale to make it register a lesser amount than the actual number of coins weighed. The skimmers then took the extra coins to the auxiliary slot change booth on the casino floor. At the start of each shift, the slot change girls in the area of the auxiliary booth would withdraw coins needed for their change belts. As the slot change girls accumulated cash in the course of making change for slot players, they deposited the paper money in the auxiliary slot booth. By doing so, they unwittingly were converting the skimmed coins from the hard-count room into cash. The paper bills were then converted into larger bills at the casino cage and returned to the slot booth in the larger denomination. At the end of each shift, the slot manager simply walked into the auxiliary slot booth and pocketed the large bills. Even the control board had to admit that it was a masterful skim.

The mobsters who benefited from the Stardust skim operation— Joe Aiuppa of Chicago, Nick Civella of Kansas City, Frank Balistrieri of Milwaukee, and Moshe Rockman of Cleveland—were brought to justice nearly ten years after the control board's raid of the Stardust. A federal strike force team in Kansas City charged them all with conspiracy to defraud the government of taxes through illegal and unreported income from a casino skim operation. All the gangsters were sentenced to prison. Frank Rosenthal was not indicted because he apparently agreed to provide information to the government in exchange for immunity from prosecution. The state also forced Stardust owner Glick to sell his casino holdings in Las Vegas.

The federal government also cleansed the Teamsters Union of mob influence, which had been a goal since Robert Kennedy's time, when he went after Jimmy Hoffa. For a while in the 1980s the Central States Pension Fund was overseen by a federal supervisor, and the fund was barred from making casino loans.

By the time the denouement of the Stardust saga was played out, mobsters and mob associates had become nearly extinct on the Las Vegas Strip. What finally drove the mobsters out of the gaming business was not so much the efforts of the control board or the FBI but the development of a new way of doing business.

Publicly traded corporations had come to town. Since they had the power to sell stock on national money markets, these corporations could raise money to buy, construct, or expand casinos on a grander scale than mobsters ever could. A corporation's ability to sell stock gave it a way of raising money that was not tied to mobster influence. Publicly traded corporations made mobsters obsolete in Las Vegas.

Before 1969 publicly traded corporations had been discouraged from entering the gaming industry because every stockholder would have been required to go through the ordeal and expense of obtaining a gaming license. The Gaming Control Board insisted on licensing every casino owner in order to screen out mob associates among the shareholders. Most casino ownership groups up to 1969 were either partnerships or closely held corporations (companies with only a few stockholders such as Del Webb Corporation). But how would the control board deal with a corporation that had hundreds upon hundreds of shareholders?

In 1969 the Nevada Legislature passed a corporate gaming control law that permitted corporations to enter Nevada's gaming industry without requiring each shareholder to submit to individual licensing. The Gaming Control Board adopted a new policy of licensing only the major corporate shareholders, those owning 10 percent or more of the stock. Individuals who held from 5 percent to 10 percent of the stock could be called in for licensing at the discretion of the board, but it was not mandatory. And those individuals owning less than 5 percent of the stock, which is to say the majority of shareholders of typical publicly traded corporations, did not have to be licensed at all.

The need to reexamine the state's policies toward corporations took place at the same time that the eccentric tycoon Howard Hughes lived in Las Vegas. Hughes began buying casinos with abandon until he became the single largest casino owner in the state. Never was any man so welcomed by the state of Nevada. "Mr. Hughes' involvement here has absolutely done us wonders," said Governor Paul Laxalt at the time. "I just returned from a trip to the East where I spoke to some industrialists in mid-town Manhattan, and their questions no longer are concerned with the Mafia, the skimming, the underworld. . . . People come here now feeling they can come here in a respectable, safe circumstance."

The licensing of Howard Hughes himself was just as zany as the billionaire's habits. Hughes was the sole stockholder of his corporation, and ordinarily this would have been an easy licensing procedure. Hughes, however, would not come out of his penthouse suite atop the Desert Inn to be fingerprinted and photographed, to fill out his application, to make a detailed financial statement, or to appear before the Gaming Control Board at all. Governor Laxalt, a major benefactor of Hughes's political contributions, waived all these requirements in Hughes's case out of respect for his privacy.

In 1970 Hughes abruptly left Las Vegas. He also fired Robert Maheu, his chief executive in Nevada, and replaced him with Chester Davis and Bill Gay, who were put in charge of the newly created Summa Corporation to handle Hughes's holdings in Nevada. The Davis-Gay faction had been vying with Maheu for control of the Nevada operations. This faction moved its personnel into the casino cages to take over the money and the records of Hughes-owned casinos. Maheu challenged the takeover in court, claiming that the state had no way of knowing if Hughes had indeed approved the takeover. After all, who had even seen the man? Maheu himself had never met him and had communicated with him only through handwritten notes and telephone calls.

To quell the furor, Hughes telephoned Governor Laxalt and told him that he had indeed authorized a new executive team for Hughes's casinos. In the next two years, the stories about Hughes became wilder and more worrisome to the gaming authorities. According to some rumors, Hughes might not even have been alive.

The pressure to have a face-to-face meeting with Hughes intensified, and the issue landed squarely in the lap of a gregarious Irish Democrat, Mike O'Callaghan, when he became governor in 1971. "I asked for a meeting with Hughes because I wanted to make sure the new people in charge of his corporation were picked by Hughes. That's all I wanted to know," O'Callaghan recalled. "The Hughes organization at first tried to stall me. Two of Hughes's personal physicians came to see me and assured me that Hughes was living and of sound mind. Then Chester Davis and Bill Gay talked to me. But this still wasn't enough. Davis had never seen Hughes, and Gay had not seen him in over ten years. I had to see Hughes for myself. I insisted on it. After all, the state would in a very embarrassing position if the guy turned out to be dead."

After considerable negotiations, a meeting between the governor and Hughes was arranged in Nicaragua, where Hughes was living. But that meeting had to be postponed because of the terrible earthquake that hit the country's capital city, Managua. Finally, in 1973 Governor O'Callaghan and Gaming Control Board chairman Phil Hannifin flew to London to meet Hughes.

"The meeting was set up for 2 A.M. at the Inn of the Park," O'Callaghan said. "Hughes came out dressed in a bathrobe and slippers. He was frail looking, but his eyes were bright and his appearance was neat. He exchanged a handshake with Phil and me, and after a few pleasantries we got down to business. He revealed a grasp of his situation in Nevada. At one point in our conversation I needled him about some minor point, and he answered with a mild joke. That showed me he had a sense of humor. The meeting lasted about an hour."

What O'Callaghan did not know was that Hughes resented having to meet with anyone. Hughes agreed to the visit only after his confidants convinced him that he could lose his Nevada holdings by not seeing the governor. Whereas Hughes had been cozy with the Republican Paul Laxalt when he was governor, the Democrat O'Callaghan owed Hughes no favors. Hughes dreaded talking to people over whom he had no influence.

Also unknown to O'Callaghan, Hughes's personal aides had spent hours prior to the meeting making Hughes look presentable, clipping his long, curlicue fingernails and trimming his shoulder-length hair. The hour-long chat must have been an ordeal for Hughes, who was deeply disappointed by his Nevada experience. In Nevada he had hoped to build a private empire unruffled by meddlesome government officials. The reclusive billionaire thought he could acquire enough assets in the state to merit being left alone.

Hughes, who made a rational impression on his Nevada visitors, told them he had personally authorized the executive changes in his organization. On the basis of this representation, Nevada gaming authorities approved the reorganization of Hughes's company.

Nevada had bent the rules for Hughes, but it was never to happen again with the corporate licensings that followed in his wake. His was a special case. Corporations that followed him reaped a revolution in Nevada's gaming industry, and when casino gaming spread to other areas of the country, these same corporations would dominate the field. This might have never happened if not for Nevada's pioneering efforts to tame a wild enterprise.

Tycoons and magnates replaced mobsters. Wall Street replaced the Teamsters Pension Fund. College business majors ruled the erstwhile turf of con artists. The pariah industry became more respectable, more profitable, and more popular than ever. Perhaps the crowning touch came in the 1990s when mega-corporation ITT invested in Las Vegas by buying two premier properties, the Desert Inn and Caesars Palace, which in their infancy were the domain of mobster associates.

The Gaming Control Board would grow in size and regulatory responsibilities. The board would go on to tackle such matters as cash reporting requirements when money is exchanged for chips (a possible avenue for money laundering); gaming license investigations for applicants who were citizens of other countries; computer chip technology used to power slot machines and the newfangled, high-tech scams resulting therefrom; the illegal drug habits of gaming licensees; casino hosts and the sometime suspicious friends they ask to frequent their casinos; stock "shelf" offerings, stock assignments, junk bonds . . . and what not.

Just like every other business, only more so, Nevada's "peculiar institution" now functions amid a mind-numbing blizzard of red tape. Although still haunted by the specter of federal gaming taxes, Nevada's gaming industry finally has found its place in the sun—now that the Titans of old have been put to rest.

For more information on Nevada's gaming control history, see:

1. Skolnick, Jerome H. *House of Cards: Legalization and Control of Casino Gambling.* New York: Little, Brown, 1978.

2. Reid, Ed, and Ovid Demaris. *The Green Felt Jungle.* New York: Trident Press, 1963.

3. Wiley, Peter. *Empires in the Sun: The Rise of the New American West.* New York: Putnam, 1982.

4. Glass, Mary Ellen. *Nevada's Turbulent '50s*. Reno: University of Nevada Press, 1981.

5. Turner, Wallace. *Gambler's Money*. New York: Houghton Mifflin, 1965.

6. Sawyer, Grant. *Hang Tough!* Reno: University of Nevada Oral History Program, 1993.

7. Glass, Mary Ellen. *Robbins E. Cahill: Recollections of Work in State Politics, Government, Taxation, Gaming Control, Clark County Administration, and the Nevada Resort Association*. Reno: University of Nevada Oral History Program, 1977.

8. Shipperson, Wilbur S. *Mirage Land: Images of Nevada*. Reno: University of Nevada Press, 1992.

9. Goodwin, John R. *Gaming Control Law—the Nevada Model*. Scottsdale, Ariz.: Publishing Horizons Inc., 1985.

Cliff Jones: "The Big Juice"

Sergio Lalli

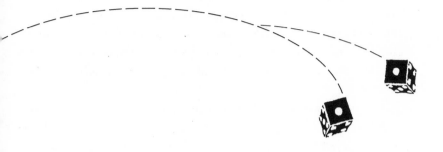

Clifford Aaron Jones was the youngest lawyer in town when he returned home from the University of Missouri in 1938 to practice law
in Las Vegas. The twenty-six-year-old attorney—who would become
known as "the Big Juice"—established a modest office on the second
floor of the Beckley Building, above a clothing shop and amid the
retail stores, service stations, casino saloons, and hotels on Fremont
Street, within a block of the Union Pacific railroad station.

Jones's downtown neighbors included the four major gambling
houses in Las Vegas at that time: the Northern (whose owner, Mayme
Stocker, had obtained the first gaming license in town just after Nevada legalized casinos in 1931), the Hotel Apache, the Boulder Club,
and the Las Vegas Club, all of which were owned by local businessmen. The owner of the Las Vegas Club, for instance, was J. Kell Houssels Sr., a Las Vegan since 1929, who was the leading voice for casino
interests downtown and influential with businessmen and politicians. Houssels was a proponent of limiting casino development to
several blocks on Fremont Street, and for a while that restriction held
sway. This sort of influence, or clout, carried a special name in Las
Vegas, as the city increasingly adopted the jargon of gambling. Influence became known as "juice." If you had "juice," you were someone who could get things done.

Gaming law at that time consisted of a state statute that declared
casinos to be legal in Nevada. If you wanted to open a casino, all you
had to do was apply for a gaming license from a county board composed of county commissioners and the sheriff. If the casino was in

a city, you also had to get a city license. But the county license dominated. There were no licensing investigations, and the body of rules and regulations governing gaming was not to be fully implemented until 1959. The process was akin to obtaining an ordinary city business license today. A casino was assessed a special fee, however, depending on how many tables games and slot machines it contained. If the casino was located in an incorporated municipality, the county shared some of its fee with the city. The fees were relatively small. The Northern Club, for example, paid $1,410 for its original gaming license.

The system worked well enough for those times because everyone knew everyone else in town, and also because a gambling business in those days was mainly an offshoot of an existing business, such as a saloon or a hotel. Casino operators were referred to as gamblers. This term was not meant to imply that casino owners played cards or shot craps. The language of the day, as well as the economic reality of the situation, recognized that establishing a casino was a gamble. Not all casinos succeeded, and more often than not casinos went through boom or bust cycles. The biggest hurdle any casino owner faced, especially as casinos became larger and fancier, was finding the money to finance the property. No respectable bank would lend money to a gambler. So the early gaming pioneers banked themselves, pooling their money in partnerships to provide the seed money for new enterprises.

Not many casino owners in Las Vegas in the 1930s were outsiders. Tony Cornero, a Californian, had obtained a gaming license in 1931 for the Meadows Club on the road that led to Boulder Dam. Cornero's casino, which catered to locals, closed after the dam was completed.

The gambling business did not take off in the 1930s because the country was rife with illegal gambling houses tolerated by local officials, in much the same way that speakeasies were allowed to operate during Prohibition. Californians, for example, did not have to come to Nevada to gamble because gambling was readily available near where they lived.

By the end of the 1930s, however, authorities in California, particularly in Los Angeles, cracked down on illegal gambling houses and offshore casino boats. Gambling operators increasingly began to look at Nevada as a place to do business unhindered by the law. It might be said that Nevada owed its initial good fortune to the moralistic fervor sweeping the nation. The more that state and federal officials elsewhere inveighed against the gambling vice, the better it was for Nevada's economy.

In 1938 another Californian, Guy McAfee, opened his Pair-O-Dice Club on a deserted stretch of road outside the Las Vegas city limits. It was just a roadhouse south of town along Highway 91, the road to Los Angeles. In California, McAfee had been a Los Angeles police vice commander who had had to hide his ownership interest in various illegal casinos. In Las Vegas, he was considered a businessman who did not have to hide what he did. (He later established the Golden Nugget casino downtown.) Pair-O-Dice, a pun on the word *paradise*, was the whimsical name McAfee chose for the forlorn area in the county where his saloon-casino was located. In the same spirit of irony, McAfee liked to call the road in front of his joint "the Strip"— a facetious reference to the Sunset Strip in Los Angeles.

A glorious enterprise hatched in the unseasoned mind of Cliff Jones about this time. He and his friend Dr. Roy Martin (who with several other doctors operated a medical clinic, on Eighth Street, that became the city's first hospital) planned an entrepreneurial venture with the flamboyant aim of building not just a roadhouse but a gambling resort on Highway 91. It would have a swimming pool, and swamp coolers would ventilate every room.

But where would they get the money for such a grand project? They knew of only one man up to the task: A. P. Campbell, a local rogue who was in prison for having persuaded several ladies in California to part with their money so he could drill an oil well at Arden Dome outside Las Vegas. Martin and Jones secured an early release for Campbell by obtaining a job for him at a local hotel. Then the two men approached Campbell with their idea.

"Oh no," the reformed swindler told them, "speculation's not for me. I've learned my lesson."

Instead of becoming a resort builder, Campbell continued to tap women for funds. He persuaded a rich woman to buy him a house in the country, where he lived happily ever after. He never married the woman.

Gambling, however, was not yet foremost on the mind of the young Cliff Jones. As he went about building his law practice, he yearned to participate in the city's civic and business life—a passion that was to dominate his outlook for the rest of his life. He wanted to be part of things—everything. He was a tall, lean, and handsome fellow who liked to wear cowboy shirts, cowboy boots, and calfskin vests, even to his law office. He fit right in with the town's western heritage and wide-open frontier disposition. On weekends he would join his friends to ride horses or to participate in rodeos. He excelled as a calf roper. During Helldorado Days, Jones would be in the parade on his horse, at the head of the Lions Club contingent. He had co-founded the club in 1938 and served as its first president. Although a "cowboy" at heart, he was not uncouth or vulgar. He had a knack for getting along, but he could also display a sharp edge when forced to do so. Jones did not drink, smoke, or gamble.

Most Las Vegans in 1940 (the town had about eight thousand residents and the county about sixteen thousand) believed its future was as a resort city, but not necessarily as a gaming resort city. The influx of federal funds during the construction of Hoover Dam, from 1931 to 1936, had kicked off an economic boom in the otherwise somnolent hamlet during the Great Depression. In 1931 Jones's family had moved from Missouri, where Cliff was born, to Nevada, crossing the Colorado River on the ferry owned by Big Jim Cashman. Cliff's father believed a great city would grow in the desert and opportunities would abound. The elder Jones staked his life savings on that premise. It was not to be easy, however, and Cliff Jones had to seek work on the dam, in jobs ranging from sandwich maker to crane operator, in order to save enough money to contribute to the family's finances and to pay for his law-school education. Some civic boosters thought that light industry could be lured to Las Vegas because of the cheap electric power from the dam, but that was not to materialize quite yet. Las Vegas envisioned itself as the gateway for tourists who wanted to see Hoover Dam and enjoy the Lake Mead recreation area, as well as a mecca for people who wanted quick divorces and no-hassle marriages. Gambling was a subordinate aspect of city development. The nationally publicized divorce of Ria Langham (Mrs. Clark Gable) in 1939 had caused much more commotion in Las Vegas than the opening of any casino. Jones liked to walk across Fremont Street to chat with Langham when she gambled at Frank Houskey's casino in the Hotel Apache. She was a whiff of glamour that the rough-at-the-edges frontier town was unaccustomed to.

Many a lawyer in town handled divorce cases because it was such an easy way to make money, but Jones gravitated toward politics. One of his closest friends was Al Cahlan, editor of the *Las Vegas Review-Journal*. Jones's sister, Florence Lee Jones, was a reporter for the newspaper and later would marry Al's brother, John, who was the city editor. Al Cahlan was an influential Democrat, closely allied with Senator Pat McCarran, the undisputed political "boss" of Nevada. Jones was a political worker for McCarran when the latter won his first U.S. Senate seat in 1932. Although Cahlan thought it was still too early for Jones to enter politics, he could not dissuade his friend from running for the Nevada Assembly in 1938. Jones lost.

Clark County was heavily Democratic, whereas the northern part of the state around Reno was a Republican stronghold. At that time, Clark County was grossly underrepresented in the Nevada Legislature; that was to be the case until court-ordered reapportionment of the state legislature in 1965. When Jones first ran for office, Clark County had but one state senator and four assemblymen. He won in the 1940 election, along with C. D. Baker (later to become mayor of Las Vegas) and Berkeley Bunker (later to become a U.S. senator). After Jones traveled to Carson City for the biennial legislative session, he pulled off quite a coup in a deal he engineered with a northern Democrat, Bill Cashil: Jones would support Cashil for the speaker of the Assembly position over Denver Dickerson; in return, Cashil supported Jones for the majority leader post and agreed to give him the right to appoint all the committee chairmen—a privilege usually reserved for the speaker. Jones himself, as one of the only two lawyers in the Assembly, became chairman of the Judiciary Committee. Jones's deal-making prowess endeared him to McCarran, who delved into every aspect of Nevada's political life. Jones became one of the early McCarran boys, a long line of lawyers the senator groomed for higher office under his patronage.

By the early 1940s McCarran was telling Jones that he might one day make a fine lieutenant governor. In 1940 Jones became a member of the Clark County Democratic Central Committee (a post he retained until 1972) and a delegate to the Democratic National Convention (a position he held on four occasions).

Jones became involved in the gaming business through a stroke of luck just before the United States entered World War II. Several Californians sought his help in obtaining a gambling license. They wanted to locate the casino in the clothing store beneath Jones's law office. The men offered to give Jones a 2½ percent interest in the casino if he obtained the location and the gaming license for them.

"I asked them how much would this deal make," Jones recalled in an interview. "They said about $100,000 a year. Well, $2,500 per year looked like a sum to be reckoned with, so we agreed upon those terms and I got them the license and the lease for the Pioneer Club."

The casino owners later came back to Jones and suggested revising their deal, offering $5,000 in cash to buy out Jones's interest. The men—Tutor Scherer, Farmer Page, Chuck Addison, and Bill Curland—had made a name for themselves in the gambling business in California. Now it was their turn to learn some things about the local yokels in Las Vegas.

Jones responded by making a counteroffer to buy an additional 2½ percent stake in the casino for $5,000. The men refused. Jones then used his trump card, his "juice" in the community. "I've been to the City Commission and I've been to everybody in town telling them what fair, honest fellows you are," Jones told them, "and now you've made me realize that I've made a mistake."

The Pioneer owners understood the veiled threat and quickly agreed to Jones's proposal. Thus, Jones acquired a 5 percent stake in the Pioneer. "I started learning about this business from that point on," he said.

The establishment of the Pioneer was one of the few times that Jones helped a property obtain a gaming license. Throughout the 1950s, at the height of his influence in Las Vegas, Jones did not represent any properties for licensing.

Soon after the Pioneer deal, Jones struck up a friendship with another Californian, Marion Hicks, who used to operate a gaming boat off Long Beach. Hicks wanted to build a Las Vegas casino in partnership with Johnny Grayson. Jones became Hicks's legal advisor, their friendship sparked by the fact that they were both born in Missouri. Jones bought a 5 percent stake in a partnership that in 1941 erected the El Cortez, downtown's first major resort, way out on Sixth Street.

The major gaming development of 1941, one that had the whole town abuzz, was the opening of the El Rancho Vegas, the first gambling resort on the Strip. It was built by Tom Hull, the owner of several theme hotels in California. Local businessmen, including Jim Cashman, had invited Hull to Las Vegas to interest him in building a hotel within the city limits, but to their surprise Hull chose a site just across the city's boundary. The location made sense to Hull. Land was much cheaper in the county, making possible the purchase of larger parcels. Taxes were cheaper in the county. Water costs were lower because the early county-based resorts dug their own wells and their own cesspools. There were other factors too, such as ample parking for motorists traveling on the Los Angeles highway and the convenience of a roadside attraction for guests who stopped to gamble on an impulse. But the most important reason for choosing a county location was that it lowered the capitalization costs of building a resort: It was cheaper to build in the county than in the city. (After the war, Jones became Hull's attorney, and Jones confirms this assessment from his conversations with Hull.) Raising the money to build a resort and then to maintain it on the level of its competition was the most critical factor, then and now.

Jones went off to war in 1942 and rose to the rank of major in General George S. Patton's Third Army. When Jones returned to Las Vegas in 1945, the area's economy was hopping as it benefited from the continuation of federally funded projects such as the Army Gunnery School (later to become Nellis Air Force Base) and the Basic Magnesium plant. On the gaming front, R. E. Griffith, the owner of a movie theater chain doing business in the Southwest, had built the Last Frontier in 1942, the second resort on the Strip. And another investor, Ben Siegel, had started construction of his lavish Flamingo resort.

Back home, Jones was appointed to fill a vacant seat in district court, where he served as a judge from 1945 to 1946. His friend Louis Wiener, who later became Jones's law partner, was the local attorney for Siegel's Flamingo. Although there were suspicions that Siegel's past might have been unsavory, the town accepted him at face value as the owner of a wire service that supplied racing results to Las Vegas bookmakers. Siegel was one more Californian who had invested in Las Vegas. As long as he did not break the law in Nevada, he was welcomed. Even Senator McCarran was accommodating. To help Siegel obtain building supplies for the Flamingo during the shortages at the end of the war, McCarran used his position on the Senate Appropriations Committee to relax strictures on construction materials by the War Production Board.

Jones saw Siegel but once, when he visited the Flamingo after its 1946 opening, but he never got to know the man. What impressed him most about the Flamingo was not its exotic Miami-Caribbean theme, nor the Hollywood stars in attendance, nor the high rollers, nor the tuxedo-clad employees. What stuck in Jones's mind was the Flamingo's alleged $6-million price tag, by far the most money that had ever been spent on a Las Vegas resort. Jones (now eighty-four years old) sharply disagrees with the view that holds Siegel to be the founding father of the Strip. "Development of the Las Vegas Strip was the result of many fathers," Jones said. "Siegel's true contribution to the Las Vegas gaming industry was that he was able to obtain so much money for his project." The mother lode that Siegel tapped to raise all that capital came, of course, from crime syndicates.

In 1947, with the full blessing of McCarran and his fellow Democrats in Clark County, Jones resigned his judgeship so he could run for lieutenant governor. The election of 1947 was a sweep for the Democrats. Vail Pittman was elected governor; his running mate, Jones, won as well. By that time Jones was also a member of the Democratic State Central Committee. He had become a bona fide member of the Establishment—in politics, in civic affairs, in the legal field, and in the gaming business.

The gaming property that Jones was most closely associated with was the Thunderbird, the fourth resort to open on the Strip in 1948. Jones placed the initial down payment for the land and then coaxed his friend Marion Hicks to pay the majority share. The two men, along with several other local investors, then formed a partnership to raise the money to build a hotel-casino. All told, it was a $2-million investment. Jones wound up getting 11 percent of the equity stock; Hicks got 51 percent. Hicks, however, held 90 percent of the voting stock to Jones's 10 percent—meaning Hicks ran the place and was the boss.

The property had a southwestern theme. A neon sign in the shape of a regal bird perched atop the Thunderbird tower. The bird's mouth would later hiss a vibrant gas flame over the Strip. The hotel's namesake was the Navajo Indian symbol for "the sacred bearer of happiness unlimited." For a time, the resort lived up to its name, at least for its two main partners. The hotel was noted for its innovative entertainment policy, providing a stage for such shows as the Mills Brothers, Ziegfeld Follies, and Scandals on Ice (the first show on the Strip with nude ice skaters). Jones played a major role in bringing Broadway musicals to Las Vegas for the first time. The Thunderbird hosted *Flower Drum Song* and *South Pacific.* The hotel's Topaz Room was noted for its New Orleans jazz. The all-men's Hualapai Club—a leisure group for local bigwigs—was founded and met regularly at the Thunderbird.

The Flamingo appealed to the jet set from Los Angeles; the El Cortez and the Last Frontier mainly catered to the tourists seeking a dude ranch—style vacation. But the Thunderbird became the favorite Strip hangout for the cream of local society and some famous out-of-towners. Howard Hughes, for one, used to stay at the Thunderbird. Jones recalled that even then, Hughes was a little strange. "The porters wanted a guest evicted from the hotel because he was washing his shirts and hanging them up to dry in the men's room. They described the culprit as a thin man who wore a narrow mustache. The porters said the man sometimes walked out of the restroom with a wet shirt on his back." Further examination revealed that the self-launderer was none other than the millionaire Howard Hughes. Management did not evict him.

Several Thunderbird employees later attained prominence in the gaming industry. In the casino cage was a young cashier by the name of Jack Walsh, who would later become owner of the Algiers Hotel on the Las Vegas Strip and a member of the Nevada Gaming Commission from 1972 to 1984.

Sam Boyd, who would become chairman of the Boyd Group, worked in the casino pit. Thunderbird owner Marion Hicks had become acquainted with Boyd when the young man worked on Hicks's casino ship. Hicks gave Boyd a job at the El Cortez and later at the Thunderbird. Boyd's first venture in casino ownership was engineered by Jones. When the Sahara resort was being built, Jones was responsible for finding support for the deal among several groups of minority investors. A group from Dallas wanted to make sure they received their fair share of profits from the Sahara; they requested their local attorney, Jones, to name a trusted representative who would work in the casino and make sure no money was being skimmed. Jones suggested Sam Boyd. The Dallas group allowed Boyd to purchase some of their shares in the hotel-casino. Boyd wound up owning a 1 percent stake in the Sahara, an investment he would later parlay into other casino ventures. Jones said that Boyd would go to the Sahara's count room every night to assure himself that no one was slipping money under the table.

One of the most popular nooks in the Thunderbird was Joe's Oyster Bar. The bar was named after Joe Wells, the general manager and part owner of the Thunderbird. Wells had come to the casino industry from his family-owned Wells Cargo trucking firm, which operated throughout the West. The rotund and jovial Wells was a local favorite, as was his daughter Dawn Wells—better known to the rest of the country as Mary Ann on the television show *Gilligan's Island*.

Both Hicks and Jones had strong local connections and friendships in the business community. When McCarran came to town he usually stayed at the Thunderbird. On several occasions Hicks and Jones brought legislators from throughout the state to stay at the Thunderbird to show them firsthand that Clark County needed more revenue from the state's general fund than it was receiving. When the resort owners met, it was usually at the Thunderbird; and since Jones was the only lawyer in the bunch and had a pipeline to McCarran, his advice carried weight. Hicks and Jones took the lead in persuading the Strip resorts to contribute money to Democratic candidates, such as Pittman and McCarran. Then, as now, casino owners were allowed to participate in politics and to contribute to candidates.

On the state political level, Jones became an active lieutenant governor who attended all the Senate meetings while the Legislature was in session. In 1947 he was instrumental in passage of a law that gave the Nevada Highway Patrol the legal right to crack down on casinos that cheated customers through rigged or exotic games. These unethical casinos, operating mainly along Highway 40 in the northern part of the state, were called roadside "zoos" because some of their games involved animals, such as chickens, to decide the outcome of a game.

In another legislative session, Jones lobbied for a bill that in essence prevented the Strip resorts from being annexed by the city of Las Vegas. By the early 1950s Las Vegas was casting a covetous eye on the four-mile Strip area, wanting to include it in the city's tax base. Jones helped guide a law through the Legislature that required a majority vote of the residents as well as county commission approval before a township could be annexed by a municipality. Since the Clark County Commission was not about to let go of the Las Vegas Strip, the areas known as Paradise and Winchester quickly formed into townships and thus successfully thwarted several attempts by Las Vegas to gain this valuable territory.

In 1954 Walter Cosgriff, president of the Continental Bank of Salt Lake City, assigned Jones the mission of obtaining a state charter for a new Las Vegas bank. The only other bank in Las Vegas, First State Bank, considered the gaming industry to be too risky for investment. The new bank that Cosgriff proposed would make casino loans. Jones put a deal together that resulted in the founding of the Bank of Las Vegas in 1954. He nominated the local partners who joined the Salt Lake City bankers to form this bank, choosing men he knew in the community: Nate Mack (father of Jerry Mack), Bob Kaltenborn, Jake Von Tobel, Bruce Beckley, and Herb Jones, Cliff's brother. Cliff Jones himself would have joined the group, but all his money was tied up in casino ventures. Two years after the bank's founding, E. Parry Thomas, an executive with Continental Bank, joined the Bank of Las Vegas as its chief loan officer. The bank reorganized in 1964 as Valley Bank, and under the leadership of Thomas it became the leading source of bank capital for the gaming industry. In the 1990s Valley Bank was purchased by Bank of America.

The number of deals that Jones either engineered as a legal adviser or participated in as an investor is extraordinary. At various times, he held interests in the Pioneer, the El Cortez, the Thunderbird, the Golden Nugget, the Algiers, the Westerner, and the Dunes. As a lawyer, Jones laid the financial groundwork that helped investors either to buy land or build properties at such venues as the Fremont, the Sahara, the Riviera, the Tropicana, the Hacienda, and the Royal Nevada.

"Cliff is an absolute deal maker without peer," former governor Grant Sawyer said when Jones retired from his law firm in 1993. "He can make a deal faster than the rest of us can think about it."

In the 1950s Jones was easily the most active lawyer dealing with gaming properties. In addition, the law firm he founded has been the training ground for many attorneys who went on to greater success in the gaming industry, such as William Boyd, Mike Sloan, and Mike Rumbolz.

At the height of his career in Las Vegas, Jones deserved to be called the Big Juice. This title was pinned on him by his detractors, but it is an appellation he does not disown. Attaining that position, Jones said, "took a lot of work. You had to work at it every day. In the process, I've made many friends, and these friendships are what sustains you through life."

Some of the deals in which Jones participated got him in trouble. Some of the people he trusted turned out to be the wrong kind of people. His life has been, not a smooth road to the top, but rather an adventurous ride with ups and downs. People who know him express a fondness for Cliff Jones and extol his good intentions.

"He never was money hungry," said Jerry Mack, a former director of Valley Bank and a partner in some of Jones's deals. "He always wanted to be part of everything and be buddies with whomever he was working with."

One of Jones's favorite stories is about a conversation he once had with Marion Hicks, his Thunderbird partner. Jones's whirlwind activities always puzzled Hicks. Jones was making a very good living as a lawyer and as a Thunderbird partner. A mark of his success was his house in the exclusive Rancho Circle neighborhood. Jones's house was one of the largest, if not the largest, in town. Why, Hicks asked him, did he insist on going from one deal to the next, sometimes even helping competitors of the hotel?

"I told him," Jones recalled, "that my greatest satisfaction came from helping to build a city."

Perhaps no Las Vegan has ever engaged in so many different activities on so many levels for such a long time in helping to transform Las Vegas from a railroad town to a prosperous resort city. There have been wealthier Las Vegans, more powerful Las Vegans, and more important Las Vegans, but never someone like Cliff Jones, who had his fingers in so many slices of the Las Vegas pie.

For more information on the Cliff Jones era, see:

1. Reid, Ed. *Las Vegas: City without Clocks.* New York: Prentice-Hall, 1961.

2. Paher, Stanley W. *Las Vegas: As It Began—as It Grew.* Las Vegas: Nevada Publications, 1971.

3. Moody, Eric N. *Southern Gentleman of Nevada Politics: Vail M. Pittman.* Reno: University of Nevada Press, 1974.

4. Hulse, James W. *The Nevada Adventure.* Reno: University of Nevada Press, 1965.

Moe Dalitz and the Desert

John L. Smith

Las Vegas history is replete with tales of men who crossed the desert in search of a fresh start and freedom. The transition from outlaw to legitimate citizen was more than a physical journey. Not all made the trek unscathed. The ones who kept their wits about them and packed a little extra luck not only survived but found their place in the sun.

Gambler Moe Dalitz was one of the lucky ones.

Dalitz is arguably the most important, and least understood, gambler-developer in the history of Las Vegas. Law enforcement officials tracked his daily movements from an early age to the day of his funeral and never convicted him of so much as jaywalking. To the coppers and G-men, he was a racketeer working a legal angle.

But Dalitz was much more than that. He played an integral role in building posh casinos, then investing gambling profits into mainstream businesses. Although most known locally for building and shaping the Desert Inn and Stardust resorts, his enormous influence can be traced from Sunrise Hospital to Southern California's Rancho La Costa. It is difficult to drive far in several parts of burgeoning Southern Nevada without passing an office complex, shopping center, or housing tract he had a hand in developing.

The legendary Dalitz never will be known as anything so undramatic as a developer. After all, he was a Great Lakes racketeer during Prohibition. He sparred with crime-busting senator Estes Kefauver and won, by most accounts. Dalitz was a gambler, a casino owner, a bootlegger, an associate of Detroit's murderous Purple Gang, a driving force within Cleveland's infamous Mayfield Road

Gang, a pal of Meyer Lansky, a reputed associate of the Chicago Outfit, and a manipulator of million-dollar loans from the Teamsters pension fund—anything but a builder of shopping centers and golf courses.

But Morris Barney Dalitz, in a life that spanned eighty-nine years, was all those things. Dalitz was born in Boston on December 24, 1899. His father, Barney, moved the family to Detroit while Morris was still young. Although legend would have Moe Dalitz bootlegging while still in short pants, the reality was not quite so romantic: He worked in his father's rapidly expanding laundry business.

Dalitz's family owned Varsity Laundry in Ann Arbor, which catered to University of Michigan students. James Neff wrote in *Mobbed Up*, a book on the life of former Teamsters boss Jackie Presser, that Dalitz associated himself with the Italian-dominated Purple Gang when he tried to block the city's laundries from union organization. Purple Gang thugs were hired to protect his businesses and bust up trouble. Once free of grassroots unionists, the laundry association was able to set up its own network to force operators throughout the city to pay a form of protection.

By the mid-1930s Dalitz had been introduced to Jimmy Hoffa, the future president of the Teamsters Union and one of the men most responsible for funneling millions of dollars in loans from the trucking union's pension fund to help finance Nevada casinos and projects such as Sunrise Hospital and Rancho La Costa. The total Teamster investment in Nevada casinos is said to have exceeded $230 million.

Dalitz's business soon turned from washing shirts to supplying liquor to speakeasies and outlaw casinos from Cleveland's Mayfield Road to the heart of Kentucky. His host of partners included Morris Kleinman, Louis Rothkopf, Sam Tucker, and Maxie Diamond. It was in those years that he met and cut liquor deals with a young New York bootlegger named Meyer Lansky, who headed the murderous Bug and Meyer Mob. Their relationship, from which neither man flinched, would be the point of controversy throughout Dalitz's life. Although Lansky remained an outlaw until his 1983 death in Miami, Dalitz was a legitimate, leading citizen in Las Vegas. Although they ended up in different places geographically and politically, their starts in business were not so different: Prohibition booze, and violence.

The Cleveland liquor racket of the 1930s was not a place for the fainthearted. Alvin Sutton, the director of public safety in Cleveland, described the city in dramatic terms to the Kefauver Committee in

1951: "They had their suppliers of Canadian whiskey, and their sales-men and thugs to distribute contraband and to reap the harvest of money. Ruthless beatings, unsolved murders and shakedowns, threats and bribery came to this community as a result of gangsters' rise to power."

Thanks to the Volstead Act, rise they did.

When the business was Canadian whiskey, the methods of trans-port were precarious and varied. The hooch was shipped up the St. Lawrence River, driven by truck across the border on winding roads, and floated across the Great Lakes on barges.

"I never met a man who knew more about boats or yachts than Moe Dalitz," a longtime friend said. Moe learned all he needed to know running after midnight without floodlights.

Shipping whiskey short distances from Canada to Detroit was scarcely easier. Often trucks were loaded with cases of bootleg liquor and rolled onto makeshift barges. A shoreline lookout signaled when it was safe to cross. A green light meant the shipment was to proceed as planned.

"If they didn't get a green light, they sunk the truck and returned later for the booze," an associate of Dalitz recalled. "They'd float a buoy and go after it when the coast was clear."

Two decades later, on February 28, 1951, Kefauver attempted to pin down an older, wiser Dalitz whose legitimate business pursuits had grown tenfold.

KEFAUVER: "As a matter of fact, you had been making a great deal of money in recent years, so I suppose from your profits from one investment you would then go ahead and make an-other investment. Now, to get your investments started off you did get yourself a pretty good little nest-egg out of rum running, didn't you?"

DALITZ: "Well, I didn't inherit any money, Senator. . . . If you people wouldn't have drunk it, I wouldn't have bootlegged it."

Dalitz, Lansky, Tucker, and their associates continued to bootleg even after Prohibition was repealed in 1933. Through the Molaska Corporation, the increasingly notorious fellows supplied powdered molasses to illegal distilleries from Ohio to New Jersey, according to *Little Man: Meyer Lansky and the Gangster Life*, a critical biography of Lansky written by Robert Lacey.

Booze was not the only game the young Dalitz played during Prohibition. Outside Cincinnati, his Mound Club and Pettibone Club casinos operated free of government interference. Near Youngstown, Ohio, the Jungle Inn was the center of the action. Across the Ohio River from Cincinnati, the Beverly Hills Club and the Lookout House were notorious joints that managed to do business free of law enforcement scrutiny.

An illegal dog track near Dayton, Kentucky, did not work out so well for Dalitz. The greyhounds made so much noise that local authorities were compelled to investigate. The district attorney shut down the track after thirteen days. "Not even Moe Dalitz could operate an illegal dog track without attracting the attention of the authorities," Wallace Turner wrote in his 1965 book, *Gamblers' Money*.

Dalitz's casinos remained as popular with civic leaders and chamber of commerce members as they were with less influential customers—a fact he often would point out to those who were naïvely critical of casinos. "How was I to know those gambling joints were illegal?" Dalitz once quipped to a friend. "There were so many judges and politicians at them, I figured they had to be all right."

The young Dalitz hardly lacked for legitimate businesses, however. In the 1920s and 1930s Dalitz held an interest in the Michigan Industrial Laundry Company in Detroit and the Pioneer Linen Supply Company in Cleveland and percentages in the Reliance Steel Company and the Detroit Steel Company. Other holdings included Milco Sales, Dalitz Realty, Berdene Realty, Liberty Ice Cream Company, and even a piece of the Chicago & Rock Island Railroad Company. During World War II, in which he served as a 2nd lieutenant in the Army, Dalitz put his laundry expertise to use.

Although Dalitz would be known chiefly as a gambler until his death in 1989, the record clearly shows a variety of business investments and an uncanny sense of the marketplace. Like all good businessmen, he knew when to invest and when to divest. He demonstrated this business sense in Cuba in the late 1950s.

Gambling was legal in Havana, but the island's politics were changing dramatically. Dalitz was surrounded by friends and investors at the Nacional Hotel, whose chief financial operator was Lansky. Dalitz and his Cleveland partners were poised to take over the Nacional once Lansky completed his glitzy Havana Riviera, but their dreams were dashed when Fulgencio Batista was ousted by Fidel Castro. Also, Nevada's gaming authorities, fearing federal intervention in Las Vegas casinos, had grown weary of the Cuban connection.

"Came 1958 and the Cleveland Syndicate decided to pull out of Havana," veteran organized crime writer Hank Messick wrote in *Syndicate Abroad*, a book on the spread of casino gambling to the Bahamas. "Officially, they were forced to sell the Casino Internacional because Nevada authorities decided their casinos shouldn't be linked—on record, anyway, with Havana."

Investors who failed to get out of Cuba in time were financially devastated. One man who lost a small fortune was Tampa mob boss Santo Trafficante. The widely diversified Dalitz only dabbled in Havana. His first love, and the respectability he craved, lay more than three thousand miles west in a place where gambling was legal and gamblers were not outlaws but entrepreneurs. Las Vegas was in its Golden Age, and Dalitz was a key player through his involvement with the Desert Inn and Stardust hotels.

Reno's Riverside Hotel was almost the site of Dalitz's first casino acquisition. In 1949 a crap dealer and bar owner with big ideas convinced Dalitz to invest elsewhere. Wilbur Clark had dreamed up an idea for a palatial casino resort, the Desert Inn—a name he borrowed from a motel in Palm Springs. Starting in 1947 he scraped together a $250,000 grubstake but was millions short of the money he needed to see his idea become a reality. Instead of abandoning the project or, worse, watching someone steal it out from under him, Clark met with a group of Cleveland investors—Dalitz, Kleinman, Tucker, and Thomas McGinty—and saved his vision. The Cleveland group acquired 74 percent of the Desert Inn; the rest went to Clark.

"It was Wilbur's dream. It was his idea. My husband had the foresight. He worked hard to get the hotel together. He always said the bubble would never burst in Las Vegas, and he was right," Clark's widow, Toni Clark, remembered as she sat in her home at the Desert Inn Country Club early in 1994. "The Desert Inn was all class then. People used to dress every night. It was a very glamorous place. It was a winner from the day it opened. Everybody loved being there."

Unlike some business arrangements of the day, the agreement between Clark and the Cleveland group was amiable as well as profitable. Dalitz's understated manner helped ensure a smooth-running operation.

"He was a generous man, and a kind man," Toni Clark said. "He was there with everybody every day. Moe could talk about everything. He was a very smart, brilliant man."

The Desert Inn, which Dalitz and company eventually sold to

Howard Hughes, was more than a hotel and casino; it was a place to experiment with a golf country club theme Dalitz would repeat on several occasions throughout his life. In 1952 the Desert Inn Country Club was the stage for an exclusive event in which only PGA Tour winners could qualify: the Tournament of Champions. For sixteen years the national press gave the tournament, and Las Vegas, enormous attention. Some proceeds from the event benefited the Damon Runyon Cancer Fund, and that made the Strip look all the better. The same technique proved successful at the Stardust Golf Course, which from 1961 through 1966 played host to the LPGA Championship.

Although younger casino operators are credited with revolutionizing the marketing of Las Vegas, history shows Dalitz clearly was a visionary in converting happy customers into profits.

Dalitz's success did not shield him from investigative reporters and critics from beyond Las Vegas. To the outside world, he remained a racketeer.

"In a recent interview, Ed Reid was stunned when Dalitz burst into tears," Ovid Demaris and Ed Reid wrote in *The Green Felt Jungle*.

"Why, why," he implored, his arms rising in supplication, the tears streaming from his hard little eyes, "why are they persecuting me?"

"Who?" Reid inquired.

"Them. All of them! I've fought hoodlums all my life. What are they trying to do to me?"

What eventually will happen to Dalitz may be very similar to what happened to a number of Dalitz's competitors in the old days, as Moe well knows. Meanwhile, to a corps of uninitiated magazine writers, Moe still palms himself off as a big shot and dispenses his two-bit philosophy on morality. . . . Moe said: "Let's say gambling isn't moral. Neither is drinking to excess. I think Las Vegas has given people lots of fun. Sure, some will get hurt. But listen, they can go to Atlantic City and get into more danger in a crap game than here, where there's supervision."

In *Gamblers' Money*, Turner borrowed heavily from the Kefauver Committee: "Various elements of officialdom look on Dalitz as a known quantity, a gambler they can figure is less likely to be a part of some terrible criminal conspiracy. Dalitz is widely respected among observers of the gambling scene. The Desert Inn management group is a sort of aristocracy among the gamblers who control the casinos in Las Vegas.

"In Cleveland Moe Dalitz was a bootlegger; but in Las Vegas he stands as an elder statesman of what they call the 'gaming industry.'"

Had Dalitz been content to develop the Desert Inn, he may have faded into Las Vegas history with many of the other earlier casino bosses. Instead, he became a giant.

In 1958 Tony Cornero's Stardust Hotel was unfinished, and builder Jack "Jake the Barber" Factor was without the means to complete the job. Dalitz and his investment group seized the deal, arranged the financing through various means—including $8 million from the Teamsters pension fund and Emprise Corporation patriarch Louis Jacobs—and added it to their list of Las Vegas holdings. Rumors that skimmed profits from the casino were being divided by a variety of mob families persisted from the start of business. Nearly a quarter century later, a group of organized crime figures from Chicago, Cleveland, Milwaukee, and Kansas City would receive long prison sentences after being convicted of casino skimming. By then, Dalitz officially had severed his ties with the Stardust.

Law enforcement and mob informants, including former Teamsters president Jackie Presser, believed Dalitz was far more than a mere casino operator. Several studies of organized crime make reference to Dalitz's notorious status.

"The Cleveland Mob maintained strong ties to Las Vegas and worked at making new ones," Neff wrote in *Mobbed Up*. "The Mafia's ruling commission had declared Las Vegas an open city, so each crime family was entitled to stake out different casinos as their exclusive territory. The Cleveland family got in early with the Desert Inn. Its principal owner, Moe Dalitz, served as an informal referee in territorial disputes among the different Mafia crews, as Jackie [Presser] informed the FBI in 1978."

Although the Stardust would be the subject of persistent law enforcement scrutiny, for many years it also was one of the most popular and progressive properties on the burgeoning Strip. Its one thousand rooms rented for $6 a night; its Lido de Paris can-can show, with its French showgirls and elaborate sets, revolutionized Las Vegas entertainment. "We planned a variety-type show where we could have ice skating one moment and a full production number in another," Dalitz said in 1983.

The property at 301 Fremont, which Dalitz and company would

buy and sell more than once before it would be the site of the Sundance Hotel (now Fitzgerald's), is another example of his developer's vision.

It was Dalitz who helped arrange for the purchase of the land on which the Las Vegas Convention Center would stand. Dalitz worked closely with Joe W. Brown Sr., who owned the land and conveyed it for use as a convention facility. Today, Joe W. Brown Drive runs at the back of the Las Vegas Convention Center. Early county officials as well as Dalitz's former partners credit him with developing the idea of catering to conventioneers, an act that alone would have given him a place in local history.

With a consistent source of financing through the Teamsters and its local lending conduit the Bank of Las Vegas (later Valley Bank), Dalitz had plenty of venture capital. After assembling a group of loyal, dynamic partners—Irwin Molasky, Allard Roen, and Merv Adelson—and forming what now is known as Paradise Development, his empire was poised for rapid expansion. Sunrise Hospital was built in 1959 with the first of several $1 million Teamsters loans. The Winterwood Golf Course, centerpiece for a sprawling housing development, opened in 1965 and marked the start of the city's perennial housing boom. The Las Vegas Country Club was built on a 640-acre tract of real estate previously owned by Joe Brown. Paradise Development surrounded the country club with homes, apartments, and shopping centers. The Boulevard Mall was the first super shopping complex in Las Vegas.

While other of his associates were tracked by the law in illegal jurisdictions, Dalitz surrounded himself with fresh air and friends and began investing in the community. Even the cynical Kefauver admitted as much back in 1951: "They have been engaged in rum running and other types of activities, gambling and so forth, and then go into legitimate businesses or get into whatever they can. Of course, gaining respectability as they go along, or trying to."

But how did a former bootlegger and illegal casino operator, who submitted to scrutiny by the celebrated Kefauver Committee—which went a long way toward solidifying the image of Lansky as a criminal mastermind—go about gaining respectability? Dalitz took the same approach that many other American capitalists did: He donated generously to political causes and wrapped himself in the tailored suit of corporate citizenship.

Moe Dalitz (center) with Al Sachs (left) and Herb Tobman (right), in 1981.
(Courtesy Las Vegas News Bureau)

Dalitz was quietly influential with Nevada's elected leaders a generation before anyone spoke of the nuances of political science. Acting on behalf of Dalitz and lesser casino men, Nevada senator Pat McCarran worked long hours to attempt to slow Estes Kefauver's sensational rackets investigation. Three decades later, Senator Paul Laxalt gave his impression of his political benefactor: "My general opinion of him, as a citizen of Nevada, is favorable. He's been a good citizen, and his dealings with gaming authorities over the years . . . they too have been favorable."

Part of that favorable reading was a result of Dalitz's undeniable charity. He truly was fond of Las Vegas and its people, many of whom, like him, had traveled to the desert in search of a chance to reinvent themselves.

"He never turned me down for anything charitable," said former Stardust Hotel general manager Herb Tobman, who proudly recalls meeting, in 1970, the man he refers to as Mr. Las Vegas: "I was in awe of meeting him. As far as I'm concerned he was a great man. . . . Moe's charity is legendary around this town. There has never been a greater influence on this city."

Roen, a multimillionaire whose career skyrocketed after joining Dalitz in Paradise Development, echoed Tobman's sentiment: "He was always in the forefront of charitable and civic drives. I to this day do not remember him ever turning a charity down. It was always his contention Las Vegas has been good to us, we want to give something back to Las Vegas."

Dalitz was named Humanitarian of the Year by the American Cancer Research Center and Hospital in 1976. In 1982 he received the Torch of Liberty Award by the Anti-Defamation League of B'nai B'rith. In 1979 he set up the Moe Dalitz Charitable Remainder Unitrust, a million-dollar fund to be divided upon his death. When Dalitz died a decade later, fourteen nonprofit organizations split a $1.3-million fund. The United Way was handed a check for $670,114. The Las Vegas Variety Club received $268,045; the City of Hope and the *Las Vegas Sun* Camp Fund received $67,011 each. From the Salvation Army to the National Parkinson's Foundation, the Saint Jude's Ranch orphanage to the Opportunity Village work center for handicapped adults, the money was generously divided.

"Moe was always such a gentleman," Las Vegas advertising executive Marydean Martin said. "He gave back to the community. When the Maude Frazier Building [at the University of Nevada, Las Vegas] was built, it had no furniture. He bought all the furniture and didn't want anybody to know about it. He was that kind of person."

Although history shows he maintained associations with many notorious characters, and law enforcement authorities believed that profits from his casinos found their way into the pockets of La Cosa Nostra, Dalitz defined himself differently. "I was never a member of any gang," he said in a 1975 interview. "I never considered myself a gangster or a mobster. I was always in the business that threw me into meeting all kinds of people."

In the 1950s one of those people was Irwin Molasky. Their relationship defined the notion of venture capital. Dalitz had plenty of capital. Molasky and Adelson provided the ventures. The result was a wide corridor of development stretching across much of the Las Vegas Valley.

"Moe was an innovative thinker," Molasky recalled. "He said, 'Let's build a golf course. Give them something else.' He was a good thinker. He was a good investor. Moe never went against the tables. He gambled on people. He was a keen observer of character. It was one of his long suits."

Some of the people he met, including Lanksy and Hoffa, wound up in a *Penthouse* exposé, by Lowell Bergman and Jeff Garth, on Califor-nia's 5,600-acre Rancho La Costa Country Club south of Los Ange-les. La Costa was financed with Teamsters pension fund loans and was developed by Dalitz and his partners. "La Costa: Syndicate in the Sun" resulted in a half-billion-dollar libel suit against the magazine and the freelance writers for describing the multimillion-dollar development as a playground for the mob. The article stated that La Costa was the dream project of Meyer Lansky. The plaintiffs included Dalitz, Roen, and Molasky. After months of litigation, the suit was resolved in the magazine's favor. If the article had been recklessly researched in places, a court ruled it had not demonstrably libeled Dalitz and his younger partners.

Not long after the article was published and the lawsuit broke, Dalitz became the subject of a state Gaming Control Board suitabil-ity investigation. Dalitz, the fellow who had been licensed to oper-ate casinos under a grandfather clause and who was now in his eight-ies, suddenly found himself the subject of investigative scrutiny. Mob informant Aladena "Jimmy the Weasel" Fratianno accused Dalitz of being "owned" by the Chicago Outfit. Although not founded in fact, such allegations only reinforced what some people and much of law enforcement suspected for generations: that Dalitz, who had survived America's bloody bootlegging era and intense federal scru-tiny and had emerged as a master developer of the fastest-growing city in the country, was not his own man. There was one problem with that theory: Not even everyone in the mob shared it. New Jersey mob boss Angelo "Gyp" DeCarlo had just the opposite impression. His awe of Dalitz's success was recorded in a wire-tapped conversation. Dalitz had powerful associates, including those who had access to the Teamsters Central States Southeast and Southwest Area Pension Fund, but was nevertheless a power unto himself. Dalitz tapped the Teamsters like no other Las Vegan. As one longtime acquaintance carefully put it, "If Moe told them to make somebody a loan, they made the loan."

There was another side of Dalitz, a side that reflects his rough-and-tumble days and is perhaps best illustrated by the often-re-peated story of his showdown with heavyweight champion Charles "Sonny" Liston. When threatened, the slight, pleasant Dalitz was capable of intimidating almost anyone. As the story goes, Dalitz was in the dining room of the Beverly Rodeo Hotel in Hollywood when

Liston approached. Liston had been drinking and had words with the sixty-four-year-old Dalitz. When Liston raised his ham-sized fist, the soft-spoken Dalitz bristled.

"If you hit me, nigger, you'd better kill me, because if you don't, I'll make one telephone call and you'll be dead in twenty-four hours."

The mob-owned champ was stunned, dropped his fist, and immediately checked out of the hotel. Moe Dalitz, then retirement age, stopped Liston faster than had any opponent.

In an interview, Dalitz recalled his early days with a simple line: "Tough times call for tough people." Obviously, he remained tough long after departing Cleveland.

For all his notoriety, Dalitz never was convicted of a major crime. He was indicted for bootlegging in Buffalo in 1930 and for tax evasion in Los Angeles in 1965. Both charges were dismissed.

"Moe never did nothing wrong that the government could get him for," said one friend of the Las Vegas patriarch. If gambling was legal and taxable, Moe Dalitz would pay his share.

At La Costa, where whispering visitors were awed by an occasional Dalitz sighting, he was sharing lunch one day with Las Vegas advertising executive Marydean Martin, who handled public relations for Paradise Development. It was during the *Penthouse* libel trial, and Dalitz reflected about his reluctant role as media devil.

"Moe almost never complained, but he was feeling down. He said, 'I'll bet your grandpa drank whiskey,' and I said that he did," Martin recalled. "'I'm the guy who made the whiskey, and I'm considered the bad guy. When does the time ever come that you're forgiven?'

"I said, 'I don't know.' It was one of the very few times he ever said anything about it," Martin said.

People who knew Dalitz return time and again to his sense of humor, his love for his daughter, Susan, his fascination with mountain-lion hunting and sport fishing. The iron-handed former bootlegger, the man who once intimidated a heavyweight champion with a single sentence, the fellow who knocked around with the most notorious names in the history of organized crime, lived nearly nine decades, drove a canary-yellow Volkswagen Beetle through the streets of Las Vegas, and was content to sit alone at a small table in the corner of the restaurant at the Las Vegas Country Club—a place he was instrumental in developing. Although he could afford to travel anywhere,

Dalitz customized a Greyhound bus and spent weeks touring the nation. The man commonly called "first among equals of the Cleveland Mob" professed an undying love for his country.

"He tried to be low-profile, believe it or not," Molasky said. "These dimestore novels and myths written about him . . . he was tarnished with that all of his life."

In rare interviews, Dalitz was philosophical about his rise from laundry boy to multimillionaire. "When I left home it was during Prohibition in Ann Arbor, Michigan, and I went into the liquor business while it was illegal," he said. "Then when the Repeal came along, we went into the casino business in Kentucky and Ohio where it was illegal. I learned everything I know there."

He applied that knowledge in Las Vegas, the desert place where he found a fresh start and the respect of a community he was instrumental in building. In the process, he made a different kind of history.

When Moe Dalitz died, more than three hundred mourners attended his funeral service. In the audience were former governors, judges, sheriffs, casino men, and no doubt a few FBI agents. In death, Dalitz was praised as a man of great vision and charity. He had crossed the desert, defied the odds with which he was so familiar, and carved out his own brand of paradise.

The fact that this final gathering was the subject of law enforcement surveillance was not mentioned. After all those years, the coppers were still trying to solve the mystery of Moe Dalitz.

Benny Binion: He Who Has the Gold Makes the Rules

A. D. Hopkins

In 1946 Texas seemed too hot for Benny Binion. He packed his wife and five kids and his cash into a Cadillac and took a "vacation" to the Southern Nevada desert, which seemed, in the sense that concerned Binion, as cool as life would ever get.

He found here an opportunity made for a man of his talents. And with the exception of three and one-half years spent at Leavenworth Penitentiary, Binion called Las Vegas home the rest of his long life. For nearly forty-four years, Binion defined high-limit gambling. Binion and his wife and his sons invented tournament gambling as it is known today, resuscitated the dying game of craps by changing the rules, and fostered a national image of Las Vegas that was simultaneously sinful, dangerous, and user-friendly.

Until a year or two before his death on Christmas Day in 1989, Binion was a familiar sight in Binion's Horseshoe Club. The first thing you noticed about him as he entered from the parking lot was his white cowboy hat, worn cocked forward like gunfighters sometimes wore them to make sure the sun was not in their eyes when it counted. From under the brim gazed piercing blue eyes, locked in a sizing-you-up squint. His carried his head unusually erect, and on his round face he wore an almost-permanent, cocky smile. Not particularly tall, he was pudgy but powerfully built in the chest and shoulders, with the short, sturdy neck that resists auto accidents and uppercuts. He wore western-cut suits of gray and other conservative colors, but the buttons on his shirts were made of real gold coins, and his favorite overcoat was of buffalo hide, with the fur on. He did not like neckties and did not shave every day.

His eyes never seemed to quit moving, darting about the casino as he walked through, darting about the casino's restaurant as he sat alone, sometimes for hours, drumming his fingers on the table. "We would be walking through the casino," said Harry Claiborne, who was Binion's friend and his lawyer for thirty years before becoming a federal judge in 1978. "We'd be talking about something important, and he would see something wrong at a table, and go over and talk to the pit boss. Then he'd come back and pick up the conversation in a way that showed he hadn't lost track of it. I never knew anybody else who could do that."

Binion was a study in contradictions. His reputation as a killer, which he acquired in his youth, followed him to his grave in 1989; but by then he had gained the active affection of thousands of Las Vegans, who saw also a philanthropist, a generous and fair employer, and a brilliant innovator in the city's key industry. Binion and his wife, Teddy Jane, owned a large home, built in cattle-baron style of stone and timber, but spent most of their last three decades in a modest apartment over their casino. Surviving into an age when resorts were usually run from corporate offices, Binion operated mostly from that restaurant booth, where virtually anybody could get at least a minute of his time. He was on speaking terms with presidents and mafiosi, and at any given moment the man sitting opposite him might be a senator or a judge or simply a broken-down cowboy who could say something perceptive about horses.

Binion's Horseshoe, the Fremont Street operation he began in 1951, exhibited the same democracy that characterized Binion himself. Binion's has seen the biggest bets in casino history, but they were not made in some private second-story casino where oil princes wager undisturbed by the presence of peasants. They were made out on the everyday green table, with ordinary folk looking on, and the public nature of these events has cemented their stories like gems into the rich metal of American legend. It can be documented that a Japanese investor dropped millions at the Dunes, but when the kid put a suitcase full of money on the don't-pass line at Binion's, or bet $1 million on a comeout roll, somebody just like you probably saw it.

"He was an extraordinary person his whole life," said Binion's son, Ted, who followed him into the casino business. "My aunt is as

Horseshoe owner Benny Binion (right) with actor Chill Wills and an unidentified reveler at a downtown block party, 1968. (Courtesy Las Vegas News Bureau)

far as I know the only person still alive who knew Daddy when he was a little boy. And she told me that by the time he was eight years old everybody around there knew he was special, and by the time he was twelve, grown people would ask him for advice!"

Binion's personality was shaped by a childhood unusual even for a Texan born in 1904. "I never went to school, not even grade school, because I was sick a lot as a kid," Binion told an interviewer in the 1970s. "I suppose if I had it to do over again, I would almost certainly be a gambler again, because there's nothing else an ignorant man can do." Asked by the same interviewer what he might have become with an education, he grinned and said, "There's more than one kind of education, and maybe I prefer the one I got."

The Binions were from Grayson County, about sixty miles north of Dallas, and the family business was trading stock, mostly horses and mules. Because of little Benny's repeated bouts with pneumonia, his family made the desperate decision to let him travel with his father, hoping the fresh air and robust horseback life would heal his lungs. "And from a real small kid, I'd go with horse traders, and became a pretty good horse trader," Binion told a University of Nevada oral historian in 1976. "They all traveled in wagons, and they had some of the wagons fixed kinda like trailer houses now. . . . So they had known campin' places. And they'd all get together, and sometime there'd be ten or fifteen there at the time. So they'd gamble, and play cards, and do this, that, and the other, and trade horses."

Benny's father, however, was not good at holding on to money. "So Benny Binion, when he was about fourteen or fifteen, became the breadwinner and kind of the head of his family," said his son Jack, who is president of Binion's Horseshoe and habitually speaks of his own father using both first and last names.

After that, nobody had authority over Benny Binion, so he did as he saw fit. The results quickly spawned a legend. "He was driving a Model T by a church parking lot when a car came out and hit his," recounted Ted Binion. "Two guys got real pushy with him and came at him both together. He saw he couldn't lick them both so he grabbed a piece of the bumper that broke off when their car hit his, and he hit them both with it, and broke something. And then some of their friends come on to help them, and they kept coming till there was fourteen of them with broken bones. That got written up in the newspaper, and that's when he actually got to be famous."

Jack, however, says that while his father's legend was mostly about his toughness, "he wasn't really all that tough a guy. He was, " Jack said, pausing to search for a word, "a very *practical* man. He got where he wanted to go on the basis of his personality.

"I'm going to tell you the truth about Benny Binion," said Jack. "He just liked people more than other people like people. He worked hard to make them like him. When he met somebody, he would ask questions, try to find some common ground, some interest they shared.

"He moved to El Paso when he was eighteen," said Jack. "He had a gravel wagon and some mules, and was spreading gravel on this parking lot for Model T Fords. He figured out they were bootlegging out of the booth where you paid for your parking. So Benny Binion went to Oklahoma and got a load of whiskey. And he'd come down and go to work about five in the evening. Some guy would come up and say he was looking for Joe, and Benny Binion would say 'I'll take care of you,' and sell them his own liquor. He didn't have any association with the bootleg concern that had built up the business, but the customers assumed he did.

"Another time he got locked up for liquor. They made him a trusty. One day they told him to go get judge so-and-so some liquor out of the evidence vault. I guess the police had grabbed some particularly good stuff in a raid.

"So Benny Binion went and made an imprint of the key. Sent it out and had a key made. Then he got the jailer drunk, and when the jailer went to sleep, he called up a friend with a truck, got some of the other trusties to help load it, and stole a truckload of liquor right out of the jail. They had to dismiss a bunch of cases because the evidence disappeared. And they never figured out where it went."

In the early 1930s Binion was twice convicted for bootlegging, and he told a federal judge he would quit the liquor business if the judge would not send him to prison. "Bootlegging was going out anyway," said Jack. "So he started the numbers business." It was the same sort of illegal lottery that became common in all big cities before state governments declared the racket morally pure and took it over. In Dallas it was called "policy." The name was a euphemism derived from the practice, once common in poor neighborhoods, of paying for a small insurance policy with a few coins a week.

About 1936, a political climate of tolerance emerged in Dallas, primarily because local powers thirsted to host the Texas Centennial and a reputation as a swinging town was considered necessary to obtaining it. Dallas did get the Centennial celebration, and Binion expanded into craps. "We used to operate in hotel rooms, because it was less conspicuous," Binion said years later. "Had craps tables made up in crates that looked like bed crates, and hotels always had beds coming in and out. If we had half hour's notice we were going to be raided, we could clear it out." Getting caught was not such a tragedy, either. Fines were a cost of doing business.

"What made Dad so successful was there was so much money around," Ted relates. "That 45-by-10-mile oilfield at Beaumont was said to be half the world's oil supply at the time. So they didn't really have a Depression. And the guys that owned it and profited from it liked to gamble high. Plus, a lot of people from other parts of the country, professional gamblers and bookmakers, liked to come down there. They came because Dad would run a high limit, and also because he was known to run honest games. And also because Dallas itself [was] considered just a good place to go for a vacation."

The cash flow continued through World War II, when GI payrolls were spent on good times. However, Binion's Dallas businesses were nerve-racking and dangerous. There was more loose money in a good crap game than in many a bank, and hijackers came to get it. Protecting the games required hiring men who were handy with guns and willing to use them. But these men themselves sometimes became ambitious.

Benny protected himself, in those years. He carried a .45 automatic for each hand, and in a pocket he carried a .38 S&W Terrier, a compact double-action revolver. The hammer spur on the Terrier had been cut off so it would not catch on clothes and could be whipped out of a pocket quite suddenly. In later years Benny was content with one gun, so long as it was a Colt Commander .45, and in the twilight of his life he carried only a small .22 Magnum revolver. But there was always a five-shot, semiautomatic shotgun handy, in his car or his golf bag. The scattergun barrel was cut off to fourteen inches, but it was legally registered with the federal government.

In 1931 Binion and a bootlegger were seated on a log arguing. "It was over this guy stealing whiskey, something like that," said Ted. "This guy was a real badman, had a reputation for killing people by stabbing them. He stood up real quick and Dad felt like he was going to stab him and he rolled back off the log, pulled his gun, and shot upward from the ground. Hit him through the neck and killed him.

"Dad felt it was self-defense, that the guy was really going to stab him. But the guy hadn't pulled the knife yet, even though he did have one. So Dad was convicted of first-degree murder, but he only got two years suspended because the guy's reputation was so bad."

In 1936 Binion killed a rival numbers operator, Ben Frieden. "I was told that Dad was walking down the street and Ben called him over to his car. Dad said Ben was smiling. As Dad came up real close to him Ben upped his gun; he'd had it hidden behind the door. Dad threw up his arm, I guess instinctively as if it could stop a bullet, and Ben Frieden shot him in the armpit. He grabbed the cylinder of Ben Frieden's gun so it wouldn't turn and wouldn't shoot again." Holding on for his life, Binion whipped out the .38 Terrier and shot Frieden dead.

"He told me he never thought about grabbing the cylinder of a revolver before, that it just came to him to do it," said Ted. "He said that when he saw the pistol all he could think about was how much he'd like to run."

This time Benny was found innocent because he acted in self-defense.

Binion was never officially connected to any other killing. But gang war was foreshadowed by the 1938 killing of Sam Murray, and it broke out in earnest in 1946. As friends, partners, former partners, and competitors began to die violently and with regularity, a reform administration promised an end to the rackets they were fighting over. That is when Benny packed his suitcases full of cash and brought his family to Las Vegas.

"I don't even remember how much money I brought," Benny said once, "but I made sure there was enough." Jack remembered that a particular suitcase was treated with special care on that trip. "I was about ten then and I couldn't lift that suitcase," Jack said. "I didn't know what was in it. The only one who did, other than my parents, was my older sister, who was about fourteen. If the hotel caught fire she was supposed to get that suitcase out."

Benny had picked a good time to leave. Back in Dallas, at least a dozen attempts were made on the life of gambler Herbert Noble, who was trying to expand his own turf. Noble did not take kindly to these murder attempts, and some who sought to kill him wound up dead themselves. When Noble's wife was killed by a car bomb meant for him, Noble thought Binion was responsible and dreamed of terrible vengeance. Already a pilot, he bought an airplane, equipped it with bomb racks, and acquired two large bombs—one high explosive, and one incendiary. He had an aviation map with the Binion family residence, on West Bonanza Road, marked on it. Noble never made his bomb run, though, because a policeman, intending to question Noble about another matter, visited his ranch unexpectedly and caught Noble preparing the plane. Noble was finally killed in 1951 by a bomb buried in front of his mailbox.

Binion always denied responsibility for Noble's killing and the attempts that preceded it, particularly the bombing that killed Mildred Noble. Some thirty years after the killing, reminiscing over a beer at his restaurant table-*cum*-office, the aging Binion denied it to the author of this chapter. "By then, taking over Dallas was the last thing I wanted to do," said Binion. "When I got up here and saw how good things could be here, I said to myself, 'Let 'em have Texas.'"

"So who do you reckon was trying to get him?" asked the journalist. "What that was really about, was . . ."

Binion was interrupted by a tall, middle-aged man wearing a cowboy hat with a handful of chicken feathers, dyed in Easter-egg colors, stuck behind the hatband. He wore a western-cut suit from Taiwan. "I've heard of you for years and I just wanted to tell people I shook your hand," said the drugstore cowboy. He talked a while more, without saying anything at all, while Benny nodded agreeably.

When the visitor finally left, I tried to broach the subject again, but Binion's reminiscent mood had passed. He set his grizzled jaw and responded with a silent, slow shake of the head, a mannerism that always meant, "I ain't gonna talk about it."

In early 1947 Binion became partners with J. Kell Houssels Sr. in the Las Vegas Club on Fremont Street. "Kell was about the biggest landowner and operator out here at the time, and had a piece of everything," said Jack. "He was a dead serious guy, just the opposite of Dad, but he liked Kell all his life."

Binion did not get along so well with some other early casino operators. The primary point of difference, explained his sons, was that competing with Binion forced casino operators to get into the gambling business. He kept raising the house limits.

"Up till that time," said Jack, "gambling around here had been more of a taking business." The odds always favor the house, but when the limits are low, the house has an additional and substantial advantage.

"But Daddy had been used to dealing high," said Ted Binion. "At his better places, even way back in the '30s and '40s, he was dealing $200 and $400. And a lot of his best customers came to him for that very reason." The higher limit gave customers what Binion always called "a lot of gamble for their money."

At the Horseshoe, which opened in 1951, Binion had a limit of $500 on crap games, while the rest of the town would not take a bet over $50.

All gamblers dream of hitting a hot streak and snowballing a small stake into a large one. When playing the "pass" line at craps, which pays even money, many a player will double his bet each time he wins. Winning a $10 bet, he will bet $20—his original $10 and the $10 he won. If he wins that time he will bet his entire $40. But until Binion raised the limits, the player could not have doubled his bet again: $50 was the maximum bet. Even if he enjoyed a run of seven straight winning bets, he could have won only $270.

Under Binion's $500 limits, the same run of luck would have let him win $1,130.

"A lot of 'em felt you shouldn't let a guy beat you like that with your own money," Benny Binion explained in the 1970s. "But it isn't your money. Quick as he's won it from you, it's his money, and you're trying to win it from him."

How mad did it make his competitors?

"One of 'em actually threatened his life over it," said Ted. "He was going to raise the keno limit to $500. Davie Berman said if he raised it, he'd kill him!

"And you know what Dad said? He said, 'Well, I believe I'll deal $200 a while longer.' He said there wasn't no doubt Berman would've done it. Berman was one of the guys who came into the Flamingo with Siegel, and he was a known killer. Wasn't Siegel, or none of them guys, tough like Berman!

"So six months later, Dad raised it anyway."

Ted thinks that some condition probably changed to allow that—perhaps a different attitude among the faction Berman represented—but Benny never told him what had altered. He suggests that Berman would not have made the death threat unless he was himself out of alternatives, and Benny knew better than to challenge a man with his back to the wall.

Other operators fought in different fashions. "He never had any trouble getting licensed at first," said Harry Claiborne, Binion's lawyer. "But there was a lot of trouble when it came time to renew it. That was just about the time he had started double odds on craps, and I have no doubt there was a connection."

"Double odds" were another better deal for the customer. Once the comeout roll has established the point a shooter must try to make, any player with a bet on the pass line may put up an additional bet that the player will make his point before sevening out. (A player with a bet on the don't-pass line may similarly make an additional bet that the shooter will not make his point.) It is called an "odds" bet because it is the only bet a casino ever pays at true odds—that is, in direct proportion to the risk involved. Since this is the least risky bet possible, every crapshooter who understands the game will bet all he can at odds. Therefore the amount of the odds bet is limited according to the size of the original bet on the passline.

Binion realized that no matter how much he had to pay off in odds bets, he would collect just as much in the long run. So he let gamblers bet twice as much as customary at true odds. This brought gamblers to the table in droves, vying for a few inches of passline to lay down bets on which Benny *would* collect a little more than he would pay out.

"Benny Binion was the man who put the gamble into Las Vegas," said Bill Friedman, who wrote the first book on casino management and managed one himself. "From the day they arrived the Binions pushed the limits up, and they still do."

Many other casinos have followed the Binion lead on limits and craps odds, but the Binions are still known for "giving a lot of gamble for the money"—more, in fact, than any other casino operation. Their original double-odds practice has been liberalized, step by step, to ten-times-odds at this writing. Since the house limit is $10,000 on line bets, a player may bet $100,000 at odds. Blackjack limit is $25,000, and you can play all six hands on the table. Baccarat is $25,000.

Leo Lewis, a Gold Coast executive who worked for the Binions in the 1960s, repeated a sentence he learned there by rote: "Sir, your first bet is your limit." It meant a player could bet any amount, so long as he did it immediately. The current offer is that one can bet $1 million on the first bet.

William Lee Bergstrom took the Binions at their word and found it good. Back in 1980, Bergstrom asked the Binions if he could bet $1 million if he could get it together. The Binions took him seriously, for he had dropped $47,000 in the casino that very day. They said he could bet a million if he could get it.

A few months later he showed up. He had not been able to get $1 million, but he would like to bet $777,000. It took a suitcase to carry the money, and he had another suitcase to carry away the money if he won.

Ted Binion, who was then casino manager at Binion's, approved the bet, and Bergstrom laid the money on the don't-pass line. The woman holding the dice rolled a five-ace, establishing six as her point. Then she rolled a five-four, and then a five-two, seveningout in three rolls. So Bergstrom the don't-bettor won his bet. He packed another $777,000 into the empty suitcase, and Ted Binion escorted him personally to his car.

Bergstrom would be back. "He bet that $777,000 and won," recalled Ted Binion in 1994. "Some time later he bet $590,000 and [won] it; $190,000 and [won] it; $90,000 and [won] it.

"Then he bet a million and lost it.

"He put the million on deposit at [the] cage. And I said you can bet it anywhere. He run a few feet ahead, up to a crap table, put his finger on the table and said, '$1 millon on the don't-pass!' The shooter picked up the dice and looked at me and said 'Is this on the square?'

"I said it was. And he rolled. It was the comeout roll so the shooter wanted a seven, and they come ace-six. It was all over in one roll.

"I felt like electricity run through me.

"And Bergstrom pulled his finger off that table like it was on fire!"

Three months later, Bergstrom committed suicide in a Strip hotel room. "But you know, he was still [a] $400,000 winner when he quit," pointed out Ted Binion. "Fact was, I knew him pretty well by then, and his reasons for suicide were more romantic than financial."

There is some kind of story behind every gambler who risks six-figure amounts, says Ted. There was Bernard Gould Murphy, an heir to the fortune originally built by railroad tycoon Jay Gould. "Murphy owned all kinds of buildings and the Union Pacific Railroad, or a great deal of it. He had hung around this town till he was sixty-eight years old, and never made a bet. Then he found out he had cancer, and took off and bet $6 [million] or $7 million. He was worth a lot more than that, but I believe that was all the ready cash he could put his hands on, so you could say that was kind of a suicide trip for him. But he did not in fact commit suicide; cancer killed him.

"He had been staying at the Sands for eleven years, before he decided to bet. And he wanted to put $55,000 on the don't line. And they said '*Bull shit!!*'" So he tried at Caesars, and then the Stardust. And a busboy steps up and says if you want to bet high, why don't you go to the Horseshoe?

"And this old sonofabitch comes up to dad wearing a bathrobe and slippers. Dad and him sat at a 21 table and talked about fifteen minutes. Then Dad come over and said, 'See that guy over there? Give him all the money he wants. He'll pay Tuesday.' I mean, this guy looked like a bum.

"He [lost] $875,000 that week. And he paid Tuesday.

"Dad could tell, just talking to people a very short time, whether they were who they said, whether they would do what they said. He made mistakes in extending credit, but darn few."

Benny said once that knowing when to extend credit was perhaps the hardest decision to make in the casino business. "When you look into a man's eyes and you can see he intends to pay you—that ain't enough," Benny explained in an interview in the 1970s. "A lot of people are poor judges of their own ability to pay. The same guy who fully intended to pay you may tell you three weeks later that he can't, and he really can't."

Benny Binion opened the Horseshoe in 1951, as a family operation. Besides his wife, the only partner was Robert Caudill, known to one and all as Dobie Doc. Doc had been in the construction business as the Adobe Doctor, which was subsequently abbreviated into his nickname. Doc had made part of his fortune by collecting and reselling western antiques, including a full-sized railroad train of doubtful title. He was taken in as a partner because he had helped smooth out some licensing bumps for Binion and also because he could stay awake through the count after every shift, day after day and year after year, sleeping three times a day between the counts.

Binion was forced to sell controlling interest two years later to pay the legal expenses of fighting rackets charges in Texas and for his unsuccessful fight to avoid prison on income tax charges. He was sentenced to five years in prison and served three and one-half years in Leavenworth Penitentiary. He never was licensed as an operator again, but the family was able to regain control of the casino in 1964. Teddy Jane Binion died in 1994. After the settlement of her estate, Jack Binion in 1996 owned a controlling interest of 43 percent of all Binion's Horseshoe stock, Ted Binion owned almost 20 percent, and the Binions' two surviving daughters, Becky Behnen and Brenda Michael, owned close to 19 percent each.

Benny Binion did not own stock after returning from Leavenworth and was technically a consultant. "But he got the biggest salary of any of us," said Ted. "And that was right because he started it and taught us how to do it."

Long after Ted and Jack had reached manhood and were actively running the operations, Benny would brag that "they mind me like a couple of six year olds."

Ted said he never resented the extended years of parental control.

"It's easy to give somebody his way when he's nearly always right," he explained.

Benny Binion trained his sons by requiring them to deal every game in the house and work their way up through pit boss. "You didn't get to keep the job, either, if you couldn't handle it," said Ted in a 1974 interview. "He wouldn't tolerate bad work from anybody—not even himself." The Binion boys adopted methods much like their father's, and these methods served them well.

One of the biggest decisions they ever had to make was to purchase the adjoining Mint in 1988. This $27-million purchase doubled the size of the Binion's Horseshoe casino and put the Binions into the hotel business in a significant way. (The Horseshoe had only 80 rooms; the Mint had 296.) Yet Jack says his father barely asked a question about the proposed deal. "If I had come to him and said 'I'm gonna buy the Taj Mahal'—not the one in Atlantic City but the tomb in India—he would have said, 'If it's a good deal go ahead.' He would get cranky if the chili wasn't good, but he didn't concern himself much with the big stuff."

The Horseshoe was a conservative operation, not because Benny was conservative, said Jack, but because the family operated on the principle of unanimity. Every Binion in the operation had to agree to a financial move or it did not happen. Some of the decisions were achieved only with much argument. The arguments rarely became public, but in early 1996 Becky Behnen filed suit in an effort to replace Jack Binion as president of the Horseshoe. The issue was unresolved in May 1996.

Annual reports of the privately owned casino are not available, but Ted said the Horseshoe made $350 million in one 15-year period. "The best year, in the early '80s, was $28 million. That isn't too bad for a place we only paid $3 million for and would have sold for $8.5 million in 1969. But Aristotle Onassis wouldn't give us but $5.5 million, so we kept it."

Gene Moehring, a University of Nevada, Las Vegas, professor who writes on urban history, explained Binion's extraordinary success as the fruit of playing the game he knew best. "He epitomized the non-corporate approach. With all this talk that Las Vegas now deals to families, Binion's remains a stone gambling joint. And to certain kinds of Americans that image is very appealing."

Benny Binion bucked the tide. In the 1940s and 1950s, said Jack Binion, most casinos considered big-name entertainment essential to attracting visitors. "But Benny Binion was anti-entertainment. He said, 'I'm not gonna let some s.o.b. blow my bankroll out the end of a horn.'"

"All the Binions knew how to market to gamblers, and they invented new ways to do it," said Bill Friedman. "Other casinos brought in people all kinds of ways, and hoped some of them would gamble. But when your primary attraction is a better gamble, everybody you attract is a gambler." In a casino, the latter method is clearly the more profitable.

One attraction they invented was the gambling tournament. The World Series of Poker was actually begun by Tom Morehead of the Riverside Casino in Reno, who ran it as an invitational. Benny, Jack, and Ted were all invited. "We had so much fun that when Morehead got out of the business, we decided to pick it up," said Ted.

It was a curious vehicle for Benny Binion to ride to further fame, for Binion himself was admittedly not a good poker player. "He lost $400,000 at poker when he first came out here in 1946," said Ted. "And damn, that was a lot of money in those days."

Jack was a good poker player, but Ted preferred craps. The Binions did not even offer poker at the Horseshoe, primarily because the Horseshoe, despite its success, was physically small and floor space was at a premium. (After the Horseshoe acquired the neighboring Mint in 1988, they finally found space for a big, permanent poker room.)

Nor was poker completely respectable. Unlike other games played in casinos, poker pits players against one another, not against the house. This makes poker more difficult to police and regulate than other games. It is also played widely in places that have no effective gambling regulation. Long after all other casino games were universally dealt on the square, poker tables remained the natural habitat of the card cheat. Many casinos did not have poker tables because they did not want that kind of gambler around, and others offered it only as a service to customers, hiding it in some nook so remote that the player had to ask directions to find it.

Promoting a casino with poker was, in short, a revolutionary idea. The Binions, however, managed to do it. They cleared enough space to set up a small poker room, then lured in shark and sucker alike with the prospect of a big win. All you had to do was bring $10,000, and everybody would play until one guy had it all. When somebody did win it all, it was apt to be some colorful individual such as Amarillo Slim Preston or Puggy Pearson, champions made to order for media coverage. Within a few years, the tournament was covered extensively on national television.

Until the Binion tournament, most of the world's legendary poker games had been marathon confrontations involving men of great skill and deep pockets, and sometimes they had gone on for months before one called it quits. The Binions needed an event, not an institution, so they introduced tournament rules that would force a resolution in some finite length of time.

In tournament poker as devised by the Binions, antes and blind bets increase significantly at predetermined points in the play. A tournament player must participate in most pots or he will soon be in a $500-ante game with a nickel-ante stack of chips. Winning a couple of those rich pots will put anybody in the lead, and pursuing a couple to the showdown, and still losing, can put him out of the running. This introduces into tournament play an element of luck that is not present in the ordinary game, where a player may bide his time as long as he has the money to ante.

These changes meant any good player—not necessarily the best player there—might win a tournament. Amateurs who could never hope to beat a Johnny Moss or Doyle Brunson in a regular game saw the possibility of glory. For $10,000, they would take the chance. In 1993, 220 people put up the money. The winner that year was Jim Bechtel, an Arizona cotton farmer. In 1995 there were 273 entries and the winner was Dan Harrington, a former attorney who became a professional player in 1981.

Of course, poker players who spent eleven months of the year in Charlotte or Nome without seeing a crap table might try their luck at that game too. Soon poker tournaments modeled on Binion's blossomed all over town and, eventually, everywhere that poker was legal. Variations of the idea have been applied successfully even to banking games and slot machines. And the exposure brought on by national publicity helped wipe out the last lingering stigma attached to poker. Today casinos are proud to offer the game.

While they worked hard to make sure most of their promotion money went to attract true gamblers, the Binions treated every customer like a live one.

"Everybody comped big players, but Benny Binion was the first I ever knew who comped little ones," said Leo Lewis, Binion's former controller. If somebody had $50 to spend on an evening of playing the slots and a few drinks, it did not matter if Binion's Horseshoe sold the drinks or gave them to the players. The casino would usually get the whole $50 either way.

Benny Binion, however, did not explain that policy in terms of economics. "'If you wanna get rich, make little people feel like big people.' That was how he put it," said Lewis. Today, free drinks for players are a standard casino attraction.

"He was the first in Las Vegas to have limousines," remembered Jack. "I think one of the Strip hotels started meeting people at the airport with a station wagon. He started sending a limousine.

"He believed in operating with class," said Jack. In the casino business, a "carpet joint" is a casino with some aspirations to presenting an atmosphere of refinement and elegance. A "sawdust joint" is anything that does not try to be a carpet joint. When Binion came to Las Vegas, some downtown casinos had actual sawdust on wood floors, and the rest had linoleum. "He put the first carpet in a downtown place," said Jack. It touched off a race toward refinement, and in 1956 there was enough confidence downtown—directly across Casino Center street from Binions—to open the ten-story Fremont Hotel, then the tallest building in Nevada and one of the finer hotels.

"Another thing Benny realized was the importance of repeat business," said Lewis. "We ran the place on the theory that every customer in there was somebody we were trying to get to come back. Being rude to a customer was completely unacceptable in there, but I've been in corporate casinos where they roughed up people emotionally just for sport!"

Binion's staff would rough up people physically, if the occasion demanded it. Historically, getting caught cheating in any gambling house meant getting slapped around. Since the business was illegal most places, pit bosses could not call police; they called a burly bouncer instead. Even after gaming was legalized in 1931, it was many years before law enforcement agencies learned the games well enough to police them. In the meantime, problems were handled "manually."

Benny Binion honored the tradition much longer than most. While some who cheated were merely banned from future play, others paid in pain. As late as the 1970s Benny made it semipublic information that purse snatchers and room burglars caught at the Horseshoe could expect thorough and expert bruising. Most, understandably, plied their trades elsewhere.

But the Binions also paid. In 1985 two gamblers claimed they were beaten up and robbed of winnings after they were caught "hole carding," or peeking at the dealer's hidden card in the game of blackjack. The Binions settled a lawsuit with the two for $675,000. A district court jury convicted two Binion employees—one of them Benny's grandson, Steve Fechser—of felonies in connection with the incident, but a judge set aside their convictions. The charges were finally dropped in 1995 because questions arose about the accuracy of a transcript from the initial trial.

The same incident was one of several that led to federal racketeering charges that Fechser, Ted Binion, and six security guards had an ongoing practice of beating and robbing "undesirables." Those charges, however, were dropped in 1992 because of what Interim U.S. Attorney Douglas Frazier called "insurmountable" problems with evidence. In their motion to dismiss, prosecutors said that "the Horseshoe since 1986 has taken action to insure that activities as alleged in the indictment do not occur."

One of Benny Binion's gifts was being able to make quick decisions. "He never wanted to sleep on anything," remembers Claiborne. "He'd make the decision now. And he could do it because he could see right to the crux of a complex issue. And he could express that point in fewer words than anybody I ever met." As a result, Binion's gnomic wisdom became the principles by which many in the casino industry operate: "Good food cheap, good whiskey cheap, and a good gamble. That's all there is to it, son."

Explaining the difference between his operation and a posh Strip competitor, he said, "We got a little joint and a big bankroll, and all them others got a big joint and a little bankroll."

He said the gambling industry was apparently immune from recessions because "lazy people don't gamble." People who stayed up late looking for action, he would explain if prodded, were apt to be folks with plenty of energy. And energetic people tend to be the ones still employed after the layoffs brought on by recessions.

Some of his sayings made it onto wall plaques, such as the one often labeled the Golden Rule: "He who has the gold makes the rules."

Jack likes another one. "I don't know what everybody's got against inflation and corruption," Benny said. "If you got those things there's always plenty of money around."

In 1975, almost thirty years after Benny left Dallas, the syndicated columnist Jim Bishop mentioned to him that, according to a recent estimate, one out of every three men in Dallas carried a pistol. "One hundred percent of the armed robbers carry guns but you tell me only one out of three citizens walks the streets with protection," exclaimed Binion. "Son, it ain't a good sign."

"I think one reason he was such a good judge of situations and people was that he didn't read well," said Ted. "He didn't read at all, until he went to prison and learned some there. But when you get down to it, a lot of what there is to read, isn't true. It's just a theory that somebody put down on paper. So Dad wasn't exposed to much of that misinformation. He had to go on what he observed, and because he was a good observer, he came up with some truths."

Even though there was a long tradition of secrecy in the gambling industry, Binion shared his truths with anybody who asked. Many in the profession thought that casino management had to be learned on the job, as Benny had done, and resisted any change in that tradition. But Benny helped in the first effort to teach casino managment in college.

"Originally, I was writing a history of the casino industry," said Bill Friedman. "I just walked in off the street and told them I was interested, and he and Jack proceeded to teach me the casino business. Later, the dean of the hotel college at UNLV, Jerry Vallen, proposed that somebody teach a casino course. He knew that I was working on the history. You have to remember that while there were any number of people with more professional experience than I had, everybody was a specialist in some aspect or another, and they needed somebody who knew something about each aspect.

"I had been a dealer, and when I started looking at what had been written on the subject, realized it was completely distorted. So I went to Jack and Benny, yelled 'Help!' They sat me down—and Leo Lewis had a big part in this too—and taught me how to keep a set of books for a casino, and anything else I would need to know to teach the course."

Eventually Friedman would record the principles they taught him in the first textbook on casino management, which is still widely used today. And by getting himself hired to run the Castaways, a tiny and unsuccessful Strip resort then owned by Howard Hughes, and turning it around, Friedman was able to demonstrate that the Binions' success with these principles was no fluke.

Benny Binion never lost the love for horses that had made him able to trade them profitably at an age when today's boys can barely manage baseball cards. Ted notes that he loved his Montana ranch so dearly that when he needed cash to pay his lawyers in the early 1950s, it was the casino, and not the ranch, that he sold.

The ranch at one time owned more than one thousand head of horses and today produces about four hundred a year—fine quarter horses and rodeo stock. For a horseman and rodeo fan, Binion may have enjoyed one of life's greatest pleasures. He once owned Midnight, a bucking horse so famous that there are songs about him.

It took him fifteen years of lobbying, but Binion helped lure the National Finals Rodeo from Oklahoma City, where it had been for years, to Las Vegas, bringing hundreds of rich customers to the city in December, a traditionally slow month for tourism.

Binion had two ambitions he never realized. The first was a presidential pardon for his felony tax conviction. After Ronald Reagan's Republican pals hit him up for donations to the cause, Binion let his faded hope gleam anew. If he had become respectable enough to help support the party of law and order, he reasoned, might he not be respectable enough to have his civil rights restored? So he wrote a $15,000 check for a fund-raising dinner, even though he was ill at the time and could not attend. A few days later he was notified: Sorry, no pardon.

That created a new ambition for Binion, also involving the Gipper. "I have to outlive him now 'cause I wanna be there to [expletive] on his grave."

He did not. Binion died of congestive heart failure on Christmas Day in 1989. A thousand people packed into Christ the King Catholic Church to bid him farewell. A great many of them were surprised to learn, when the presiding priest mentioned it, that Binion had given much of the money to build that church.

Not many knew it, but Binion had religion, much of it acquired during his stay in the federal penitentiary. "It's too big a mystery to doubt," he said later.

He had another reason for believing: He had personally seen Jesus, or at least thought he had.

It was 1985, and Binion was in the hospital with heart trouble—trouble enough that his heart flat stopped.

As he later related to me, he found himself in a white room. And Jesus himself looked toward him and called to him, gently but insistently: "Benny?"

Then the defibrillator brought him back.

Much later, when Benny told me the story, I asked what Jesus looked like. "He had long hair, like you see in the pictures, and I don't believe he was a very old man," said Benny. "You have to remember, I wasn't there long enough to see much. You die longer than a second, you stay."

"Well, I guess you'll see him again," I said.

Benny looked away. "From what I've been told, I'm supposed to go the other way."

At that moment, my identity as a journalist seemed a lot less important to me than my identity, in common with Binion, as a believer.

"If it was Jesus talking to you," I said, "that's who said it doesn't matter what you've done, so long as you repent."

"That's the problem," said Benny. "There's some of it I can't repent. I've tried, and I just can't!"

Sportsman's Paradise

John L. Smith

Separated by time and technology, two generations of bookmakers stand at opposite ends of the history of the multibillion-dollar Las Vegas sports betting.

On one side are the venerable old-schoolers, street-smart men who broke into the business by working out of their front pockets and glancing over their shoulders for signs of the law. Men like Bob Martin, Jackie Gaughan, and Mel Exber made the transition from the street to the legal Las Vegas sports parlors despite recurring headaches from Washington bureaucrats who did not know a long shot from even money.

The younger generation got its start in licensed sports books and today supervises enormous operations for megaresorts. They know plenty about computer programs and just as much about the politics of the corporate world. The industry has moved from smoky back rooms to the opulent emporiums that handled more than $2.4 billion in bets in 1995.

One constant is shared by the hall-of-famers and the corporate directors: an eternal love of the action.

Although betting probably has been around as long as men have held different opinions, a one-time Connecticut math teacher, Charles K. McNeil, is credited with developing modern bookmaking. In the early 1940s in Chicago, McNeil penciled the first point spread. It was a variation on a handicapping system he had developed, and it rapidly replaced the standard system of odds as the preferred method of wagering on football and basketball games. McNeil drove the competition out of business and prospered until 1950, when the Chicago Outfit attempted to enter into a partnership. McNeil retired, but his system remained. In fact, point spreads and future innovations are what helped Las Vegas sports betting prosper.

Mel Exber was a cocky kid from Brooklyn, his pockets bulging with Army Air Corps mustering-out pay, when he drove into Las Vegas on July 4, 1947, bent on busting the town wide open. The son of a tailor, Exber had been betting sports since the stickball games of his childhood. He played back-alley craps and basketball for two bits a game. If it moved, he bet on it. But few beat the odds for long in Las Vegas, and Exber lasted a week before taking a $15-a-week job as a ticket writer at J. Kell Houssels's old Las Vegas Club sports parlor. It worked out for the best: In partnership with Jackie Gaughan, Exber went on to own the Las Vegas Club.

The very thought of computerizing a sports operation was the stuff of science fiction, if it was imagined at all. In the West, live radio sports broadcasts were rare. Pacific Coast League ballgames were more popular with bettors than those played by American or National League teams. Ballgames and horse races were commonly recreated, making Al Capone and Ben Siegel's Trans-America Wire Service indispensable for bookmakers and players. Siegel had been dead less than a month when Exber unpacked his bags and bankroll and made his play for Vegas.

"In those years there wasn't much action on sports," Exber says. "Remember, there were no big-league baseball teams on the West Coast at that time. And the books weren't what they are today. They were hole-in-the-wall operations. They might take big bets, but they weren't much to look at."

Exber eventually hooked up with Gaughan, who gradually acquired downtown properties like hotels on a neon-lit Monopoly board. Gaughan, best known as one of the most successful casino operators in Las Vegas history, was an Omaha bookmaker before he was a casino boss.

"All the early people in gaming in Nevada all came from where they had gaming in other places. A lot of people came from Stubenville, Omaha, and Palm Springs," Gaughan says. "Most of them were bookmakers at one time."

Take, for example, Benjamin "Bugsy" Siegel, one of the most celebrated figures in Las Vegas history. Although Siegel enjoyed a repu-

Las Vegas club owner and sports betting wizard Mel Exber, 1983. (Courtesy Las Vegas News Bureau)

tation as a New York rum-runner and ultimate tough guy and hit man—some old pals estimate he killed at least a dozen men—the man only fools dared call Bugsy was a bookmaker and race-wire operator. Fronted by his associate and bodyguard Fat Irish Green, Siegel operated the horse parlor at the Golden Nugget during World War II. Horse parlors were a part of downtown casinos until the imposition of a 10 percent wagering tax and pressure from federal law enforcement during the Estes Kefauver era of the early 1950s drove operators into stand-alone books and slowed the legitimate industry's growth. It should be noted, however, that federal intervention only encouraged the expansion of illegal bookmaking.

By 1951 Gaughan and Exber were operating the Derby Racebook on First Street near Fremont on land now occupied by the Golden Nugget. They bought a piece of Sammy Cohen's Saratoga across the street from the Derby and were partners in a going concern until being slow down by the wagering tax. Cohen, Gaughan recalled, was the first booker of horse racing in the city.

They were by no means the only bookies occupying betting parlors downtown. In 1953 Demetrios Synodinos, better known as Jimmy the Greek Snyder, opened the Hollywood horse and sports book. In the mid-1950s, Jimmy the Greek booked out of the Vegas Turf and

Sports Club and is said to have handled as much as $2 million a week in action.

Although Snyder was the first Las Vegas bookmaker to seek publicity in the daily press, he was not the last—and not all the news was good. Bookmaking has had a long, stormy relationship with federal law enforcement. Because most of the nation's bookmakers plied their profession illegally, they were easy marks for mob strong-arm "partnerships." Unsophisticated cops and headline-hungry G-men made much of the relationship between the boys in the back room and the bent-nose set. What they rarely acknowledged is that the majority of the nation's illegal operators were free of such organized crime pressure and that many of the bona fide mob bookies often were the victims of extortion by thugs who knew that the bookmakers could not run to the police.

Jackie Gaughan, Jack Binion, and Mel Exber (left to right), 1982. (Courtesy Las Vegas News Bureau)

There were exceptions, to be sure. In fact, Las Vegas has been home to many illegal bookmakers, including Ron "the Cigar" Sacco and Frank Masterana. Perhaps the most notorious of the bunch, Frank Rosenthal, plied his trade legally for a few years at the Stardust Hotel before being caught up in a multimillion-dollar casino skim connected to the Chicago mob and other midwestern organized crime families. The scent of the mob only added to the intrigue for law enforcement and the media.

"It wasn't a hard call to make," says Bob Martin, the dean of America's oddsmakers. "Nobody's going to shoot at them. They can say it's an $80-million ring. It might have been $500,000, but it's automatically $80 million. But how much has prosecution cost the government? How successful has it been? How much has bookmaking gone down?"

Las Vegas offered sanctuary for diehard players and bookmakers wary of increasing federal interest in their activities. So they arrived in small waves. Barbary Coast oddsmaker Pittsburgh Jack Franzi moved to Las Vegas in 1971, settled in, and prospered. "The bottom line was, 95 percent of what I was doing back in Pittsburgh was 5 percent legal," Franzi says. "Nowadays, if you don't do 99 to 100 percent legal here, it's your own fault."

Prior to 1951, law enforcement occasionally pursued bookmakers, but the government did not tax the profession. A groundswell of opposition to sports gambling, led in part by mob-busting senator Kefauver, resulted in the 10 percent tax on betting transactions. With the average football season often netting as little as 3 percent profit, the tax threatened to devastate the fledgling legal industry. The tax drove some bookmakers out of business and many more into the illegal side of the ledger. The ones who stayed in business passed along the expense to the customer.

The tax came as result of a compromise crafted by Nevada senator Pat McCarran. Faced with the reality of a tax being slapped on either keno or betting, McCarran opted to salvage the former. "The keno game was very similar to bookmaking. In those days they called it racehorse keno," Gaughan says. "Pat McCarran, he made a deal with the government not to tax the keno but to tax the horses and the sports. The 10 percent tax closed all the books in all the hotels."

After more than two decades of opposition, Congress lowered the wagering tax to 2 percent on October 15, 1974. That, many experts agree, helped lead to a resurgence in legalized bookmaking activity in Las Vegas. On January 1, 1983, the tax was trimmed to .25 percent, and it appeared legalized sports gambling finally had come into its own. Only in 1985, when the federal currency transaction reporting law went into effect in an attempt to detect potential money laundering, did the handle decrease at legalized books.

Like many other bookmakers of his generation, Martin operated illegally until being chased out of town by federal authorities. In Martin's case, the town was Washington, D.C., and the fed was Attorney General Robert Kennedy. "They wanted to make me Secretary of Bookmaking in Washington," Martin says, laughing. "Politicians don't understand gambling. They really don't know what it's all about. And they could care less. That's the biggest thing."

Lowering the federal tax in 1983 helped make the books more palatable propositions for the image and profit-conscious resorts. "That's when it started to catch on," Martin says. He was the oddsmaker in 1975 when the Union Plaza opened the first sports book of the modern era inside a casino. The Stardust followed less than a year later. "It's overwhelming the volume you do now," says Martin.

Martin was convicted in 1983 of illegally transmitting wagering information, which forced him into an early retirement from his position as the nation's leading oddsmaker. His departure and the technological advances that occurred about the same time changed the face of bookmaking forever. Before computers, there was Bob Martin's brain. ("I just have always known what was the right number," he says. "The right number fits like a glove.") Although Martin remains the most respected of the city's old-school oddsmakers, not even his phenomenal mind could keep up with expanded sports seasons and the latest in computer technology. "It's too big now if you're going to put basketball in there," Martin says. "One man can't do it alone. It takes three months just to prepare for the basketball season."

Longtime Las Vegas sports book boss Sonny Reizner is a Boston native who turned to sports betting and oddsmaking fulltime after his 1945 Air Force discharge. Finding a bookie in Boston was easy; gathering accurate and timely information was not. In the days before computers, players and bookies relied on newspaper stories and the latest rumor.

"There was only one place in Cambridge, Massachusetts, that had out-of-town newspapers. But if I needed Tuesday night's basketball results, they might not arrive until Friday. I had to figure out where

Bob Martin, the man who set the Las Vegas betting line, 1978. (Courtesy Las Vegas News Bureau)

to get all this information plus have time to look things over and be ready by the time the line came out on Friday," says Reizner. So he dispatched a runner to Logan International Airport to gather discarded newspapers from arriving flights.

"This guy would drive like crazy, because the time was so important—get to my house with no time to spare, and get those newspapers to me like clockwork. I was prepared, where other bettors had nothing but secondhand information and were not really prepared," Reizner says.

Enter the microchip.

Computers changed everything, not only for the bookmakers but for the bettors as well. The latest advances in personal computer technology were immediately integrated into the complex matrix of sports and horse wagering. The new reality of bookmaking did not exactly fulfill the romantic vision of the professional betting wise guy with his pocket full of c-notes, unwavering intuition, and impeccable inside information. By tapping a few keys, even mediocre players had access to the fickle odds, updated injury reports, and weather conditions from Seattle to Foxboro. No more swiping out-of-town newspapers from airline seats; no more wondering about the mysterious information available to those stonehearted bookies.

"I think it's definitely a case of evolution," says Art Manteris, co-author with Rick Tally of *SuperBookie: Inside Las Vegas Sports Gambling*. "I have nothing but respect for the older bookmakers, but I definitely think the world has changed. There's a vast difference between a bookmaker and a corporate bookmaker. A corporate bookmaker has to alter his strategy around a corporate mentality. You have to limit your exposure. It doesn't mean anything to the corporation if you have the best of it and lose a quarter-million dollars."

Manteris's uncle is Jack Franzi, who laughs at the thought of becoming computer-literate at his age. "I'm definitely not one of the computer elite," Pittsburgh Jack says. "From what I can see, there's no question it's the way to go. But I've done everything this [old] way. My style and my system, in its own way, have been very successful."

Presuming bookmaking's halcyon days ever existed outside the pages of Damon Runyon's short stories, computerization made earning easy money booking straight sports bets a thing of the distant, stogey-fogged past. If a bookmaker's betting line is slightly out of focus, the best bettors in the world know it in seconds. The information revolution has made corporate bookmakers wary and the public more knowledgeable than ever.

Vic Salerno of Leroy's Horse and Sports Place downtown, on the site of the old Saratoga sports book, is credited with franchising satellite sports parlors through an advanced computer link up. Salerno operates thirty-five minibooks throughout Nevada. Each one is dialed into the home office at Leroy's, which truly is the last of the Runyon joints in a city that has gone high-tech and sports-book crazy.

But strip away the machinery and corporate suits, and the younger generation is not so different from the older generation. Although they gained their formal training in legalized sports books, people like Las Vegas Hilton sports book director Art Manteris and Caesars Palace sports book director Vinny Magliulo are not so different from their street-wise uncles. For his part, Manteris booked parlay cards at Pittsburgh's Churchill High. ("Some of our best customers were teachers," he says.) About the time Manteris was booking parlays to classmates and faculty, Magliulo was wagering at Saint Joseph's Junior High in Brooklyn.

"I bet Sister Mary Catharine that the '69 Mets would beat the Baltimore Orioles in the World Series," he says. "I was a fanatical Mets fan. The nuns were tremendous baseball fans. There was a lot of excitement in New York with the Mets. The nuns had attended their novitiate in Baltimore. I can remember being on the playground that afternoon in my uniform. I bet a month's worth of lunch money. They were the best lunches of my educational life."

But to compete in a rapidly expanding market, the new bookmakers had to learn about and keep up with changes. That is something Michael "Roxy" Roxborough knows plenty about. Roxborough is the man behind the numbers in the new Las Vegas. He has largely filled the vacuum left when Martin stopped oddsmaking fulltime in 1980. Today, his Las Vegas Sports Consultants provides odds for 80 percent of Nevada's sports books as well as for betting and lottery operations in Oregon, Canada, Mexico, Ireland, England, and Australia. Although his company is on-line and linked to dozens of sports books, he did not start out with an advanced knowledge of computers. He was just another professional player trying to earn enough to keep the lights on and his shirts pressed. As late as the mid-1980s, oddsmakers calculated their opinions by using pencil and paper.

"I think what happens is you respond to what's happening in the real world," Roxborough says. "If the bettors hadn't gotten computerized, we probably never would have gone that way. They became more sophisticated in their approach. The result is a better line. We have to have it. The players make better selections. The information we have is incredibly superior to anything before."

The players may be sharper than ever, but the industry is not exactly struggling. In fact, it enjoys unprecedented success. How can that be if the bettors are smarter and faster?

Technology is not all that has improved. Parlay cards, wild proposition bets, and tempting futures odds have become a staple of the modern sports book.

Although known as sucker bets among sharp players, parlay cards offer small-money players a chance at big payoffs. Picking a five-team parlay pays 20-to-1. Although the true odds of hitting a five-teamer are 31-to-1, making the bet a poor value for serious gamblers, parlay cards are enormously popular—and profitable for the books. The hold averages around 20 percent (as opposed to as little as 3 percent for football).

Futures bets also appeal to player cravings. A generation ago, a gambler could not bet on a professional football game until Tuesday morning. Now, he can bet on next year's Super Bowl a day after this year's spectacle. The World Series, National Basketball Association Championship, and Breeder's Cup Thoroughbred races are a few of the events a player can get down on months ahead of the first pitch, jump shot, or post time.

"Proposition bets have become more creative," Magliulo says. "Propositions on the dice table have been around since the game itself. Those wagers on the dice table are a game within a game. I equate that same theory to proposition bets in sports wagering. When you have a bet on the Super Bowl and your team may be getting blown out, you might have three or four proposition bets that you're going to win. I think that's very appealing to the player."

Standard propositions range from predicting the number of first downs in a football game to the total yards a star running back will gain. Then the action gets a little crazy.

When Manteris was at the Caesars Palace book in 1985, he offered this strange proposition at 20-to-1 odds: Would William "Refrigerator" Perry, the 330-pound defensive tackle for the Chicago Bears, score a touchdown against the New England Patriots in Super Bowl xx?

Bettors went bananas, piling so much money on the possibility Perry would score that the odds fell to 2-to-1. In the third quarter with the game well out of reach, Perry lumbered onto the field and bulled his way into the end zone from the one-yard line. Caesars Palace had gained national publicity with the proposition, but the book lost $120,000 on one play.

Do you remember who shot J. R. Ewing? Sonny Reizner does. One of the most creative operators in the city's history, Reizner has been coming up with headline-grabbing gadget bets for years. In 1980, when the television soap-opera *Dallas* was one of the most popular programs on television, Reizner placed odds on the most popular question of the day. Treacherous capitalist and infamous Texan J. R. Ewing, played by Larry Hagman, had taken a bullet. The national press made a beeline for Reizner's office, television viewers tore themselves away from the set long enough to bet on the various possibilities, and the Castaways Hole-in-the-Wall Sports Book gained international attention. (Trivia buffs can stop wondering: J. R. Ewing's wife's sister, Kristin, did the deed.)

Gaughan grabbed the nation's attention in 1979 when he set a line on where the Skylab space station would hit the earth. Different countries brought varying odds. When Skylab slammed into a remote area of western Australia, lucky bettors won their wagers at 3o-to-1 odds.

The 1994 Winter Olympics in Norway were marked by the exploits of figure skaters Tonya Harding and Nancy Kerrigan. Harding was suspected of concocting a plan to eliminate Kerrigan from the competition by having her physically assaulted. Although the Olympics traditionally draws relatively little betting action, gamblers were interested in Harding and Kerrigan, who eventually garnered a silver medal. Harding wound up in eighth place and later accepted a plea bargain in the conspiracy case regarding the attack on Kerrigan. Interest was high, so the Kerrigan-Harding line on who would place higher was posted.

Before the state Gaming Control Board put a halt to nonsports wagering, the Academy Awards attracted lively bets. The line is posted today for publicity purposes only.

The books have changed as well. Only the lines remain the same. Although they were sometimes known as parlors, the early sports books were no place for a lady. They were dingy places filled with smoke, the floors strewn with cigarette ends and discarded betting slips. There was no flash, no neon, certainly no giant television screens, delicatessens, or cocktail service.

"Even in the mid-'70s when I got here the books were full of a bunch of cigar-chewing guys spitting on the floor. It was basically a men's social club. Tourists didn't want to show up, and you sure wouldn't bring your wife to one of those places," Roxborough says. "I think the industry's so much better now than it used to be. What the casinos have done is turn these books into giant entertainment complexes."

The Las Vegas Hilton Race and Sports SuperBook, for example, cost $17 million to build. The Hilton, Caesars, and Mirage sports books bear a closer resemblance to mission control at the Kennedy Space Center than to a traditional pony parlor. The SuperBook not only has attracted sports bettors but also has led to increases in casino slot and table play. Room occupancy rates and food and beverage percentages also have increased. The same is true at the Mirage and Caesars Palace.

"We try to provide an experience," Magliulo says. "I think that's the key. People just don't come to some small, smoke-filled room and feel intimidated. They come here to experience the excitement in comfort."

If all that sounds like so much slick marketing and unabashed hucksterism, well, it is—because it all leads to the bottom line. That is where the numbers are. And the numbers are staggering.

According to state Gaming Control Board figures for 1995, Nevada sports books handled $2.43 billion in bets. The hold, or percentage of dollars retained by the book after paying winners, was 3.27 percent before the .25 percent federal excise tax. The true hold for the year was 2.49 percent. Put away your calculator: All those numbers translate into a $79.4-million profit statewide.

You want a growth industry? Eight years earlier, the handle was $989.1 million, the net win $39.3 million. In 1981 to 1982 it was $384.9 million, with a $12.8-million after-tax profit.

If everyone bets, what are they betting on?

More than $1 billion of football bets were placed in 1995. (By comparison, the construction cost of the 3,000-room Mirage was approximately $630 million.) Professional and college basketball garnered approximately 30 percent of the action, which pencils out to $700 million wagered. Baseball's handle was $533 million. Horse racing totals for the same period were $575 million, approximately a 15 percent hold. Parlay cards are the biggest winner for the books, and the biggest sucker bet for the player. In 1995 thousands of optimistic fans wagered $71 million trying to correctly guess three-, five- and even twelve-team winning combinations and in the process donated 28 percent, or approximately $20 million, to the sports books. Nevada horse and sports betting is on track to be a $3-billion industry by the end of the century.

With all that potential revenue, and with many states scraping for tax sources, the push to legalize sports betting would seem like a natural. Is it possible in the immediate future?

Don't bet on it. In one of his last acts as president, George Bush signed the Professional and Amateur Sports Protection Act in 1992, a law prohibiting the spread of legalized sports betting beyond its current jurisdictions, namely Nevada. The bill was lobbied hard by the National Football League and National Basketball Association, with Arizona senator Dennis DeConcini playing the role of political point guard. Sports betting was a scandal waiting to happen, De-

Concini and company bellowed. The future of amateur sports was at stake, they cried. Passage of the bill did not hurt Las Vegas bookmakers' feelings one bit, but it gave them pause.

After all, who were the NFL, NBA, and a few esteemed senators trying to fool?

According to 1991 estimates Americans wager from $30 billion to $100 billion illegally on sports. Dominican Republic–based bookmaker Ron Sacco is estimated to have personally handled more than $1 billion annually before his operation was interrupted by the FBI. Veteran Las Vegas bookmakers and players know more money is wagered in the bars and back rooms of Chicago and New York than in all of Las Vegas sports books combined. And the illegals do not pay taxes. Prohibition has not exactly been successful so far.

"Pete Rozelle [former NFL commissioner] would never have admitted it, but [wagering on games] definitely helped attendance," Martin says.

The younger generation concurs. "It sounds preposterous to me," Manteris says. "Are they actually saying that by making a law they're going to stop it? I don't think that's what they're thinking. There's absolutely no question in my mind that privately the NFL and NBA know that without gambling their revenues would diminish drastically. If I was an illegal bookmaker, that law clearly would be the best thing that would happen to my business. For the foreseeable future, legalized sports betting will be unique to Nevada."

That makes Las Vegas America's sportsman's paradise.

The old-schoolers and corporate operators would not have it any other way.

The Ghost of Ben Siegel
John L. Smith

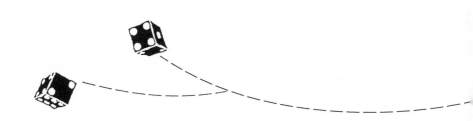

Look quickly and you might catch a glimpse of him on scorching July afternoons around the Flamingo Hilton pool. He will appear briefly in the shade of a tall palm tree, or over by the place his rose garden used to grow. Handsome but harried, forever young, forever wandering.

It is the ghost of bloody Ben Siegel.

Some will call it a super-heated mirage; others say it is the kind of apparition tourists will see after a few too many tropical drinks. But if you look long enough, you will see Siegel's ghost at his Flamingo, along the Strip, and all the way downtown. It is only fitting, considering how Siegel's image has shaped Las Vegas for generations. In life, he was a handsome hoodlum. In death, he remains a legend taller than any Las Vegas resort.

Ask almost anyone. They will tell you all about the infamous Bugsy. He dreamed up the idea for the Flamingo. In fact, he raised Southern Nevada from sand and sage with his partner in crime, Virginia Hill. The Strip? He thought of that one, too. Why, Las Vegas is the town Bugsy built.

Right?

Not exactly.

If anything, Siegel inadvertently contributed an aura as unique as neon to Las Vegas. All it took was his sociopathic personality, the lure of celebrity, a brassy dame named Virginia Hill, and a couple of .30-caliber slugs in the head. America did the rest.

In his psychotic world, Benjamin Siegel was an overachiever from New York's Lower East Side. Born in 1905 Siegel operated his own street gang by the time he was fourteen. On the street he befriended a rat-faced Jewish kid named Meyer Suchowljansky, better known as Meyer Lansky. Together as the Bug and Meyer Mob, Siegel and Lansky led a cast of young felons who carried out murder contracts for New York's most notorious bootlegging outfits. Blood flowed almost as freely as Prohibition hooch.

With Repeal and what might be described as a series of violent corporate takeovers in the New York underworld, Siegel and Lansky emerged as young powers with their Italian partners Joe Adonis, Albert Anastasia, Charles "Lucky" Luciano, Frank Costello, Vito Genovese, and Thomas Lucchese. The group had plenty of money to invest in legitimate and illegitimate business.

One racket was the horseracing wire service, a radio transmission system that relayed thoroughbred information across the country on behalf of avid equestrians and illegal bookmakers. Contrary to popular belief and Hollywood legend, it was the ponies—not the poker tables—that first attracted Siegel to Southern Nevada in 1941. Gambling, a sin from coast to coast, had been legal for a decade in Nevada, and the state legislature had legalized the racewire business months earlier. Las Vegas was close enough to Siegel's first love, Hollywood, to make a relatively easy day trip across the desert. Siegel had come to California for four basic reasons: to secure the racewire business, to shore up the West Coast rackets, to beat the 1939 murder of Harry Greenberg, and to avail himself of certain celebrities. Siegel was a childhood pal of ultimate screen tough guy George Raft, who eventually would lose his bankroll betting on the Bug's ability to build the Flamingo.

When he arrived in Las Vegas, Siegel saw the Wild West version of a wiseguy paradise: downtown with its rows of smoky gambling halls, U.S. Highway 91 with the El Rancho Vegas, the Last Frontier, and thousands of acres of undeveloped desert. Siegel, Lansky, and their partners made early investments in the El Cortez, Frontier Club, and Golden Nugget. The small joints generated easy money, but the big time were situated just off the highway on what would become known as the Strip.

Siegel cut a handsome figure in his tailored suits, and after latching onto Virginia Hill, the former girlfriend of fellow New York mobster Joe Adonis, the infamous Bug became a constant source of Las

Siegel was known for his dapper dress.
(Courtesy Las Vegas News Bureau)

Vegas gossip. Longtime Southern Nevada tourism executive Herb McDonald remembers being impressed with the man only a fool ever called Bugsy. McDonald was a young assistant general manager for the El Rancho when Siegel surfaced on the site of the Flamingo project. To the naïve McDonald, Siegel was just another man on the make.

"We played gin rummy, and I won twenty-eight bucks," McDonald said. "When I saw Ben Siegel again [at the El Rancho], he asked me when I was going to give him a chance to win some of his money back. I said, 'Any time you think you're good enough.'"

Bugsy's girlfriend, Virginia Hill, at whose Beverly Hills mansion he was murdered. (Courtesy Las Vegas News Bureau)

McDonald merely was cracking wise, but an El Rancho casino employee overheard the comment and, when Siegel had gone, quickly brought the young assistant general manager up to speed. "The casino man said, 'That's Bugsy Siegel, the president of Murder Incorporated.' My knees buckled. Had I known that, I would have dumped." But McDonald maintained his composure and his friendship with the Bug.

Others were less fortunate. The late Las Vegas attorney Lou Wiener Jr., Siegel's local spokesman, often told the tale of the unfortunate fellow who was so pleased with the Flamingo that he just had to inform the boss in the casino. "He said, 'Great place, Bugsy.' Ben just glared at him and said, 'Have we been introduced?' The guy didn't know what to do. Ben said, 'My name is Ben Siegel.' He had a temper, but I rarely saw him get angry."

Similar stories about Siegel are common. Apparently, he never thought to change the nickname he grew to hate so much.

His philosophy of violence is probably best captured in his much-chronicled conversation with Flamingo builder Del Webb, the Phoenix contractor who had expressed concern about Siegel's clients. Webb had nothing to worry about because "we only kill each other," Siegel told him, admitting to a dozen homicides.

Siegel was also a lady killer. Although a string of starlets always were close by, foremost in his life was auburn-haired hussy Virginia Hill, a former member of respectable southern society who gained a national reputation for bedding gangsters. As legend has it, Siegel and Hill were truly in love. Siegel planted and tended a rose garden at the hotel in her honor, and he even named the Flamingo after her nickname. Either that, or it was named after the brightly colored birds at Miami's Hialeah race track. His love for Virginia aside, Siegel was said to have had four girlfriends staying at the Flamingo when it opened.

Do not sob for Virginia, though. She also had a relationship with New York rackets prince Joey Adonis. Other benefactors included Capone lieutenant Joseph Epstein, Rocco and Charlie Fischetti, Tony Accardo, Murray "the Camel" Humphreys, Frank Nitti, and Frank Costello. In the press, Hill was the Queen of the Mob. In truth, she was a part-time bag woman for Lucky Luciano, who flaunted her relationships with bad boys and was not above playing one suitor against another. Before the 1951 Kefauver Committee, she revealed the secret of her success: "Senator, I'm the best goddamned cock-sucker in the world." During a break in the hearings, Hill punched out a female crime reporter. But in 1946 she was the woman Siegel loved most.

Try as he might, Siegel was a gangster, not a developer. His first thought was to buy his way into the El Rancho Vegas, but owner Tom Hull was not interested in a partner with a reputation. When that failed, he looked for another opportunity, which presented itself in the form of a slick-talking big-idea man from California named Billy Wilkerson. The founder of the *Hollywood Reporter* and the creative force behind the Café Trocadero and other clubs along what would become known as the Sunset Strip, Wilkerson had bumped into the Bug in the movie mecca. Wilkerson had an idea for a casino that would turn the Old West–themed operations upside down: a glamorous, Beverly Hills–style carpet joint just oozing with class. Gourmet food, big-name entertainment, the works. Most of all, Wilkerson's dream would have something every other club in town lacked: movie stars and starlets in the casino day and night. After all, Wilkerson had the contacts.

What he did not have, however, was enough cash to make his dream come true. During World War II, building supplies were heavily rationed; major construction projects were out of the question until months after Johnny came marching home from Europe and the Pacific. But money has a way of talking even in tough times, and Ben Siegel's bankroll could sing Carmen. Besides, Wilkerson and Siegel figured their casino would cost no more than a few hundred grand, $1 million at most.

So they went to work in the months following the end of the war, and piece by piece the Flamingo was born. Material appeared from all parts of California, much of it purchased at exorbitant prices. The tons of steel reinforcement bar used to frame the four-story concrete palace came directly from a Navy ship. With the fall of Germany and Japan, a generation of gamblers who learned to play craps in the American armed services was turned loose on society. The potential was great. But the Flamingo would not come cheap: Siegel, Lansky, and their partners bought 67 percent of the project for $650,000. Lansky predicted the rise of peacetime airline travel that would make places such as Las Vegas, Miami, and even Havana easily accessible.

The Flamingo immediately experienced cost overruns. Materials not only were hard to come by, but they kept disappearing from the construction site. In months, Siegel's investment was spent. Far worse for him, his partners' money also was gone. Luciano and the bunch did not understand the nuances of construction. They were contractors of another sort. They did, however, understand the value of a dollar—or, in this case, a *million* dollars.

Siegel was a hitter, not a builder. But he was not as arrogant as he often has been portrayed, Wiener said. He may have preferred spending wild weekends in Hollywood to days on a super-heated construction site, but he knew more was at stake than the future of his desert oasis. Wiener knew the Bug as a friend given to great generosity, occasional flashes of rage, and painstaking detail.

"He used to carry a pocket secretary with him," Wiener said. "He'd ask me four or five [legal] questions and want all of them answered on a separate piece of paper. He'd say, 'If you're right, it's going to be in writing. If you're wrong, it's going to be in writing.'

"He was meticulous about expense accounts. You had to be right to the penny on expenses. He didn't care what you spent, but it had to be exact."

Siegel's eye for detail did not keep the Flamingo from using up buckets of Syndicate cash. Concrete walls and pillars left no room for error. Tearing out multi-ton chunks of the hotel took time and money.

In Siegel's fourth-floor master suite, complete with side exits, three-foot-thick concrete walls, and trap doors in the closets leading to his basement garage and a waiting getaway car, one beam proved too much for the Bug to bear.

"He called me up to the penthouse," Wiener said. "I didn't see anything unusual. I'm only five-six. I could walk under it. He was so mad he couldn't see straight. He bawled out the architect." Siegel had the beam replaced. Nothing was going to make the boss duck.

"A lot of contractors, I think, duped him," Wiener said. "They'd go in through the front gates with materials and drive out the back."

His $1-million desert dream ballooned into a $6-million nightmare as 1946 wore on. Siegel knew gambling far better than construction and was eager to open the casino and recoup some of his associates' lost investment. Thanks in large part to Wilkerson and Raft, half of Hollywood was invited to the premiere. And although Siegel was hounded in New York, he enjoyed favorable press in Las Vegas. Upstart publicist and newspaper publisher Hank Greenspun, fiery future publisher of the *Las Vegas Sun*, was just breaking into the fledgling local market with *Las Vegas Life*. Greenspun's pen captured the image Siegel wished to project:

"Youngish, baby-blue eyed Benjamin 'Ben' Siegel has spent a great deal of his 40 years running around the periphery of big-time respectability. The few encounters he has had with it were either head-on or passing through.

"It was obvious after a few years that you don't get in the blue book by making book, so Ben decided to go into the hotel business. Result of this Siegelian course of action is the Flamingo—the world's most lavish conception of hotel resort, casino, cafe and playground all rolled into one."

With such positive press, how could the Flamingo lose?

Unfortunately for Siegel, it takes more than one favorable feature—or even one hundred—to make a casino operate.

The Flamingo opened the day after Christmas in 1946, but the premiere was filled with Dickensian omens. The weather was awful, the movie stars stayed home. And in the hotel's signature fountain,

An early mug shot of Ben "Bugsy" Seigel.
(Courtesy Las Vegas News Bureau)

a black cat had given birth to kittens. It was considered bad luck to move the brood, so the fountain remained dry. The hotel was not ready, but Siegel's partners had run out of patience. Not all the stars would be in attendance, but Xavier Cugat and his popular band complemented Jimmy Durante in the showroom for the black-tie festivities.

"You never saw so many black-chip gamblers in all your life," Wiener said—or so many lucky ones. That was the problem that first night. Above everything else, too many gamblers won too much money from their gracious, quick-tempered host. Also, the Flamingo's hotel rooms were not ready, Wiener remembers. The gamblers walked across the street, booked rooms at the El Rancho Vegas and Last Frontier, and wound up dropping most of their Flamingo winnings at the rival hotels. In the days that followed, the Flamingo, already mired millions in debt, lost $300,000 in the casino.

Siegel shut down the casino and scrambled to raise enough capital to complete the seventy-eight rooms. The Flamingo finally reopened March 1, 1947, with the Andrews Sisters headlining in the showroom. This time, Siegel finally appeared to have beaten the curse of the pink bird.

But Siegel could not rest easy. He knew the debt was large enough to make him expendable with his longtime friends.

"He used to go down to Los Angeles about every two weeks," original Flamingo engineer Don Garvin said. "He'd have me change the locks on the door of his room almost every week. He and Virginia would sit in the hall while I worked. He was a little leery. It got to where I would pretend to change it and hand him the same key."

As spring faded, so, apparently did the smiling, supremely confident fellow searching for respect that Greenspun and others had chronicled.

But Wiener remembers those final days in a slightly different light. "I saw him every single day," Wiener said. "I saw him the day he left for Los Angeles. If he was nervous, I never saw it. The hotel was just really starting to take off when he got killed."

Had he been a conventional developer, Ben Siegel would have faced angry creditors, embarrassment, and bankruptcy; but there was nothing conventional about him. It can be safely surmised the mob did not care for a lot of paperwork, and its definition of bankruptcy is not to be found in any dictionary. Benny Siegel, whose splendid "Nevada Project" was collecting debts even faster than it was collecting dust, would have to be retired.

According to one version of events, syndicate bosses met in Havana in December 1946. Luciano, who is said to have been most upset with Siegel's big idea, was adamant that Siegel had to be killed. Lansky, Benny's boyhood friend, attended the meeting. Lansky denied being in on the decision to kill his old New York running mate. "If it was in my power to see Benny alive, he would live as old as Metusula [sic]," Lansky said in 1975 to an Israeli reporter.

But it was not in Lansky's power. In the psychopathic world of the syndicate, the decision had been made. Ironically, the Flamingo had begun to show all the signs of turning a profit. But $6 million was an enormous sum in the years shortly after World War II, and it was commonly held in some mob circles that Havana—not Las Vegas—was the place to build for the future.

On June 20, 1947, Siegel was at Virginia's Beverly Hills home on North Linden Drive. She was in Paris; they were on the outs. He had just returned from a late dinner. As he sat on the living room sofa picking through the *Los Angeles Times*, the first of nine shots roared through the neighborhood.

One slug from the .30-caliber Army carbine entered through the back of Siegel's neck and ruined his handsome face forever. Another shot knocked his right eye across the living room, where it was found fifteen feet from its socket.

Before the police had finished collecting pieces of the victim, California-based hitman Frankie Carbo, who would so successfully corrupt the nation's boxing racket, was being blamed for the Siegel murder. It was a familiar story: Carbo and Siegel were friends, but business was business. The case never was resolved.

"When he got killed, the chief of police of Beverly Hills came to see me and wanted to know if Ben had any enemies in town. I said he was well liked, and he could ask anyone. He came back a few days later and said I was right. Everyone liked Ben," said Wiener.

Everyone to whom he did not owe money, at least.

"It makes me feel bad because that was the origin, really the start of Las Vegas as a resort town," Wiener said. "This was the first real jewel in the desert."

Just as quickly as Benny Siegel had died, Phoenix-based bookmaker and betting wire service operator Gus Greenbaum packed his bags and made the winding, bumpy journey by car to Las Vegas. He was unpacked before anyone was the wiser, carrying out the orders of his sponsors and keeping a closer accounting of their cash. The Flamingo's turnaround was dramatic, but Greenbaum's luck was not all good. In 1958, on a trip to Phoenix, Greenbaum and his wife were murdered: their throats were cut.

But that grisly double murder was quickly forgotten by a nation enamored of Las Vegas and the legendary Ben Siegel. Locals could remind visitors of the truth about the infamous Bugsy, but no one was listening. The legend was more fun.

The Las Vegas press has been more than willing to play along. When Siegel's old floor safe was uncovered in 1972 at the Flamingo, the *Las Vegas Review-Journal* and *Sun* speculated about the potential fortune in mob money contained inside. A dozen reporters and an NBC television camera crew invaded the city. When the safe was opened, it contained only a few scraps of wood. In fact, the money had been removed from the safe a few hours after Siegel's demise.

Hollywood producers have made a fortune romanticizing the life of Siegel and men like him. The most expansive effort was the 1991 movie *Bugsy*, starring Warren Beatty in the title role and Annette Bening as the luscious Virginia. It was a pretty picture, to be sure, but it only perpetuated the myth.

"Ben Siegel did not invent the luxury resort-casino," Robert Lacey writes in *Little Man: Meyer Lansky and the Gangster Life*. "He did not found the Las Vegas Strip. He did not buy the land or first conceive the project that became the Flamingo. But by his death he made them all famous."

By dying so violently, bad Ben Siegel won a kind of Vegas immortality.

So wander through the new Las Vegas, and you will see Siegel's ghost in every glittering façade and exotic waterfall, each gourmet room and opulent suite. The city has become the class operation that had disturbed his maniacal dreams all those years ago.

And when you see him, do not forget to call him Ben.

Jay Sarno: He Came to Play
A. D. Hopkins

When he hit town, some called him a visionary and a huckster. But in the decade after his death in 1984, Jay Sarno's most radical philosophy—that a casino should not be merely a hotel with gambling tables but an island of fantasy in a mundane world—has become gaming industry dogma.

Sarno expressed his fantasy so well that its two original manifestations—Caesars Palace and Circus Circus— remain on every tourist's must-see list nearly thirty years after he built them.

"We had a chance to buy into Caesars Palace and didn't take it," admitted Ted Binion, whose family usually does not make bad decisions in the gaming business. "But he wanted to dress his security guards as gladiators. He wanted to put his pit bosses in togas! In 1966, who'd ever heard of such a thing?"

In retrospect, it does not seem so strange that America bought into Sarno's idea of how to have fun. He knew how. In fact, Sarno was a world-class good-time Charlie whose creativity at making money was born of his joy in spending it. He lived like a Caesar in some Cecil B. DeMille movie and spent his life helping other Americans do the same.

"A lot of what made him tick was recoiling from his youth," said his oldest son, Jay Jr. "He didn't like being poor."

The rest of his family did not enjoy living in poverty, either. Jay Sarno's father, a Missouri cabinetmaker, and his homemaker mother managed to save money to help all their seven children attend college. One became a doctor, while Jay and a brother became hotelmen.

Sarno was hustling a buck even at the University of Missouri, where he majored in business. He started a laundry delivery service and sold corsages for campus events. In the Pacific during World War II, his government job was operating the communications system on an airplane. On his own time, he cut hair and ran a crap game.

After the war he looked up a classmate from Missouri, Stanley Mallin. They became tile contractors in the Miami building boom and expanded into office buildings and motels.

Born in 1922, Sarno was thirty-six when he met Joyce Cooper, the twenty-three-year-old operator of a beauty and charm school, who was vacationing in Miami Beach with her parents. "He spotted her and four days later they were engaged," said their daughter, September, who would be born in 1959. "He wooed her parents to get permission to marry her.

"That was typical of him," September added. "When he set his sights on something he liked, he liked to close the deal." The couple were married a few weeks later in Jackson, Mississippi.

In the late 1950s, September pointed out, the downtown motor hotel was coming into vogue. "Before that you could stay in a motel out on the highway, but if you wanted to be downtown in most cities, you had to stay in a traditional hotel with all the expense. So he built one of the earlier motor hotels."

The Atlanta Cabana not only pioneered the new motor hotel concept but also marked the first time that Allen Dorfman, the controversial money manager for the Teamsters Union, arranged a loan from its Central States Pension Fund. Sarno met Dorfman and Teamsters boss Jimmy Hoffa through a Dallas Teamsters official and became friendly with both, said September. "He was better pals with Dorfman because Dorfman's lifestyle was more similar: He liked to gamble and play golf. Hoffa wasn't like that; he never had any fun. But he loved my father all the same; he wouldn't take calls from most people, but he would from Dad."

While the arrangements were usually made with Dorfman, resort and motel investments were a policy originated by Hoffa himself, said former Teamsters vice-president Allen Friedman in *Power and Greed*, his book about the union.

Hoffa had a good business sense despite his corruption. He always said the pension fund backed a larger number of financial winners than most banks, and I think that was true. But his real genius was understanding what was happening in America.

Hoffa wasn't only getting better contracts for the working-man. He knew what the extra money would mean for their families. . . . The new contracts meant that people could afford to take a real vacation. They could stay in hotels. They could eat in restaurants. They could gamble a little in Las Vegas. . . . Bowling alleys were built in record numbers. Companies like Holiday Inn were expanding. . . .

Hoffa began looking for real estate investments that would match the leisure-time interest. He wanted the Central States Pension fund to invest money in casinos, hotels, and resorts, among other properties.

The $1.8 million Sarno got to build the Atlanta Cabana in 1958 would be followed in 1959 by a $3.6-million loan for the Dallas Cabana. By 1962 there was also a Cabana in Palo Alto, where singer Doris Day was Sarno's partner. And Teamsters money would finance his later ventures, Caesars Palace and Circus Circus, as well as Las Vegas hotels built by others.

Flying from city to city in the course of managing their budding motor hotel chain, the Sarnos often stopped in Las Vegas, where Jay would assault the crap tables. Crap tables, however, were about the only thing Jay liked about Las Vegas hotels.

"He was a man who loathed plain vanilla, and Las Vegas hotels at that time just oozed mediocrity," said September. The few that evoked any identifiable atmosphere at all were stuck in the western-movie era, which in the popular culture of the 1960s had already ridden into the sunset. "He was building slick, gorgeous hotels and making a modest living. Then he saw modest hotels here making money hand over fist. He realized he wasn't building the wrong kind of hotels; he was building them in the wrong place."

Las Vegas Strip hotels in those days bore names like the Desert Inn, the Dunes, the Sahara. "But those desert themes couldn't be extrapolated into the kind of luxury he wanted," said Jay Jr. He adopted a different theme for the hotel he began building in 1964. "The Roman theme at Caesars fit his fantasy of life."

"He wanted everything around him to be beautiful," said September. "He felt the necessity of eating should be and could be made exciting. He designed the Bacchanal restaurant, the concept of wine goddesses massaging the gentleman diners as they ate. And people would travel from these faraway places just to get a shoulder-and-neck massage from these goddesses."

Despite his popular image as a man with more money than education, Sarno was a serious student of architecture. "He read about it constantly, and when we went to Europe, that was what he went to see," said his former wife, Joyce. "I don't think he ever went anywhere without a camera. He was always saying, 'Stop the car. I want to take a picture of that cantilever.' I don't think any architect ever presented him with an idea; they took his idea and made it work."

Sarno tried out many appropriated ideas before coming to Las Vegas; the Palo Alto Cabana looked like a miniature Caesars.

The hotel Sarno built on the Strip won the admiration of many architects, including Alan Hess, who wrote about it in his book *Viva Las Vegas: After-Hours Architecture:*

> The motel prototype used for most Las Vegas resorts since 1941 called for buildings to be arranged casually on the site. A sign or facade was likely shifted to face oncoming traffic. Caesars faced the Strip with a royal presence and bulk that established its own organization in its own domain. It disdained accuracy in favor of vigor. Technically speaking, the wings that marked the entry were more Baroque Rome (they took the parabolic shape of St. Peter's Square) than Imperial Rome. The statues and fountains evoked the Villa d'Este and other summer villas of Baroque cardinals in Tivoli. Such lapses have to be excused; a resort more accurately named Popes Palace would not have drawn as many gamblers.

Miami architect Melvin Grossman worked out details but was helped by Jo Harris, a designer who had worked at all the Cabanas and would later help design Circus Circus. "I believe very strongly that when you select a theme for a hotel, you ought to follow that theme in every aspect of the operation where it is possible to do so," she said in a 1975 interview. "Even your stationery, for instance, ought to bear out the theme." Caesars writing paper looked like weathered Roman parchment.

The casino was full of features that appeared to be architectural whims but were actually planned carefully, said Harris. "The main feature that makes it so good is that the hotel is laid out like a wheel with the casino as hub," she explained. "This means the guest has to walk by the casino to get anywhere. Now, of course this makes it easy for him to gamble, but there's a second important reason for that feature. It gives the guest a sense of being where the action is all the time, and it's one of the reasons people love staying at Caesars."

The famous floating lounge, Cleopatra's Barge, came about because Harris and Sarno were trying to make use of a dry wash on the property. "We thought originally we would make the wash into a pond and float the barge on it. Once we understood this wasn't feasible we thought the barge idea was too good to abandon, so we moved it indoors."

Sarno loved ovals, and according to his former wife, he never built a rectangular bar in any motel. He thought that they inhibited conversation and that they had a cold feeling about them. He even had dice tables built with specially rounded corners.

Caesars made money from the day it opened in 1966. And Sarno and his family became Las Vegas royalty. "Oh, it was fun. Our little rear ends were sore from everybody kissing them," said September, who was almost seven years old then.

"My brother and I were chubby and Dad thought we should swim some laps before breakfast, so we had to do that before the pool opened. There would be lifeguards and pool boys out there, all these people looking after two little kids."

Heidi Sarno Straus, the youngest of the Sarno children, was born the year Caesars opened and followed her dad into the hotel business, though she later left it to open a flower and gift-basket shop. She said that running a hotel cost the Sarno family some of the closeness it might otherwise have had. "He knew my birthday was in April, and that was about it," she said wistfully of her father.

Jay Jr. credits the opportunity of growing up in a hotel with giving him some of the business acumen that made him a successful designer of slot machines and biomedical equipment. But a normal home life just was not feasible, he admits. "The business did not peak between nine and five. When Dad came home from the office, he was on the phone constantly, because something important was happening at the hotel. He was not a delegator, so it constantly pervaded his existence. The family would go to see Dad because it wouldn't work the other way around. We would go live in the hotel about a month every summer, on holidays, on weekends."

Having kids underfoot at the hotel seemed to work fine for Sarno. "We would run into his office and jump on his lap and draw on his

The innovative visionary of Circus Circus and Caesars Palace, Jay Sarno, 1966.
(Courtesy Las Vegas News Bureau)

papers, and it did not distract him from whatever he was doing," remembered Jay Jr.

He used much the same incentive in home life that he used in business. An "A" on a report card, said September, was worth $100.

Sarno had no interest in the simple life. "I wanted to go camping once," said Jay Jr. His father tried to indulge him by getting Pug Pearson, a professional card player, to loan him Pearson's twenty-six-foot Winnebago. Sarno had it brought to the hotel, where Jay Jr. and one of his buddies filled it with provisions. The Sarnos set out for Zion National Park with a chauffeur at the helm. "When we got down in Arizona he insisted I drive. I had just turned fifteen. So the first vehicle I ever drove was a twenty-six-foot Winnebago, out of state and unlicensed, with my whole family in it," remembered Jay Jr.

Sarno was cordial to other businessmen but informal to a point many found disconcerting. "He was capable of waking up from a deep sleep and immediately talking business. There was no transition," said Jay Jr. The trouble was, he would actually do this during the time he lived at Circus Circus after he and Joyce were divorced in 1974. "He would run straight from his bed to a breakfast meeting with his hair going off in these Einsteinesque directions," said Jay Jr.

"He was a diabetic and had to give himself shots. And in the course of breakfast, without stopping to explain, he'd rub a little alcohol on his tummy and just jam the needle in. That would distract people."

Mel Larson, who was vice-president in charge of marketing at Circus Circus, remembers being in Sarno's suite when four visitors arrived to discuss funding for a huge hotel Sarno wanted to build. The visitors were Wall Street banking types and wore three-piece suits. Sarno received them in his underwear. "They looked a little shocked, but they acted like it was an everyday occurrence," said Larson.

Jay Jr. remembers his father watching ball games with friends in the hotel health club. Everybody was sitting around nude, or nearly so. "He'd have a cocktail waitress sent in there to order us a round of bitter lemon sodas. He didn't know whether any of the other guys minded a woman coming in there, or whether she wanted to come in there. He simply did not think about it."

Sarno had other things on his mind. He always did. Some say he started thinking about a new casino as soon as Caesars opened its doors. Three years after they built Caesars for $24 million, Sarno and his partners sold it for $60 million to Lum's, a Miami-based restaurant chain. "I know Sarno regretted selling it later," said Ted Binion. "But lord, that was a lot of money in 1969. Anybody would have sold it."

The sale of Caesars gave Sarno a chance to build a new place. The man who let his children romp through the plushest adult hotel in America had decided to build one that would serve a family market as well as high rollers.

Circus Circus exploited the excitement of the traditional circus and followed that theme right out the window. Gamblers played while trapeze artists swung overhead, and they were the best trapeze acts in the business. "My dad raped and pillaged the big tops for their best acts," said September. "Everybody wanted to work for him because it was the first chance they'd had to live in one place and have normal lives." There was a midway full of sideshows and carnival games that even children could play. There was a baby elephant, named Tanya, who would pull the handle on an oversized slot machine. There was a bar built into a merry-go-round. You could get to the casino floor by sliding down a fireman's pole or a slide.

Don Williams, who was Sarno's assistant in the early days there, remembered that Sarno also demanded an elephant that would fly. "So we had some steel boots made to fit a particular elephant. The boots were pink and we painted the elephant to match. The boots were cabled to this monorail that ran around the big top, and this pink elephant would fly through the air against the dark background, and it was something to see!

"But it wasn't successful. The elephant loved flying when we tried it experimentally in a barn, but it didn't take to the heights in the actual casino. Also, the elephant wasn't housebroken. We had a big diaper made for it, but we finally decided it wasn't a big enough draw to be worth the trouble. We probably wasted $50,000 or $60,000 on that project, but it was fun to try."

Sarno was so proud of Circus Circus that for a while he charged admission just to come in and look. He was so confident of his idea's drawing power that he opened the casino without hotel rooms, figuring people would be drawn from all those plain-vanilla resorts. He planned to build the hotel rooms later.

This time Sarno bet too strongly on himself. Circus Circus was an instant loser.

Maybe because his own powers of concentration were extraordinary, Sarno failed to realize that many high rollers did not want the distraction of trapeze acts. Some dealers also were unable to keep their eyes off the acrobats only a few feet above their heads, and card cheats soon learned to make their moves when the dealer looked away.

Sarno had sold midway concessions and had not been particular who bought them. Some of the midway games were dishonest, as carnival games sometimes will be, and their operators lacked discretion. One Las Vegan remembers stopping at a midway game, on the way in, and winning. His prize turned out to be a deck of cards—with every card cleverly marked so it could be read from the back. Flagrant disrespect for the honest game, flaunted only a few feet from the casino, did not inspire $1,000 bets. That gambler never bet another $2 at Circus Circus.

In 1974, after losing money for more than five years, Sarno turned over the resort to William Bennett, a gaming executive who had worked for the Del Webb organization, and William Pennington, who had manufactured gaming equipment. It was a complex deal that did not result in a complete transfer of real estate until 1983.

Meanwhile, the new operators proved that Sarno's ideas would work, with just a few modifications. They brought the midway under the hotel's direct control, replacing the more ribald sideshows and the sleazier games. They rearranged the floor plan to give gamblers easier access to the pits, moved out the more distracting acts or moved them farther from the tables.

Most important, they recognized that Circus Circus had been trying to do too many things at once, seeking to attract high rollers with high limits and credit, yet driving them away with distractions. The real potential of a casino that bathed the senses with excitement, they saw, was to attract the casual gambler who would risk a few bucks while taking in the sights. Concentrating on the middle-class market, they put the operation into the black in two months. Circus Circus set the trend of marketing to whole families. When the corporation went public, it became one of the most successful gaming stocks.

Sarno, meanwhile, had an even bigger dream—so big he called it "the Grandissimo." He never got to build it, however. Teamsters pension funds had bankrolled Sarno visions ever since the Atlanta Cabana. While most of their Las Vegas investments had paid off handsomely, the Teamsters in the mid-1970s were under heavy pressure to diversify. Sarno never found another source to fund something so big. His dream called for the largest resort ever built—six thousand rooms. It would have had lots of fountains, waterfalls, moving sidewalks, roller coaster rides in the casino.

Sounds a bit like the Mirage, doesn't it?

Steve Wynn's Mirage reflects his own tastes, just as Caesars expressed Sarno's extravagant appetites. But the Mirage—and the MGM Grand, and the Excalibur—are all logical extensions of ideas Sarno pioneered.

Without a casino to run, Sarno found even more time for his hobbies. According to all who knew him, those hobbies were women, food, golf, and gambling, all pursued to joyous excess.

One of the mysteries of Jay Sarno was how a balding man in his 50s, who stood five-feet-eight and weighed more than two hundred pounds, could repeatedly attract beautiful young blondes whom other men only dreamed about. Part of his success was making a great first impression. "If most men meet you and like you, they buy you a drink," explained one woman. "If Jay Sarno met you and liked you, he bought you a mink. He really did that, more than once, on a first meeting."

His skirt-chasing was something the women who loved him simply came to accept. Joyce, who remarried after their 1974 divorce, said, "When we were married I couldn't have a boyfriend, but he wanted me to play golf with his girlfriends. I had to divorce him so we could double date."

Even after the divorce, Joyce was an honored guest at dinner parties given for Jay's girlfriends. He continued to buy Joyce splendid presents—a full-length mink, even another Rolls-Royce. And he never married anybody else. He told friends, "Making one woman unhappy was one too many."

Sarno pursued golf almost as intently. His younger son, Freddie, born in 1961, was his frequent partner. "He was a club-buying maniac," said Freddie. "In his suite at Circus Circus he had a walk-in closet, and he called it his pro shop. There was one bag in there with nothing but putters—about thirty in all. There was one with wedges, one with drivers."

Classy pro shops used to own special golf bags as big as a garbage can. "They were strictly for store display, made to hold dozens of clubs at one time," said Freddie. "But he actually strapped one onto the back of a golf cart. It was his usual bag."

Jay Sarno once wanted a new angle on a club face, and he paid a dentist to grind it.

Despite his rotund build, Freddie said, Jay Sarno was a good athlete. "He had wonderful hand-eye coordination, and was a great Ping-Pong player. He had played high school basketball, and I think he ran track." In his youth Sarno was a scratch golfer and won the state amateur title in Georgia. His handicap was only nine when he died.

When he meant to play golf, Sarno would do it though the heavens burst. "I can remember him and his buddies chartering a jet to go somewhere else and play because it was raining here," said Freddie. Once he wanted to play in Pahrump, a little more than one hour from Las Vegas by car. That was too long for Sarno; he hired a helicopter to drop his foursome on the first tee.

"It was commonplace for him to win or lose $10,000 or $20,000 on a round," said Freddie. "He was personally trustworthy at golf, but he sometimes played with people who weren't because the action was good enough. And he also said he felt sorry for people who played so badly they had to cheat. But I would say those guys probably got the better of him, eventually."

They did indeed. Good golfer though he was, Sarno's usual opponents were better. They let him win just often enough to think he could beat them on his best days. This is the classic hustle because it works, and it worked on Sarno too.

If Sarno happened to be winning legitimately, on a day when the script did not call for him to win, some of his opponents were not above gaffing the game. The story is told that during some games these players had a crony lurking in the rough to note where Sarno's first shot landed on dogleg holes. If Sarno's ball was positioned well to land near the cup on the next shot, the confederate would run onto the green with a holecutter and relocate the cup behind a sandtrap or a water hazard.

Freddie probably understates Sarno's golf losses out of respect for his father. A scratch golfer remembers that he was told, immediately upon his arrival in Las Vegas, "Your goal in life should be to get into Jay Sarno's foursome. If you ever get a regular spot there, you won't have to work."

Sarno also lost heavily gambling in casinos, including one he had built, Caesars. In the divorce action, Joyce Sarno claimed he had lost more than $2.7 million gambling at three casinos between 1969 and 1971. In an unrelated suit, Sarno admitted losing another million between 1972 and 1974.

Ted Binion was the casino manager at his family's downtown casino, Binion's Horseshoe, but when Sarno walked in, Ted dealt the game personally. "It was the only way you could play as fast as he wanted to play," explained Binion. "I mean, he didn't want the dice to quit rolling! We didn't pay every bet as he won it, like you normally do; we just kept track of it with table markers. You can't do that unless there's trust on both sides. But you could trust him. He started out a $20 player, and he ended up a $2,000 player by '68 or '69. He'd win or lose $80,000, $100,000, or $150,000 a night, and if it was lose, he'd pay you the next day."

Sarno was a pass-line shooter, said Ted. The odds are better on "don't pass," but Sarno did not like betting on failure.

He loved food about as much as action. "He was not of the 'wait until everybody is served' school of thought," said Jay Jr. "He was more attuned to the 'don't let it get cold' philosophy."

Sarno's preferred breakfast was filet mignon. "That was when he was on a diet, which was most of the time," remembered Joyce. "When he wasn't dieting, he had salami."

His diet worried his friends. "After he had open heart surgery, I tried to get him to take care of himself better," said Lem Banker, the famous Las Vegas oddsmaker. "But I'd see him down at Baskin-Robbins, with a double-dip ice cream cone. One in each hand, different flavors."

Freddie said, "He had plenty of warnings about how he could live longer, but he seemed to make a distinct choice to live like he wanted, instead."

The odds caught up with Sarno in 1984. He died in a suite at Caesars Palace. Legend has it that he was sharing the suite with a couple of girls—beauties less than half his age. It would not have been beyond Sarno to start that rumor himself. He wanted to be remembered, and it fit his self-image.

Sarno did not leave a lot of money when he died, and his children all work for their livings. "But I don't resent that a bit," said Freddie. "It was his to do what he wanted. And if you knew him, you know that spending it was the only reason he took the trouble to make it."

Sam Boyd's Quiet Legacy
Jack Sheehan

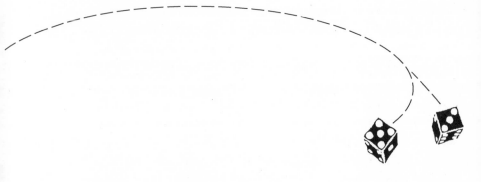

In his own way, Sam Boyd was an amalgam of many elements that transformed Las Vegas into the quintessential American dream city it has become in the last half century.

Boyd was raised in the Dust Bowl, in a family forced to struggle for subsistence, yet died an immensely wealthy man.

He was a gambler down to his toenails, but he understood that the better odds for success lay on the dealer's side of the table, so he learned everything there was to know about all the games and, more important, how to keep the customer smiling and coming back despite the inevitable losses.

He was a cowboy, but not the kind that shod horses or branded steers. He was an urban cowboy, with the ever-present Stetson hat and string tie, the handshake that meant more than any bulky legal document, and the courteous manner toward ladies that would not allow cussing or off-color stories in their presence.

He knew that you could not just take from a community, that you had to give back. So he got deeply involved in civic affairs and charitable causes and lent his time when it was needed to a growing university and to youth organizations and to all who were in need of a hand in the city that would make him rich and famous.

Sam Boyd was all work and very little play. Everyone who worked with him or for him will tell you that he demanded a lot of his employees but that he never asked for more than he was willing to give himself. His life was consumed by his work. Hours on the job meant nothing to him. He would work for days and nights at a time, taking only an occasional catnap. And there was no task too menial for him. Long after he had become a millionaire many times over, Sam could be found clearing tables in a busboy's apron, or dealing craps, or helping out at the casino cage.

Sam Boyd never wavered in his belief that Las Vegas could be as big and bawdy as it wanted to be. All it took was a strong work ethic and common sense, and he was long on both.

Boyd's legacy will be perpetuated as Las Vegas charges ahead into the next century, because he bequeathed his work habits and values onto his son Bill, who today runs the burgeoning Boyd Gaming Corporation.

From nickel bingo games on the Long Beach harbor all the way to a publicly traded company bearing his name on the New York Stock Exchange, that is how high Sam Boyd lifted himself up.

Sam was born in Enid, Oklahoma, in 1910. His father, Bill, made a decent living for his family as the owner of a cab company, and his mother, Lotta, was a nurse. But when Bill Boyd died of typhoid in 1919, he left behind five children and a business that quickly went belly up. Lotta Boyd was forced to head west in search of a better life. After a one-year stop in Albuquerque to work as a nurse and save up money, she moved her family to California—first to Monterey Park and eventually to Long Beach. This was not the first down-on-its-luck family to leave Oklahoma for what was perceived as a better life in California. John Steinbeck wrote of hordes of others in *The Grapes of Wrath*. But unlike many of those poor folk, this family would find a way to persevere.

It was on the pike at Long Beach that Sam Boyd, then a strapping teenager, helped out the family by working as a pitch man for various games of chance. His salary was ten cents an hour. He also toiled in the fun zones on the pike, working as a carny and a barker. He learned at an early age that half the battle for any business is luring customers into the house.

Later on, when Sam would operate his own "fun houses" in Las Vegas, there was no gaming operator as savvy about marketing his properties and enticing the public to come inside. "Sam never got over being a carny," says Perry Whitt, who first earned Boyd's trust by working under him at the Flamingo in 1947, then later became a director of the Boyd Gaming Corporation. "In a lot of ways he'd junk the place up, but it always drew a lot of people in. He'd have flags and

*Newlyweds Sam
and Mary Boyd.*
(Courtesy Bill Boyd)

balloons and coupon books and huge birthday cakes. And Sam didn't care if you had twenty dollars in your pocket or twenty thousand. He just wanted masses of people, and he got them."

After a year on the pike, Boyd was asked by his boss to work on a gambling ship anchored off the California coast. He was put in charge of the bingo games on a liner appropriately named the *Monte Carlo*. On this and other ships, Boyd learned how to deal 21, craps, and the roulette wheel. He should have paid his bosses for the education, because this accrued knowledge, combined with his innate business sense, would make Sam wealthier than most of the leisurely Southern California gamblers who frequented the ships.

During this period Sam was dating Mary Neuman, a girl from Salt Lake City whom he had met in Long Beach. They were married in 1931, and within a year Mary gave birth to a son they named after Sam's father. Bill Boyd was to be their only child, and he would take their shared knowledge and help turn it into a gambling empire.

"Both my parents stressed the importance of a formal education," Bill says. "When I was young, Dad always said, 'You don't want to go through life being a dealer like I am. If you get an education, no one can ever take it away from you, and you'll have some independence.'"

Of course, another path to independence was hard work and tremendous focus, and it was that road Sam arduously followed as one opportunity grew into the next.

Sam spent the early 1930s working as a bingo agent in Los Angeles, where bingo parlors would open and close at the whim of whoever was in power in local political circles. Working with him at a parlor at Sixth and Rampart was Al Garbian, who would become a lifelong friend.

"As bingo agents, we collected for each game," Garbian recalls. "They ran twelve to fourteen games an hour, and it was ten cents a card, with a minimum of two cards on up to ten to fifteen. We had mainly a movie clientele—directors and their wives, and some actors. Two months after I met Sam, they closed the parlor. But I remember him being frugal. I did a little singing on the side back then, and one day I asked Sam to fill in for me because I had a job singing for a funeral. We made eight dollars a day at the bingo parlor, so that's what I paid him. But when Sam found out that I made much more than that singing, he demanded a raise."

By being a conscientious worker, and proving to his bosses along the way that he was upwardly mobile, Sam continued to find new opportunities. He spent five years, from 1935 to 1940, in Hawaii, where he established bingo in Honolulu and Hilo for Hisanaga Palace Amusements. While there, he came to appreciate Hawaiians as honest, gregarious people who loved to gamble. The many friends he would make on the Islands would prove invaluable to him years later when he was establishing a customer base for his pride and joy—the California Hotel.

It was not until Labor Day 1941, just after the state of California and the federal government stopped offshore gambling operations, that Sam moved his wife and young son to Las Vegas. He loved the dusty, isolated town immediately and, unlike others, saw it as the future of gambling. When people would complain about the desert heat, he would argue that the lack of humidity was a great drawing card. It was a case of an up-and-coming young man recognizing a city very much at a similar juncture—on the cusp of realizing its tremendous promise.

Sam's first job in Las Vegas was dealing penny roulette at the Jackpot Club, located downtown on the plot of land now occupied by Binion's Horseshoe. Both Mary Boyd and Sam's sister, Myrtie Lee, also took jobs dealing there. Sam also worked at the Savoy and the El Cortez, and eventually at the El Rancho Vegas, which until the Last Frontier was built in 1942 was the only resort on the Strip.

Bill Boyd remembers those early years in Las Vegas. "We lived in a motel behind the Green Shack out on Boulder Highway," he says. "Dad was dealing at various places, including the supper clubs where people would pay for dinner and then gamble afterwards. Typically, there were about three blackjack games and a crap game and a roulette wheel. And there was no entertainment.

"In those days, my dad got six to eight dollars a day, paid out in silver dollars, and tips would be less than that. The thing that impressed me as a kid was when Dad would come home and bring his earnings in silver and stack it on the dresser. Those stacks of silver looked like all the money in the world to me then."

Bill also remembers his father's tireless nature. "He would work every day they'd let him. He couldn't understand why somebody who worked only six days a week wouldn't want to work on the seventh. To him work was the fun in life. He saw it as an opportunity to learn more about the business so that he could advance in it."

But another Sam—Uncle Sam—was to delay Sam Boyd's upward climb by drafting him into the Army in 1944. He was assigned to the Medical Corps at Camp Wheeler, Georgia. He almost did not survive basic training, where he contracted double pneumonia.

"My mother got a call that she needed to come to Georgia, that Dad probably wasn't going to make it," Bill recalls. "They gave him sulfa drugs [a precursor to penicillin], and it saved his life. After the war, he always showed a great love for medicine, and working with surgeons gave him an even greater appreciation for the benefits of a formal education."

Upon his return to Las Vegas in 1946, Sam jumped back into a dealing job, more determined than ever to advance his position in life. He got the chance at the old El Rancho Vegas, where his talents were recognized by one of the controlling partners, Charles Resnik, who died in his nineties (shortly after being interviewed for this book).

"I had heard Sam was a good, honest man," said Resnik, "so when we had the El Rancho I watched him closely for about a month just to make sure. He never made a bad move in that time. He handled customers well, and he was a hard worker. Later, when we bought the Flamingo after Bugsy Siegel 'got sick' [i.e., took a bullet in the head], we brought Sam over and made him a shift boss. He was with me about six years, first in Vegas and then in the summers up in Reno at the Club Cal-Neva and also at Lake Tahoe at the Cal-Neva Lodge."

During those summers up north, Bill, who was attending college at the University of Nevada, also worked at the Cal-Neva Lodge, parking cars and putting up signs promoting the new resort. He spent his weekends working as a change boy at the Club Cal-Neva in Reno. Bill did not realize it at the time, intent as he was on a career practicing law, but he was accruing ground-level experience in the gaming business that would prove invaluable in the coming decades.

Resnik took a paternal pride in how much both Sam and Bill Boyd would accomplish in later years. "I took care of Sam and he saved his money and the bonuses I gave him, and that's how he had a stake to eventually buy into the Sahara," he said. "I like to think that if I hadn't taken him under my wing like that, then none of these things would have happened with the Boyd Corporation. It was a case of giving a guy a chance, and having him take full advantage of it."

Sam's next job in Las Vegas was at the Thunderbird, working for Marion Hicks. The Thunderbird would prove to be a troubled property, since Hicks's lack of capital led him to borrow money from Meyer Lansky. In effect, the mob ran the place. Sam worked as a floorman/pit boss and got to know some of the underworld characters who were regular patrons.

In 1952 Boyd got his big opportunity to become a stockholder in a Las Vegas hotel. A Portland man named Al Winter was opening the Sahara Hotel, and Sam was given a chance to purchase 1 percent for $16,000. He put up $6,000 of his own money and borrowed the rest from a friend, Nick Zar. The owners of the Thunderbird were begging Sam to stay on, so before he made the most important investment of his life, he consulted his son.

"I remember feeling really good that Dad would ask my opinion," Bill recalls. "I was just out of college and about to start law school, and he was consulting me on the biggest business decision he'd ever made. I told him it wasn't even a close call. If he stayed at the Thunderbird, he would have owed his soul to those guys and it would have been trouble. Thankfully, he made the right decision and got out. I honestly believe that was the pivotal moment of my dad's life."

Sam Boyd was forty-two when he made that investment, and once he had a piece of the action, his long-established work habits grew into an all-consuming passion. He ate, drank, and slept the Sahara during the four years he was there. As a shift boss, he quickly grew comfortable with making all the important decisions when he was on the property and seeing to it that customers were treated right. The place was a hit from opening day, and within a year Sam was able to repay the $10,000 loan and reap a handsome profit to boot.

In 1957 the Sahara Hotel Corporation built the Mint downtown, and Sam purchased 3½ percent. The Sahara brain trust knew the best watchdog for his investment was Sam himself, so they named him vice-president and general manager. At long last, Sam would be able to run a property exactly as he saw fit. The old carny in him would come into full play at the Mint.

"He was the best promoter you ever saw," says Rita Taylor, who started at the Mint in 1959 as a change girl working for eight dollars a day and is now the corporate cage manager for the Boyd Gaming Corporation. "His ideas for keeping the place busy hadn't been done in Las Vegas before. It was always like a carnival, or a party, with people in hats and balloons everywhere. He'd have a giant birthday party for the Mint each year, and they'd bake this enormous cake, weighing about five tons. I thought no one would want to eat it, but people lined up around the block to get a piece of that cake."

The Merri Mint Theatre—featuring a splashy variety show—played to packed houses nearly every night, and Sam brought in big-name country and western stars, like Johnny Cash.

He also published fun books and coupon books for free meals, and many of the poor people downtown used them for subsistence. But Boyd did not mind; it was his way of giving something back. Longtime employees tell stories of how Sam would allow less fortunate folk to smuggle food out of the restaurant.

Rita Taylor recalls kind gestures her boss made to many employees, but always with the proviso that they be kept secret. "Sam was always giving money to workers who had a sick child, and each Christmas he'd have me bring in three single mothers who worked for us, so he could give them extra money to buy Christmas gifts for their kids. Another time, he called my sister to inquire about her son, who was ill. It was only later we found out that Sam's brother had died that very morning, yet he still took the time to call."

Virginia Torres, who was Sam's executive secretary for more than two decades, remembers that he was totally consumed by work and community events. "His day would usually start with a function around 7 A.M., then he'd work till 3 P.M., maybe go home or take a nap

Sam Boyd in 1957. (Courtesy Las Vegas News Bureau)

for an hour, or just rest on the sofa in his office, then shower and change clothes and work until two or three in the morning. He'd sleep for a couple more hours, then start his day again. He worked every day, and he thought everyone else should too."

Although the Mint had gambling limits, Torres says Sam never really sweated the action. "He wasn't afraid of big players," she says. "One time a gambler was up a couple hundred thousand on us, and Mr. Boyd stayed very calm. He said, 'Don't worry. There's more where that came from.'"

Bill recalls a time when his father quickly went from philosophical to concerned, however. "Dad was in Europe, on one of his rare vacations, and he got a call that someone had hit a $25,000 keno ticket, which was the top limit then. And he said, 'Good, you have to have winners to have players.'"

Ten minutes later the phone rang again, to inform Sam that someone had hit another $25,000 winner on the very next game. "Well, his benevolence turned to concern," Bill says. "He became instantly suspicious that something was up. He spent the next hour on the phone, getting all the details. He had a feeling maybe we were getting scammed."

In 1962 Sam and Bill Boyd and two partners purchased the Wheel, an established casino in Henderson. They renamed it the Eldorado Club, and it was the first of the casinos owned and operated by the Boyd family. Three years later they acquired the Royal Club, located next door, and doubled the Eldorado's size. With its small-town flavor, Henderson reminded Sam of his early days in Las Vegas, where customers were greeted by name and casinos offered a relaxed, down-home atmosphere. It was a style Sam would imprint in every place he ran.

Around this time, Sam started a Boys Club in Henderson, the seed for all the boys' and girls' clubs in Nevada. Many people say it was the cause closest to his heart.

In 1966 the Sahara Hotel Corporation merged with the Del Webb Corporation and became a wholly owned subsidiary of Webb. Sam agreed to stay on as the Mint's general manager for about a year—two expansions had already been completed or were under way at the time—but he left shortly after the merger was completed. Bill remembers his father saying that the Webb company's style was to give someone a title rather than a raise. Sam was a bottom-line guy. He knew from his years of struggling that money meant a lot more than a title.

Perry Whitt speculated that the Webb decision to build a high-rise hotel with a gourmet restaurant on top, which did not fare well in the early going, also was not to Sam's liking. "Sam was used to making all the big decisions," Whitt says. "He was most effective when he was in complete control, and that may have caused the rift." Whatever the reason, Boyd left for new challenges, but not before he had gained many new admirers, including E. Parry Thomas, the powerful banker who had financed Del Webb's expansions into the Las Vegas gambling market.

"Sam was a terrific manager," Thomas recalls. "And he just had the most pleasing personality. He was salt of the earth, very comfortable to be around, and had the respect of everyone from his contemporaries in gaming to his employees. And there was no one more civic-minded. He was on just about every community-oriented board we had in those days."

Longtime Las Vegas mayor Oran Gragson concurs. "Sam's down-to-earth, homey personality never changed," he says, "whether he was speaking with the King of England or a floor sweeper in one of his properties. He was especially effective as a promoter of the city because he wasn't what people expected of Las Vegas. It just wasn't in his nature to act uppity or more important than anyone else."

In 1971 four different ownership groups, led by Frank Scott, Jackie Gaughan, J. K. Houssels Jr., and Sam Boyd, opened the Union Plaza at Fremont and Main Streets. Sam was the single largest stockholder in the Plaza, with 12½ percent. Bill Boyd was still practicing law, but he was a stockholder in the corporation and served as its secretary.

At the Plaza, Sam started using women exclusively to deal 21 to attract more business. He thought they were generally friendlier to customers, but the idea met with resistance by men dealers and many other executives in the gaming business who could not understand why Sam was changing the rules. Neither could some of Sam's partners, who expressed their concerns to Bill when the first couple of months' casino counts were low.

"I went to Dad with their complaints," Bill recalls, "and he was very calm. He just smiled and said, 'It's okay. Nearly all the women dealers are new and they're making some mistakes. As long as they make them in favor of the customer, and not the house, the customers will be happy. We're just building a customer base and they'll keep coming back, thinking they can beat us. Eventually, we'll win it all back.'"

And that is exactly what happened. The Union Plaza turned the corner shortly afterward and became a big success. Contributing to the hotel's popularity was Sam's innovative entertainment policy of providing Broadway hit shows. Again, many traditionalists questioned Sam's wisdom, but musicals like *Fiddler on the Roof*, *The Music Man*, and *South Pacific* played to packed crowds and started a Plaza tradition that continued into the 1980s.

Sam had a way of keeping employees on their toes. Jerry Filipelli was a casino host at the Plaza, and in a meeting about comps he expected to be chewed out for his liberal comping practices. Instead, Sam surprised him by encouraging him to comp even more. "That's how we'll get them coming back," Filipelli recalled Sam saying. "What he didn't approve of was giving comps to friends and relatives," Bill says. "He felt you should do what you could to take care of players, but only because they would inevitably return and bring more money to the bottom line."

Sam often shot from the hip in making decisions, relying on his instincts. While Filipelli happened to find Sam in a beneficent mood, others might catch Sam feeling especially frugal.

Warren Nelson, another long-term friend of Sam's and a director of the Boyd Gaming Corporation, remembers a time when a Union Plaza department head complained to Boyd that he needed more help. "The man said that he couldn't get the job done unless he hired three more employees," Nelson recalls. "So Sam asked him how many were currently beneath him, and the man said, 'Ten.'

"'Okay,' Sam said, 'we're cutting your staff down to eight.' And that's exactly what happened."

Perry Whitt chuckles at the story. "You didn't want to tell Sam that something wasn't working. He'd bang the desk and say, 'It's gonna work and you're gonna make it work.' I learned that you never disagreed with him right away when he had an idea. But if you came back at a later time, he'd discuss it rationally with you. He just trusted his instincts, and looking back, he was almost always right."

After a few years at the Union Plaza, with all the strong personalities involved in the ownership wanting a bigger say in the decision making, Sam got frustrated. He was willing to listen to input, but he wanted to make all final decisions. After going back and forth on who would buy out whom, Sam and Bill sold their interest to the other three groups at a nice profit.

As always, Sam had other irons in the fire, including the building of the Hotel Nevada on Main Street, in partnership with Bill, Jackie Gaughan, and others, and what would become his favorite project, the California Hotel, on First and Ogden.

All the money Bill and Sam had made at the Union Plaza was put into the California. The price for 1 percent of stock was $20,000, with the stipulation that another $20,000 be loaned to the company on a ten-year promissory note with interest only for ten years. The Boyds each purchased 26½ percent, and the rest was bought up by about thirty partners, men like Perry Whitt and Jerry Filipelli, who had been with the Boyds for years and would be involved in management of the California.

"Everybody who invested with us was taking a gamble," Bill says, "myself included. I left my law practice to work full time at the California. But we also knew that if we were successful, the payoff would make it very worthwhile, and Dad insisted we were going to be successful."

As at the Union Plaza, the first few months were rocky going. Sam's penny watching, while amusing at times, nevertheless reinforced his reputation as a conscientious operator.

Sam Boyd (right), with (left to right) singer Frankie Avalon, realtor Norman Kaye, actors Mickey Hargitay and Jayne Mansfield, comedian Jack Carter, and singer Johnny Mathis. (Courtesy Bill Boyd)

Warren Nelson remembers straining his eyes trying to read a book in his room at the California. "I looked inside the lamp shade and noticed that the bulb was only twenty-five watts. When I asked Sam if he couldn't beef up the lights, he said he was trying to keep the electrical bill down."

Virginia Torres recalls one morning when a bartender came into her office complaining of ants in the bar. "Well, I never did anything without authorization from Sam," she says, "but I figured he'd have me call the exterminator. When he came in I explained the situation, and he immediately turned around and walked out. About twenty minutes later, he returned with a can of Black Flag, plopped it on my desk, and said, 'Here, take care of it.'"

It was apparent after its sluggish start that the California would have to rethink its strategy. The hotel-casino had been given its name because Sam thought most of the business would come from the Golden State, but it was only after he turned to the niche market

Sam Boyd (center), with Chuck Ruthe (left) and Bill Boyd (right) at the opening of the California Hotel, 1974. (Courtesy Las Vegas News Bureau)

of Hawaii, where he had made so many friends early in his career, that things turned around.

"Dad worked that Hawaiian market like you couldn't believe," Bill says. "He contacted all the travel agents and people he'd met through the years, and he became something of a god to the people in Hawaii. They knew if they came to Las Vegas and stayed at the California, they'd have a great time and be taken care of."

As always, Sam did everything from pouring drinks to busing tables when he was shorthanded. Rita Taylor remembers an occasion when she was swamped with customers at the cage and Sam took over one of the windows. "This man wanted to cash an out-of-state check and we weren't taking them at the time," she recalls. "So when Sam showed it to me I told him we couldn't take it. He handed it back to the man and said, 'Sorry, she says we can't take it.'

"And the man said, 'I want you to know I'm a personal friend of Sam Boyd's, and if you don't cash my check I'll have your job.' And Sam said, 'Well, you can have my job for all I care.'

"He never once told the man who he was," Rita says. "Sam never had the need to brag on himself or act important. He just wanted the business to run well."

The California was on stable ground after the first several months, so, as always, the Boyds were on the lookout for new business opportunities in the city that showed no signs of slowing down.

Bill's typical day in the late 1970s was to check on business at both the Eldorado in Henderson—which the Boyds had owned since 1962—and the California. Thus he had cause to drive nearly every day on Boulder Highway. As the months went by, he noticed the increasing traffic on that eastside corridor, and it occurred to him that some barren land they owned could be put to better use. Bill talked with Boyd director Chuck Ruthe (who was also a prominent realtor) and learned that another eleven acres were available on the corner of Boulder Highway and Nellis Boulevard. As always when offered a promising opportunity in Las Vegas, Sam and his partners plunged ahead fearlessly, and their decision to build Sam's Town helped create a third major gaming area for Las Vegas.

Catering to an exclusively local market, in an off-the-beaten-path location, the Boyds once again showed that keen management and unbridled optimism could overcome the odds. Using the proven formula of down-home courtesy in a friendly atmosphere, Sam's Town has been a huge success since the day it opened in 1979.

Sometime after the opening of Sam's Town, Sam Boyd finally started to take it a little easier. His health was not what it once was, and the time had come for the Boyd empire to move from the world of string ties to business suits. Sam's efficient, hands-on management style had been so effective that it was imperative he delegate much of the authority. Gradually, Bill took the reins; and although the transition had its awkward moments, all in the current Boyd Gaming Corporation agree that it was the right move at the right time.

"Sam was as good an operator as there was from about 1955 to 1975," says Perry Whitt. "He was great for his time because there was never a doubt about who was running the show. The buck didn't go any further than Sam. But he wouldn't want to operate the company the way it has to be run today. He wouldn't want to deal with the Gaming Control Board and all the regulations with the Securities [and] Exchange Commission."

"Sam had his way and that was it," says Bobby Neuman, Sam's Town general manager and Bill's first cousin. "He would not enjoy running a place nowadays because of all the state and federal regulations. He just wouldn't put up with it. For example, when they changed the rules and banned owners from going into the cage, he went in there anyway. His attitude was that it was his money, and he was going to keep an eye on it."

"It was tough for Sam to turn over the decision making to Bill," says Chuck Ruthe. "Just after Sam's Town opened, we were discussing the entertainment at the new place, and Sam wanted topless lady entertainers, which is what we had at the California. So he was telling us about the topless band he'd hired. And Bill said, 'No, Dad, we're going with country western, not topless.' Well, they debated the issue a little while, then Bill said, 'No, we're not gonna do it.'

"And Sam said, 'If we're not, then I quit. I resign.'

"And he left the room. Well, the board consisted of just Perry and Warren and Bill and Sam and I, so the other four of us just sat there real quiet. After about ten minutes, Sam came back in the room, sat down, pounded his fist on the table and said, 'Let's continue the meeting.'"

The passing of the mantle from Sam to Bill paralleled the progression of the Las Vegas gaming industry as a whole: from the control of hands-on operators like Sam, to boards of directors, with their attorneys, accountants, and corporate CEOs.

Bill Boyd recognizes that his father was subtly grooming him for these times all along. "It would have been impossible for Dad to employ his style today, because you can only work so hard and you have to relinquish control. He was not afraid to delegate in matters where he didn't have expertise, such as the legal side, but in areas where he had knowledge he just had to have control."

Bill says he is much like his father regarding work. "Hours don't mean anything to me, so I'm not a clock-watcher. He and I both thought of our work as fun, so I don't think much about taking time off."

But he concedes that their management style is radically different. "Dad was volatile, with a temper he could lose quickly," he says. "I have a much higher boiling point than he did. And I'm sometimes accused of not making decisions fast enough. Dad had so much self-confidence, he would make a decision instantly and be absolutely certain he was right, because he was raised in the business. Perhaps because of my law background, I look carefully at both sides of an issue before making up my mind. And I get several professional opinions before I make a decision."

Warren Nelson is more abrupt about their differences. "Sam was far more outspoken then Bill," he says. "Bill treads lightly, and sometimes I feel he wouldn't step on a bug. Sam had no problems stepping on bugs, and he was that way until he died."

Without exception, those who knew the Boyds as a father-son unit remark on the exceptional closeness and respect that existed between them.

"I don't think any man ever lived who received better treatment from his son during his illness than Sam received from Bill," Nelson says. "And I don't think Sam was strict with Bill, because he had so much respect for Bill's knowledge and character that he gave him a freer hand than anybody in the organization. He always knew Bill would do the right thing.

"My association with my own son is very strong," Nelson adds, "but not as strong as theirs."

Chuck Ruthe concurs. "I've never seen a closer bond between a son and his father," he says. "When we'd be on business trips, Bill would call his father twice a day. His last stop before leaving town was to see his dad, as was his first stop upon returning. I've never seen a guy take care of his dad—and his mother, too—like Bill did."

Although the transition of power from father to son was not easy, Ruthe understood the dynamics. "Sam didn't want to let go," he says. "It's hard to understand. A father wants his son to take over but he just can't let go. But after the transition was over and completed and accepted, Sam admired Bill like he was a god."

With Sam Town's Las Vegas, Sam's Town in Tunica, Mississippi, and Sam Boyd Stadium, and with Sam's three grandchildren (Sam J. Boyd, Marianne Boyd Johnson, and William R. Boyd) all holding important management positions in the Boyd Gaming Corporation, it is not likely that anyone will soon forget the contribution Bill's father made to Las Vegas.

"When we first came here, the city had about ten thousand residents," Bill says. "Nowadays, we have more employees than that in our organization."

From his well-appointed office just off the Las Vegas Strip, Bill tilts his head and looks up at a framed portrait of his father.

"Whenever I have a tough decision to make, I always ask myself, 'What would Dad do?' When I feel I know the answer, I go with it."

Jackie Gaughan: Keeping the Faith on Fremont Street

Bill Moody, with A. D. Hopkins

It is a crowded midday in the El Cortez, the unpretentious downtown hotel that Jackie Gaughan calls home. A journalist, trying to interview the aging but hyperactive Gaughan, is hard put to keep up as Gaughan walks purposefully through his casino, sidestepping slot players and change girls, quarter machines and cocktail waitresses, with the surefooted, rolling gait of a lifelong sailor walking a complicated deck. Suddenly he turns aside, picks up two empty beverage glasses left beside a slot machine by some player, carries them to a station where busboys collect dirty dishes to be washed, and continues on his mission.

Gaughan did that reflexively, rather than to make a point, but it made one all the same. Knowing an operation from the busboy to the boardroom makes for a consistent and successful business.

Other operators have been unashamed to imitate the methods that Gaughan learned by experience. Steve Wynn, who operates two of the most famous Strip casinos, praises Gaughan and his low-key downtown operations. "Gaughan's entry signaled the beginning of mass-marketing Las Vegas hotel casinos to middle America," Wynn says. "The contests, the promotions, the giveaways—Jackie is really the prototype guy for all of that, and he's a colorful character on top of everything else."

Gaughan's legend is not about sheiks dropping millions at baccarat; Jackie Gaughan stories run in the opposite direction. There was the customer who won $76,000 playing a penny slot machine.

That's right—a penny machine, forgotten by most of the industry before most of today's casinos were conceived, but still in use at Jackie's. Gaughan casinos are full, not of fashion and the fashionable, but of loose shirts and freebie hats and couples who care that a $5.95 steak is a bargain. They are places where even nickel slot players get free drinks and where nobody gets snubbed for playing with white chips. And consequently, in a town where a lot of people do not go to work until midnight, a Gaughan casino may be crowded at 10 A.M. on Tuesday.

Gaughan may sit still for an hour-long interview, but he is usually in motion. He starts his day at five. Fueled by gallons of Coke Classic, he walks a daily beat to the properties he owns outright or in part. His walk begins at the El Cortez, which he has owned since 1963 and considers the flagship of his fleet, and ends there twelve to fourteen hours later. Throughout the day he will ask questions in every hotel, receive scores of phone calls, and trade quips with customers and employees. Then there is still time to bet one horse, perhaps have dinner with his son Michael at the Barbary Coast, and be in bed by seven or eight.

Gaughan has nailed down both ends of Fremont Street's traditional gaming area, controlling its easternmost resort, the El Cortez, and its westernmost, the Union Plaza. He also owns all or part of the Gold Spike, Las Vegas Club, Nevada Club, and the Western Hotel and Bingo Parlor, and is on the board of the Showboat, which has licenses in Nevada, Atlantic City, Louisiana, and Australia.

All except the Showboat operations are on or near Fremont Street, and that is the way Gaughan likes it. Despite the phenomenal success and recent growth of Laughlin, which has many of the homey sort of operations Gaughan favors, Gaughan has never been interested in Laughlin.

"I have so many casinos here and I have to get to them every day," explains Gaughan. "Laughlin is just too far away for me to do that. It's good, but I don't want to get involved in something that I can't get to every day."

Gaughan has also brought his Midas touch to rescue operations such as the Sundance. The Sundance's charter operators were forced out of gaming after a skimming scandal. Rather than close the property and displace workers, though, Nevada authorities appointed Gaughan as interim operator in 1984, a job he kept until the prop-

Jackie Gaughan with heavyweight champion Floyd Patterson at the El Cortez, 1965. (Courtesy Las Vegas News Bureau)

erty was sold in 1986. When Gaughan took over, the Sundance was losing $750,000 a month. When he left, it was showing a profit of $300,000.

Bill Boyd, the son of one of Gaughan's former partners in the Union Plaza and now head of Boyd Gaming Corporation, thinks success so dramatic as that comes from "Jackie's hands-on management style." He adds, "You just don't get that with a corporation. Individual ownerships, which most of the downtown properties are, mean the individual makes his home here."

In Gaughan's case, that is literally true. Gaughan and his wife, Roberta, lived in conventional middle-class neighborhoods while raising their two sons. But about ten years ago they moved into a five-room penthouse apartment at the El Cortez.

Until recent years Gaughan operated from a tiny office just large enough for a desk and one or two chairs for visitors, and the desk was buried beneath six inches of financial data, photographs, memorabilia, and peanut-butter-and-cheese-cracker snack packs. His present office in the new El Cortez tower is larger, but hardly plush by executive standards. It has a comfortable, worked-in look. The walls

A gathering of downtown Las Vegas leaders, 1985: (left to right) the Horseshoe's Jack Binion; the Four Queens' Jeanne Hood; the California Hotel's Sam Boyd; and the El Cortez's Jackie Gaughan. (Courtesy Bill Boyd)

of the adjacent conference room are hung with photos and plaques awarded for nearly fifty years of civic and charitable work.

Gaughan is not disorganized; he is just organized in a way that is not office-dependent. "He can also tell you anything about how his properties are doing with those little pieces of paper he pulls out of his pockets," says Don Williams, a public relations consultant.

Williams turned to Gaughan for advice when he happened to become involved in operating the Big Wheel Casino, a tiny joint at the north end of the Strip. "If you know enough to ask questions, it's like getting a Harvard MBA in gaming," Williams explains. For instance, Gaughan understands why a given kind of slot machine will work better at one spot in a casino than another. When manufacturers test new models, says Williams, "there's nowhere they'd rather have them tested than at the El Cortez. He'll move one six feet to the right or six feet to the left, or somewhere else in the casino to get the best return. If it doesn't work in Jackie's place, it won't work."

Gaughan is certain that he is the last casino operator in Las Vegas still using penny slot machines. But those, too, work for him, because he understands that some of the profit cannot be counted in cash. "You use them to make a place look alive, because people stay there longer playing them," Gaughan explained. "They collect the pennies people have in their pockets and want to get rid of, and they make a little money. Of course a quarter machine makes twenty-five times as much, but [the penny machines are] a drawing card." And penny machines attract people who would not walk across the room to play a quarter machine. In a uniquely Las Vegas ritual, every year or two people jug up the pennies cluttering their bureaus and lug them down to Jackie Gaughan's Plaza or Gold Spike or Western. Unlike banks, Gaughan's change booths have no rules about rolling the pennies and writing your name on each roll. Smiling women pour the pennies through noisy counting machines and exchange them for folding money, with a wish of "good luck" and the confidence that those greenbacks will soon belong to the casino once more.

Gaughan pioneered video surveillance in the gaming industry. "People will claim money or valuables were taken from their room but when we look at the tape, we find it's their brother-in-law or a friend," he says.

His hands-on touch extends beyond the properties to customers and employees. His son Michael recalls being kept waiting to deliver a $300,000 check while Jackie Gaughan held a conversation with a busboy.

Bill Boyd calls Gaughan "one of the few old-time gamblers left in Las Vegas. He grew up in the business and his word is his bond," says Boyd. "You don't need things in writing with Jackie."

Jackie Gaughan's grandfather was a policeman, born in Ireland. His father owned race horses and was a bookmaker. "That was a legal business at the time," pointed out Jackie. "But one of his brothers was a bootlegger and got shot by a deputy during a raid, and died years later as a result of the wound."

An accident of geography put the first Gaughans into casino gambling, and maybe proved that providence has nothing against gambling. The Missouri River changed course, stranding Carter Lake, Iowa, on the Nebraska side of the river, about three miles from the sporting set of Omaha but five miles and a bridge from the police of Council Bluffs. It was the perfect niche for a gambling house, and in it evolved a big healthy one called Chez Paris, which was run by Jackie's uncle.

By the time he was sixteen years old, Jackie Gaughan was a delivery boy in the bookmaking business, and he decided to take a few bets himself for the 1936 Kentucky Derby. He does not remember how much action he covered on a colt named Bold Venture. He does remember that the horse seemed to grow wings and paid about $40. But even then, Jackie Gaughan paid without kicking. "You gotta pay with a smile" is a Gaughan motto.

It was an inauspicious beginning, but Gaughan learned the business from Ed Barrick, one of the biggest bookies in the country at the time when bookmaking was widely legal and more widely practiced. Downtown Omaha alone had fifty bookie shops in those days, said Gaughan. He soon owned two of them, and they helped send him to Creighton University.

World War II intervened, and Gaughan joined the Army Air Corps. He became a gunnery instructor at the training base outside Tonopah, Nevada, a place also known for its silver mines and faro games. Gaughan soon became the Sergeant Bilko of the base, not only making book but running all the other officially nonexistent gambling.

In 1943 he visited Las Vegas and stayed at a hotel he would eventually own, the El Cortez, which was then about a year old. In 1946, after his discharge, he borrowed money from his mother to buy a

3 percent interest in the Boulder Club, a Fremont Street casino that had drawn its name from its original clientele, the workers who built Boulder Dam.

But Gaughan still had unfinished business in Omaha. He had already married his high school sweetheart, Roberta, and by 1946 she was raising their first son, Michael, born in 1943; another son, John, would arrive in 1947. Meanwhile, Gaughan wanted to finish college and do some postgraduate studies with bookmaker Barrick.

The family returned to Las Vegas in 1951 to buy another 3 percent ownership, this time in the Flamingo, an association that endured for seventeen years and would later cause Gaughan's only embarrassment with Nevada gaming authorities.

Gaughan also had the only race and sports books, the Saratoga, and later opened the Derby, which was across the street. In 1959 he got out of the business temporarily to buy the Las Vegas Club, which required renovation and did not reopen until 1961. Later the Union Plaza and the El Cortez would bring him back into the sports betting business.

In 1963 Gaughan bought the El Cortez from J. K. Houssels Sr. He got a surprise with the property, however: Fat Irish Green.

John L. Smith, a columnist for the *Las Vegas Review-Journal*, a few years ago recorded the story of Fat Irish, who was not truly Irish but was authentically fat. Green had been a trusted assistant to Ben "Bugsy" Siegel in the early 1940s when the latter was trying to establish himself in Las Vegas gaming and had managed to acquire a piece of the El Cortez and some other downtown properties. Siegel then pumped enormous sums of mob money into the Flamingo, which began to look increasingly like a financial storm drain.

Perhaps suspecting a pending reckoning, Siegel gave Fat Irish a briefcase full of mob money; reports of its contents range from $60,000 to $600,000. Fat Irish did not run with it, and he did not hide it; he simply held it and eventually gave it back to the mob. The newspaper reports of Siegel's bloody demise may have influenced Fat Irish's behavior; nevertheless, he had behaved, so he was rewarded. Green never had to work again.

When Jackie Gaughan purchased the El Cortez, he found one of his guests—Fat Irish—had not paid his room bill since the 1940s. When he asked for the money, though, Green told him, "I never paid any rent and I don't have to pay any rent."

The flabbergasted Gaughan called the Tropicana and talked to Houssels, suggesting Houssels put up Fat Irish at his classy Strip resort. "Sorry, he went with the deal," said Houssels.

But Gaughan did not give up his youthful dream of running a hotel without Fat Irish in it. He asked Benny Binion if the Texan would put Fat Irish at his prosperous Horseshoe. Binion responded, "I feed Irish for nothin'. You got to keep him at the hotel for nothin'."

And they did, both of them, to the day Fat Irish died.

In 1971 Gaughan helped open the Union Plaza, which was for downtown Las Vegas a new kind of hotel. It incorporated the Union Pacific railroad station and in those days, before AMTRAK, got much of its business from rail travelers. The Union Pacific contributed the land and about 75 percent of the money, but the project was so ambitious for the times—a $20-million deal—that it took several serious investors to make up the other 25 percent. The principals included Sam Boyd, who operated the California Hotel and would later found Sam's Town; his son Bill Boyd, then a practicing attorney; Frank Scott, a local builder and developer; J. K. Houssels Jr.; and Walter Zick, an architect.

The Union Plaza was a calculated gamble, but a gamble nevertheless. Fremont Street's biggest hotel at the time had only 350 rooms. The twenty-two-story Union Plaza opened with 504. It also opened with a 66,000-square-foot casino, largest in town and more than twice the size of the former record holder, the 30,000-square-foot casino at the International (now the Las Vegas Hilton). Conventional thinking held that downtown Las Vegas could not support the Union Plaza, but by the 1980s the partners were plowing in another $45 million to add 521 rooms and convention space. It was the first downtown hotel to get into the convention business.

The Plaza was ahead of its time with its identifiable theme, as were the most successful resorts of the 1980s and 1990s. Themed resorts provide a unique experience to the visitor by evoking the feeling of some exotic locale or activity. Just as Caesars Palace suggested the glamour of ancient Rome, the Union Plaza extrapolated a theme from its railroad origins and exploited the romance of rails. Even the cocktail waitresses wore outfits inspired by railroad mechanics' striped coveralls. Soon after the hotel opened, a visitor walked in, bought a drink, and observed, "Those *coveralls* only cover *some!*"

The Plaza had a classy gourmet restaurant and a swimming pool,

Jackie Gaughan with Vice President Gerald Ford, 1974. (Courtesy Las Vegas News Bureau)

both amenities usually associated with the Strip. It brought class to Fremont Street and set the course that would be followed further by the Golden Nugget.

Most Plaza clientele were drawn from the Midwest, says Gaughan. "We marketed to that area originally just because we had some travel agents there we could count on. And it's good to market to a specific region because you develop a sort of regional loyalty. People from that area, even if they don't happen to stay at your hotel, will visit it while they're in town, because they've always heard of it. Sam Boyd started marketing to Hawaiians years ago, and if you go over to the California Hotel today, that's pretty much who's in there." Similar traditions make other places tick, says Jackie. "The Western has its own following in California, and among bingo players. The Las Vegas Club draws from everywhere; it's been there so long that people tell other people about it. It's a tradition."

Sam Boyd moved on to other ventures in 1973, and Scott departed in 1990; Gaughan bought out the railroad's interest in 1993 to become the major stockholder, and renamed the hotel Jackie Gaughan's Plaza. But he still lives at the more humble El Cortez. Nobody who knows him would find that surprising.

Nancy Houssels pointed out that Gaughan wore his brother-in-law's suits for years after the man's death. "Jackie didn't see anything wrong with it," recalls Nancy. "He could certainly have his own tailor, but he said they were perfectly good suits. Golly, I was glad when they wore out and he finally got some new ones."

Gaughan's main concession to the 1990s is a cellular phone, and his only luxury seems to be the purchase of his own airplane. But there was good reason for that, explained Houssels. "Airplanes are not Jackie, but Birdie smokes, and Michael wouldn't let his mother smoke on *his* plane, so Jackie just bought his own."

"He hates the plane," said Michael. "I should have just let my mother smoke on my plane."

Michael, who is himself a respected casino operator, recalls that having a hotel-casino executive for a father made little difference in his childhood. "About the only privilege I remember was being able to use the Flamingo swimming pool and getting to go to a Strip show on my birthday," he said. "It's just not my dad's style to throw money around. Jackie Gaughan is one of the old-time gamblers. For him, money is just a way of keeping score."

Yet for all his frugality, Gaughan can be absentminded about money. The $300,000 check Michael was trying to give Jackie that time Michael had to wait for the busboy was his share of a successful business deal. "Then he called me several days later and wanted to know if the check had cleared because he'd lost it," said Michael. To help him remember things, said Michael, Jackie tried one of those pocket tape recorders for awhile, "but he always forgot to replace the batteries."

The same character traits bring excitement to an automobile ride with Jackie. "He forgets where he is and opens the driver's side door in traffic. I know he lost at least one door that way," Michael said.

Most likely, the car that lost its door was not a new one. "I remember him driving a 1949 Chevy well into the late '50s. His philosophy was to never drive a better car than your employees. He also had a station wagon with a gas can rattling around in the back in case he ran out of gas, but he forgot that, too. One night he and my mother were going to dinner at the Union Plaza when the car just quit. 'Jackie, get that can out and put in the gas,' Mom said. 'I can't,' my dad said. 'I already used it this morning.'"

Gaughan can remember the things that are important, however.

He knows the names of customers. He knows the names of employees. He knows the point spread on the Monday night game.

And for all his frugality, his casinos are known for what they give away. The Housselses claim Gaughan invented the "fun book," given away at motels, bus stations, airports, and anywhere else a likely visitor might pass. The books are full of coupons good for one bet on one of Jackie's blackjack tables, a few coins for one of his slot machines, a good dinner at half price, or a free drink in a lounge. "Jackie used to take them around to the motels himself. He knew everybody," says Houssels. Of course, there are worse uses of time than befriending a motel clerk who can recommend your casino to a construction worker busting to blow a $2,000 paycheck.

Giveaways are a standard technique for casinos, but Gaughan has developed them into an art. Year after year, one of his most successful promotions has been to give away boxes of candy at the El Cortez. "I give candy five times a year—Valentine's Day, Mother's Day, Thanksgiving, Christmas, and Easter—fifty thousand, seventy thousand boxes each time," says Gaughan.

Because these holidays do not normally draw big crowds to Las Vegas, the candy promotion gives Gaughan five fat weekends that other casinos do not enjoy. But there is a trick to it, warned Gaughan: The giveaway has to start before the holiday. "You want a guy to win a box of candy on the Thursday before Mother's Day so he can give it to Mom on Sunday."

Gaughan will usually buy the candy from some charity fund-raiser, building good will in two directions with the same dollar.

Gamblers like few things better than a chance to get lucky in some sort of lottery, especially if the entry is free. But trying to tap that trait by giving away door prizes is tricky because of professional contest winners. "They aren't necessarily bad people, but they will wrangle a way to have half a million entries in that drawing bowl if they can," Gaughan explained in a 1975 interview. "Give a ticket to every customer and many of the customers will throw them away, and pretty soon the pros have collected them and enter in their own names. I remember one lady who actually entered fifteen hundred tickets. The same people always were winning, and that negates what you're trying to do." Jackie's solution was a drawing based upon Social Security numbers. "There's only one Social Security number to a customer, so it gives every customer an equal chance. And ordinary customers are winning again."

He recently estimated that "a good 50 percent of people that register win something." Started in 1969, the Social Security drawing has become a famous free long shot that seems to have brought every Southern Nevada resident into the El Cortez at least once, and some of them have kept coming for twenty-six years.

Sometimes good will backfires on Gaughan. John Smith saw him spot a wallet lying on the casino floor. Gaughan muttered something about his lucky day but had casino cage workers announce the find on the loudspeaker. The owner was profuse in her thanks to Jackie. She had come to the casino to cash a check, she said, and losing the wallet would have been a disaster.

A few weeks later Smith saw Gaughan again. "You know, that check bounced," said Gaughan.

But Gaughan wins more than he loses. J. K. Houssels remembers a scamster who forgot the code of the West: "There's always somebody a little faster."

Houssels says, "I got a call one day from a guy on a car phone, said he was calling from a limo, that we knew each other. He tells me his son is a goofy gambler and wants to know if I would okay a check to provide him with money to get home. I didn't know the guy but he sounded legitimate and had enough details to make me think I did know him. Anyway this kid shows up at the Union Plaza and wants to cash a check for about $2,500. I okayed it and then thought, what have I done?"

Houssels ran into Jackie in the sports book and told him about it. When Jackie was contacted with the same story, he immediately realized the hotel bankroll was being scammed and the Mississippi River would clear before one of those checks would.

"Jackie told the guy he'd meet him at the cashier's cage at the El Cortez to okay the check. When the guy showed up, he tumbled Jackie and took off out of the casino. Jackie didn't even call security. He just took off after the guy." Jackie chased him into the arms of an off-duty Arizona policeman who produced a shooting iron and persuaded the scamster to halt. Jackie thinks he was sixty-seven the year it happened.

It is hard to find anybody who will speak ill of Gaughan. When they do, as in January 1987, defenders rush to his side. When Gaughan and partners Joe Kelly and J. K. Houssels applied for licensing in Atlantic City for the Showboat, the New Jersey Division of Gaming Enforcement called into question Gaughan's association with the Flamingo during a period when $27 million was skimmed from the resort. The experience was unsettling for Gaughan. But former governors Grant Sawyer and Mike O'Callaghan, U.S. senators Chic Hecht and Harry Reid, and fellow casino owner Steve Wynn, whom Gaughan had helped when Wynn was a young and slightly green operator at the Golden Nugget, spoke up on his behalf. The New Jersey application was unanimously approved.

In addition to the empire of casinos, Gaughan has given the gaming business a budding dynasty of solid operators. Michael Gaughan broke in as an assistant lifeguard at the Flamingo Hotel and worked as a cook, maintenance man, waiter, busboy, dealer, and El Cortez floorman before opening a school for dealers, which became the world's largest.

He was not quite thirty years old when he opened the Royal Inn Casino in an unlikely location neither on the Strip nor on Fremont Street, and lured in locals with Dixieland, consistent drinks, and good food, reasonably priced. Michael's Gold Coast casino on West Flamingo became the definitive locals casino, exploiting the space Jackie Gaughan never had in his downtown hotels to offer a bowling alley, a dance hall, and even a movie theater.

"My Dad and I have an agreement," says Michael. "He tries to get everything north of Sahara Avenue and I try to get everything south of it."

Jackie Jr., born in 1947, is general manager of the Plaza. Michael's son, John, runs a wire service for race books, marking the fourth generation of Gaughans in the gaming business.

With so many hands to take the helm, there is not much reason for Jackie, who was seventy-five years old on October 20, 1995, to keep working. But he resists retirement. He takes a couple of weeks off to go on a cruise, and he thinks about a retirement home in Sun City. Yet he is happiest when walking his beat between his hotels.

"I can't figure out what I'd be doing if I wasn't here," he said. "It's hard for me to imagine a time when I wouldn't be here every day."

In fact, a downtown without Jackie Gaughan is hard for anybody in the business to imagine, but Steve Wynn thinks he can picture it: "There'd be a lot of extra parking and half the buildings."

Howard Hughes in Vegas

Sergio Lalli

Howard Robard Hughes secretly arrived in Las Vegas in the predawn hours of Thanksgiving Day in 1966. A private train dropped him off at a railroad crossing on the northern outskirts of town; then, a stretcher carried the sixty-one-year-old Hughes into a waiting van, which whisked him to the Desert Inn. A dolly wheeled him into the hotel through a side door. He rode the service elevator to the top floor and did not set foot outside his bedroom until the day before Thanksgiving in 1970.

In four whirlwind years, Hughes became Nevada's biggest casino owner, acquiring the Desert Inn, the Sands, the Frontier, the Castaways, the Silver Slipper, the Landmark in Las Vegas, and Harold's Club in Reno. He also became the state's largest private employer, the state's largest private property owner, and the state's largest owner of mining claims. He was the recumbent, hermit king who hosed the Silver State with green cash.

"I have decided this once and for all," Hughes wrote in one of his famous memos. "I want to acquire even more hotels and to build this operation to be the greatest thing in the U.S. This is a business that appeals to me."

The story of Howard Hughes in Las Vegas is largely the account of an indomitable mind trapped in a worn-out body. The imposing Hughes empire rested on a most frail foundation. His backbone was bent, and several spinal disks were herniated as a result of a 1947 airplane crash that nearly killed him. Hughes took narcotics to ease his excruciating back pain. He developed a dependency on codeine and gave himself daily injections. Needle marks riddled his arms and thighs. When he was a dashing aviator and rakish movie producer, Hughes measured six-feet four-inches tall. His height in Las Vegas was close to six feet one inch. A bone protruded through the skin on his right shoulder. He had a tumor on his head. He had rotten gums in the back of his mouth, which ached all the time. He was emaciated, weighing from 115 to 120 pounds. He was nearly deaf, but he refused to wear a hearing aid most of the time. Because he also hated his eyeglasses, he used a magnifying glass he called his "peepstone" to read magazine and newspaper articles. Insomnia prevented him from getting enough sleep. Since Hughes refused to rest on his side or on his stomach, only on his back, his back and rump were pocked with painful bed sores. He was anemic and allergic to sunlight. The red corpuscle count in his blood was very low, depriving his body cells of enough oxygen. He had a peptic ulcer. The constant injection of dope over nearly twenty years had overworked his kidneys, which could barely purify his blood. Hughes suffered from a prostrate blockage, which made it difficult for him to pass urine. He had a severe case of piles. His unhealthy diet—for months at a time at the Desert Inn, he ate nothing but chicken chunks from cans of Campbell soup, and banana-nut ice cream for dessert—lacked roughage and rendered him perpetually constipated. He sat on the toilet for hours, sometimes falling asleep while waiting to make a bowel movement.

A portrait of Hughes during this period would show a man with sunken cheeks, whose beard reached down to his chest and whose gray hair fell to his shoulders. His long fingernails spiraled. He had by then decided to forsake clothes altogether, save for his drawstring drawers. Sometimes he would merely place a napkin or a Kleenex tissue over his genitals.

Hughes suffered from a menagerie of phobias, manias, obsessions, delusions, and an inordinate fear of germs. To insulate himself from germs, he shunned handshakes and opened doorknobs with a Kleenex tissue. His eating utensils were wrapped in Kleenex. His imitation-leather recliner was blanketed with paper towels, as were his bed sheets. And yet, he very seldom bathed and never brushed his teeth. While in Las Vegas, he went through a period when he would splash rubbing alcohol on his body in a monotonous ritual of purification. He had a litany of phobias: bacteria, dust, sewage, rats, flies, dirty fingernails, atomic radiation, and the circus at Jay Sarno's Circus Circus casino.

Howard Hughes after one of his record around-the-world flights. (Courtesy Las Vegas News Bureau)

"The aspect of the Circus that has me disturbed is the popcorn, peanuts and kids side of it," Hughes wrote in a six-page memo to Robert Maheu, the man who ran Hughes's Nevada operations. "And also the Carnival Freaks and Animal side of it. In other words, the poor, dirty, shoddy side of Circus life. The dirt floor, sawdust and elephants. The part of the Circus that is associated with the poor boys in town. The part of the Circus that is associated with the common poor man.

"It is the above aspect of a circus that I feel are all out of place on the Las Vegas Strip. After all, the Strip is supposed to be synonymous with a good looking female all dressed up in a very expensive diamond studded evening gown and driving up to a multi-million dollar hotel in a Rolls-Royce. Now, you tell me what, in that picture, is compatible with a circus in its normal raiment, exuding its normal atmosphere and its normal smell?"

Although his writings are filled with niggling trifles, quirks, vanities, and imagined wrongs, his epistles are remarkable for their lucid prose. Hughes was weird all right, but his reasoning powers were still intact. Hughes wrote his memos with a blue ballpoint pen on yellow, legal-size note pads. Memos and telephone calls were his only means of communication to his underlings. The crowning irony of Hughes's life was that the world's most secretive man left a trail of documentation so comprehensive that his life has become an open book. His extant memos chronicle his innermost thoughts in his own handwriting as effectively as any diary. Our knowledge of Howard Hughes is further substantiated by the remembrances of the people in his life—his executives, his stewards, his doctors, his lawyers, his former wife—as quoted in numerous biographies and interviews, and from their testimony in probate court proceedings (he left no will) over the disposition of the Hughes estate. In fact, we know more about Hughes than any other phantom ever to appear in Las Vegas.

Since he was self-centered, Hughes's opinion of his fellow human beings was not very high. He was anti-Semitic. He patronized blacks, stating in one memo that blacks had made enough progress to last them for another hundred years. People with bodily deformities of any kind disgusted him. He detested children, whom he sarcastically referred to as "ever lovin' little darlings." The dread of wild, snot-nosed children running amok on the Desert Inn golf course prompted Hughes to cancel the resort's annual Easter egg hunt, a highly-popular tradition among Las Vegas families. He also forced the prestigious Tournament of Champions golf event out of the Desert Inn because he did not want professional golfers, who took balls out of dirty holes, living so close to the Desert Inn for a week. He was virulently anti-Communist. In his earlier days, he shamelessly exploited famous Hollywood starlets (Jean Harlow, Rita Hayworth, Bette Davis, and Katharine Hepburn were among his many conquests) and aspiring young actresses whom he wooed with promises of signing them to movie contracts. In Las Vegas, Hughes lived the life of a celibate monk. He also ordered his casino security forces to banish prostitutes from their customary bar stools in the casino.

A typical, wealthy man who had Hughes's physical and emotional problems would have retired from business altogether. Not so Hughes, who was possessed by an infernal work ethic.

"I work around the clock, holidays mean very little to me, since I work just about all the time," Hughes explained in a memo to Maheu. "I have absolutely nothing but work. When things don't go well, it can be very empty indeed. I do not indulge in sports, night clubs, or other recreational activities, and since, in fact, I do not do much of anything else at all, except work, just what do you suggest I do, crawl off in a corner some place and die?"

The headquarters for his grand enterprise in Nevada was a fifteen-by-seventeen-foot bedroom that was extremely dusty because Hughes, despite all his loathing of dirt, would not let anyone vacuum the carpet. The hotel maids never cleaned the penthouse during the entire four years of Hughes's stay. The bedroom closet was filled with sealed Mason jars containing Hughes's urine; Hughes relieved himself directly into these jars and stored them. The windows were taped and the curtains drawn to block all light from the room. Hughes had rented out the entire eighth floor of the Desert Inn so no one could "bug" his ninth-floor inner sanctum from below.

A television set in the room was constantly on and very loud. He liked to watch late-night movies, and he badgered the television station with requests for more westerns and airplane movies. Hughes wound up buying KLAS-TV, the CBS affiliate in Las Vegas. But it was not just a whimsical purchase so he could watch his favorite movies. His memos speak of Hughes's desire to own television and radio stations in every corner of Nevada and to link the stations in a communications network. He did buy some stations in Nevada. He also made a bid to purchase the *Las Vegas Review-Journal,* the city's largest newspaper. But he then abruptly turned his attention nationally and unsuccessfully tried to buy the ABC television network. Although the viewing fare in his room improved after he purchased KLAS, for the longest time Hughes could not get rid of the detested *Sunrise Semester* program. The station wrote to Hughes that the show was needed to fulfill the station's public interest programming requirements with the Federal Communications Commission.

Hughes kept in touch with public affairs by reading newspapers and magazines, which littered his room. He stacked his returned memos next to one wall and would periodically review them. Hughes enjoyed rifling through his notes. He adopted a daily ritual of arranging his memos in precise stacks and whopping them with his long fingernails to push the papers together.

Hughes occupied the smallest room in the three-room suite. The rest of the suite was taken over by his seven personal aides who worked different shifts around the clock. These male nurses, who preferred to call themselves Hughes's "personal staff executives," attended to all his personal needs. They acted as couriers for Hughes's

Howard Hughes testifying before the Senate War Investigation Committee hearings in 1947. (Courtesy Las Vegas News Bureau)

memos and manned the "office" switchboard. A hallway partition, with a locked door, was erected between the penthouse and the security desk next to the elevator. An armed security guard was on duty twenty-four hours a day. The ninth-floor elevator button was blocked out and replaced with a lock. To reach the top floor, you had to have a key for the lock.

Hughes's avoidance of human contact, which had begun a decade before when he lived at the Beverly Hills Hotel, stemmed from his overwhelming need to hide his embarrassing physical condition from others. Even his wife, Jean Peters, who saw Hughes occasionally when they lived in the Beverly Hills Hotel but occupied a different bungalow, was denied a face-to-face audience with him while Hughes lived in Las Vegas. Hughes would call her almost every day by phone to chat. He required her to keep a careful log of what she ate and where she went and whom she talked to. He made her promise when they were married that she would never appear in another movie, unless he decided to produce a movie for her.

Hughes would later claim that he had gone into seclusion to get away from all the interruptions in his life. He could not get any work done, Hughes insisted, because too many people were bothering him. His privacy, of course, served another critical purpose. It kept

Hughes from being served with any possible subpoena to appear in court arising from his many legal entanglements. For Hughes, an appearance in court would have been the ultimate ignominy. Everybody would be able to see him and hear him. He would be exposed to embarrassment. Hughes never forgot, for instance, his unhappy appearance before the U.S. House Un-American Activities Committee in the early 1950s. Someone might even get the crazy notion that Hughes was mentally incompetent, always a thought in the back of the tycoon's mind. Hughes kept a psychiatrist on his staff but never allowed the shrink to get anywhere close to him.

Hughes saw none of his subordinates, not even the chief of his Nevada operations, during his entire Las Vegas sojourn, but he made one exception to his vows of solitude while in Vegas. That singular honor went to J. Richard Gray, a Houston lawyer whom Hughes had newly hired to assist Maheu in the legal aspects of the Desert Inn purchase. Gray's task was to present Hughes's gaming license application before the state Gaming Control Board. Hughes already had made it clear that he was not going to submit himself to a personal interview, much less a public appearance. Gray, who was new to the Hughes protocol, wanted to assure himself that he was really taking orders from Hughes. He wanted to see Hughes in the flesh. Hughes refused, but Gray persisted. Surprisingly enough, the billionaire finally agreed to see the lawyer. Hughes was negotiating to buy his first casino, his initial territory in his imperial design, and he needed Gray's services, for he would be carrying the billionaire's power of attorney to the control board.

Gray was permitted to ascend to the ninth floor of the Desert Inn and was led to Hughes's penthouse suite. His encounter with Hughes lasted about five seconds. As Gray was ushered into the living room, Hughes appeared in his bedroom doorway, dressed in a robe.

"Well," Hughes sneered, "I exist, damn it. Are you satisfied?"

Hughes then turned around and closed the door behind him.

In moments of euphoria, Howard Hughes would break into song. The lyrics consisted of just one breezy scat phrase: "Hey ba-ba-re-bop." That is all Hughes remembered of the song. "Hey ba-ba-re-bop." In his high-pitched and reedy voice, he piped "hey ba-ba-re-bop" over and over again. And Hughes had no better occasion to sing "hey ba-ba-re-bop" than the day he became a billionaire. He had just sold, on May 31, 1996, his 78 percent interest in TWA for $546 million. It was the largest single payment ever made to an individual. The original half-billion dollars shrank by about $100 million after Hughes paid brokerage fees, legal costs, and capital gain taxes. But he still had $450 million in cash to do as he pleased. Hey ba-ba-re-bop.

He ruled out remaining in California, because the state had a personal income tax. After the TWA sale, the California courts put pressure on Hughes to declare his residency. Hughes had lived in Los Angeles for some thirty years, but he listed his official residence in Houston. In 1966 Hughes flew to Boston to assess his choices for a permanent home. He seriously considered moving to the tax-free haven of the Bahamas, but he was talked out of it by Maheu because of the unstable political situation there. Hughes then chose Las Vegas. It was a sparsely populated state where it was still possible for a single person to dominate. Las Vegas and all its surrounding townships had a population of about two hundred thousand. As a bonus, Nevada had no inheritance tax, no personal income tax, and no state corporate tax. But the state's tax climate was not the main reason Hughes chose Nevada. Hughes certainly could have avoided taxes elsewhere in the world. He came to Las Vegas because he was fond of the place.

Hughes was no stranger to the city. He had often visited Las Vegas in his carefree bachelor days, beginning in the late 1940s, when he still ventured out into the world. In Las Vegas, Hughes was rarely seen gambling, and if he did sit at a gaming table he played for small stakes. He mainly came to the city to get away from the hectic pace of Los Angeles. Hughes liked the nightlife and the glamour and the adventure that was Vegas. He became a fairly familiar sight in showrooms, wearing his crumpled seersucker suit, tieless shirt, and canvas shoes. After he closed the deal to purchase RKO pictures, Hughes flew all the principals in the deal from Los Angeles to Las Vegas at 3 A.M. to celebrate. Another time, Hughes and screen star Yvonne DeCarlo checked into the El Rancho. Reporters got wind of it. When he checked out several days later, DeCarlo told the press that Hughes had given her a liberal education in aviation and engineering science. "He's a genius," she gushed, "a wonderful man." Hughes even bought a guest house in Las Vegas.

In 1957 Hughes married movie actress Jean Peters in a secret ceremony at the Mizpah Hotel in Tonopah, Nevada. The civic arrangements were handled by Howard Cannon, who at the time was the Las Vegas city attorney and later became a U.S. senator.

Hughes made large land purchases during his pre–Desert Inn era, including the 25,000-acre "Husite" area. The land was barren at the time and far removed from the Las Vegas city limits. It is now the site of an upscale, master-planned community known as Summerlin.

His fondness for the city can be seen from one of the early movies he produced, *The Las Vegas Story*, starring Victor Mature and Jane Russell. Hughes played out his fantasies in his movies, and he chose his subjects carefully. Their titles alone express themes in Hughes's life: *The Outlaw, Hell's Angels, Scarface, The Front Page*. In that symbolic pantheon belongs *The Las Vegas Story*, a romance-action yarn about a gal and a gambler. The movie's casino scenes were filmed in the Flamingo.

These were the memories that Hughes took with him when he reappeared in Vegas in 1966. By then, he had become a man on a mission. He wanted to become the undisputed king of his new domain. The process of acquiring Vegas was a supreme act of imagination and will power, and it gave him voyeuristic delight. Since he was an invalid and a recluse, he had to content himself with pulling strings from behind the scenes, like a puppet master. He wanted to control all aspects of the state's life, not just the state's gaming industry.

In his memos to Las Vegas attorney Tom Bell, whom Hughes used to disperse political contributions in the state, Hughes requested to be kept informed on every single bill introduced in the Nevada Legislature. He told Bell to encourage legislators to adopt Hughes's views to defeat bills authorizing dog racing; to stop the sales tax, the gasoline tax, and the cigarette tax; to stop the Clark County school integration plan; to prohibit governmental agencies from realigning any streets without Hughes's personal views first given; to do whatever was necessary to shield Hughes from having to appear personally in any court; to advise him on all ordinances or laws regarding obscenity and pornography; to prevent any change of the rules of various casino games, in particular, roulette; to discourage state officials from permitting Communist bloc entertainers from appearing in Las Vegas hotels; and to take whatever action was necessary to prohibit rock concerts in Clark County.

Hughes wrote that he wanted to "make Las Vegas as trustworthy and respectable as the New York Stock Exchange—so that Nevada gambling will have the kind of reputation that Lloyds of London has, so that Nevada on a note will be like Sterling on silver."

He envisioned his own private Shangri-La in the desert. "We can make a really super environmental 'city of the future' here," Hughes wrote. "No smog, no contamination, efficient local government, where the tax-payers pay as little as possible, and get something for their money." He wrote of building a new airport outside of Las Vegas that could handle supersonic planes. In a reasonable number of years, he said, there was no reason that Las Vegas should not became as big as Houston.

Casinos were the centerpieces of Hughes's grand scheme. "I feel there is something very important and very significant," Hughes wrote to Maheu, "about being in a position of 100%, admitted undisputed leadership. I am certain that there is great value in an entity which is clearly, indisputably the world's greatest and largest gambling operation."

Hughes was more than willing to use all the tricks in his bag to secure his objective. His mere presence was a sensation enough, and his carefully nurtured image—that of a powerful industrialist who had come to rescue the gaming industry from the clutches of the underworld—seduced just about everyone. Governor Paul Laxalt saw Hughes's arrival as a way to repair Nevada's tarnished image and hailed Hughes for giving the state a Good Housekeeping Seal of Approval.

To ensure support for his initial gaming license in 1967, Hughes dangled a ripe carrot before Nevada. He wrote Laxalt a letter in which Hughes pledged to donate the money necessary for construction of a medical school for the University of Nevada. Three days after Laxalt announced Hughes's generosity, the state Gaming Control Board met to vote on Hughes's license. Hughes had not filled out a financial background report, he had not been photographed or fingerprinted, and he had not appeared in person before the control board. Any other applicant would have been summarily dismissed. But Hughes was too big of a sugar daddy to let slip away. It was if every state leader and businessman in Nevada instinctively understood that Hughes had to be kept here at all costs. Both the control board and the Nevada Gaming Commission accommodated the magnate by granting him a gaming license for the Desert Inn on unanimous votes.

"Hughes's life and background are well known to this board," said control board chairman Alan Abner, explaining how the board determined its finding, "and he is considered highly qualified."

Later, when Hughes bought the Sands, he dazzled the state with an announcement to build the world's largest hotel, with four thousand rooms, on the property. The new hotel was never built; neither was the medical school (while Hughes was in Vegas) or the futuristic airport. But the politicians, to whom Hughes generously donated cash contributions, always seemed to be on his side. Hughes once enticed Governor Laxalt with the promise of bankrolling Laxalt for a run at the U.S. presidency.

Hughes's only stumbling block in his casino-buying spree was the Stardust, but it proved to be but a temporary setback. With that resort among his possessions, Hughes would have controlled one-fourth of the revenues on the Las Vegas Strip. Even Laxalt balked at the idea, but he finally relented to Hughes's wishes after Hughes promised not to buy any more casinos after the Stardust.

U.S. Attorney General Ramsey Clark, however, filed suit against Hughes, contending that the purchase of the Stardust was monopolistic and thus violated antitrust statutes. Hughes gave up on the Stardust. Nevertheless, he later was allowed to purchase the much smaller Landmark casino. And near the end of his Vegas holiday, Hughes had started negotiations to buy the Dunes. By 1970 the political climate in Washington had changed. Richard Nixon was president, and Nixon had received a lot of political contributions from Hughes over the years. Consequently, Hughes obtained assurances from Attorney General John Mitchell that the Justice Department would not interfere if Hughes bought another casino in Las Vegas. There is every reason to believe that Hughes, had he remained in Las Vegas, would have bought more casinos.

Popular lore gives Hughes credit for chasing the mobsters out of town and for ushering in the era of corporations. He supposedly pioneered the way for reputable corporations by showing Wall Street that it was safe to run a legitimate casino business in Las Vegas. None of this is true, except by happenstance, in the sense that we say Columbus discovered America, though Columbus had no idea where he was. While Hughes did bring an image of legitimacy to the gaming industry, it was only that, an image. Legitimacy would come long after Hughes was gone.

Hughes hated the buttoned-down corporate world. He saw himself as a rugged entrepreneur, describing himself as "the only example of competitive enterprise still functioning and holding out against the onrushing hordes of corporate giants. In other words, the one 'corner grocery store,' proprietor-managed type of old fashioned business activity still holding out against the overpowering pressure of the new corporations with their executives, managers, stockholders, intricacies of control, politics, proxy battles, institutional ownership, etc. etc.—all of the interlocking industrial giant—the corporation, the Establishment."

Hughes was the sole proprietor, the sole stockholder, of all his enterprises. He did not live in the corporate world, nor did he think with a corporate mentality.

For its part, Wall Street had a dim view of Hughes and considered him a loose cannon. When he owned RKO, Hughes had run the studio into the ground. In the airline business, Hughes had been forced to sell his majority stake in TWA because of a shareholders' uprising over Hughes's mismanagement of the company. The revolt was precipitated when TWA could not pay for an enormous shipment of jet planes that Hughes had ordered. Hughes took TWA to the brink of bankruptcy. New managers took over the company and guided it so well that the price of TWA stock soared from $13 per share, when Hughes ran the company, to $86 per share after Hughes was forced out. Hughes sold his TWA shares at the higher price. His half-billion-dollar payday was a fluke.

Wall Street, and the nation at large, did respect Hughes for what he truly was: the last of the great American robber barons. Hughes played the game of business ruthlessly and with the abandon of a child. His true skills in business were that of a "fixer." He could "fix" things to go his way by bullying his business opponents or by bribing politicians or by cornering a market or by obtaining sweetheart contracts with the government or by wearing people down during negotiations. These were Hughes's true tools of the trade, and Wall Street knew it.

Rather than being thought of as the precursor of a corporate future, Hughes should be seen as perhaps the greatest in a long line of wealthy individuals who anticipated a big future in Las Vegas and bought in. Hughes's contemporaries, Del Webb and Kirk Kerkorian, were of the same mold; they just did not have as much money or as many eccentricities as Hughes.

Throughout Hughes's stay in Las Vegas and for a decade thereafter, the gaming industry's financier was not Wall Street but the Teamsters Central States Pension Fund. The large hotel corporations that came to Las Vegas—Hilton, Holiday Inn, and Ramada—came here for reasons having little to do with any trailblazing on Hughes's part. The gaming operator who more than anyone invited corporate attention to Nevada was William Harrah, another Hughes contemporary, who ran a clean and profitable operation untouched by mob influence.

Hughes's mere presence in Nevada, however, did stir state legislators into action, for it was their fervent desire to attract nationally known corporations to the state. In both the 1967 and 1969 sessions, the legislature simplified the state's gaming regulations so that corporations could be licensed to operate casinos in Nevada without the need to investigate the background and financial status of every single stockholder. Such a measure had been discussed by gaming authorities throughout the 1960s, and the ensuing legislation, in fact, was a way to catch up to an already existing situation in Nevada. Corporations, such as Del Webb's, already were operating casinos through their Nevada holding companies. A corporate bill would have been passed sooner or later. In any case, the corporate gaming act was not directed at Hughes or meant to accommodate him personally. He was the sole stockholder of his corporation, and he would have faced a licensing hearing regardless of the legislation—if he had not pulled strings to be licensed *in absentia.*

The preferential treatment that Hughes received expressed Nevada's desire to remove itself from underworld influence and join the greater business world. But it is too much to say that Hughes chased the mob out of town. Mobsters, as well as everyone else in Las Vegas, tried to take advantage of Hughes at the same time that Hughes was trying to take advantage of them. Hughes had often boasted that he could buy any man or destroy any man, but Hughes was just as often exploited by those around him.

This process of dealing oneself into a Hughes deal is exemplified in the purchase of the Desert Inn. Before he arrived in Vegas, Hughes had sent Maheu to prepare the way. Maheu was a former FBI agent who had a private investigator's firm in Washington, D.C., before Hughes hired him full-time. Maheu's close friend, prominent Washington attorney Edward Morgan, also a former FBI man, suggested that Maheu contact Hank Greenspun when he went to Vegas. Greenspun was the publisher of the *Las Vegas Sun* and owner of KLAS-TV. When he was starting his legal career, Morgan had defended Greenspun in a celebrated Washington trial. Maheu told Greenspun about Hughes's arrival and enlisted the publisher's help in finding suitable quarters for the potentate. They first tried the Dunes but were denied. Then they tried the Desert Inn. The resort's majority owner, Moe Dalitz, agreed to rent Hughes the two upper floors of the DI, but only on the condition that Hughes check out in six weeks, when the rooms would be needed for high rollers arriving on New Year's Eve junkets. Hughes was dead weight as far as the casino was concerned.

As the end of December approached, Hughes had no intention of vacating the premises. He assigned Maheu the job of stalling for time. Maheu sought help from a bevy of what he called his "facilitators." Maheu contacted John Rosselli, the mobster who acted as the Las Vegas middleman for mob families throughout the country. Maheu knew Rosselli from the time both had participated in a CIA plot to assassinate Cuban dictator Fidel Castro with the mob's help. Thereafter, they saw quite a bit of each other. Maheu's children called the dapper mobster Uncle Johnny. Rosselli got in touch with one of the Desert Inn partners, Ruby Kolod, to see if he could pressure Dalitz to extend Hughes's stay. Maheu also got in touch with Teamsters Union chief Jimmy Hoffa, and enlisted his support in the matter. Hoffa controlled the purse strings of the Teamsters Central States Pension Fund, which had a loan on the Desert Inn and was considering a large loan for the Stardust, also partly owned by Dalitz. Hoffa called Dalitz and urged him to give Hughes a little more time at the DI. Dalitz agreed to give Hughes two more weeks.

During this period Dalitz encountered Greenspun at the Desert Inn Country Club. Dalitz complained about all the pressure he was feeling to let Hughes remain at the DI. He expressed his desire to sell the resort. Greenspun suggested that Dalitz call lawyer Ed Morgan in Washington to see if he could find a buyer. Dalitz asked Greenspun to make the call for him. Morgan flew to Las Vegas and was met by Maheu. The stage was set for actual negotiations.

The talks turned out to be an exasperating three-month ordeal. Hughes quibbled over every minor detail of the purchase. Since Hughes had no firsthand knowledge of gaming operations, he needed someone who could analyze the operating figures. Del Webb was contacted, and he recommended E. Parry Thomas, the president of Valley Bank in Las Vegas. Thomas would work on this deal and would go on to make many of Hughes's large real estate purchases, acting as Hughes's agent but keeping the tycoon's name out of it. Local attorney Tom Bell was selected to work with Houston attorney Richard Gray in securing a gaming license for Hughes. Bell was recommended to Maheu by Nevada's two U.S. senators, Alan Bible and

Howard Cannon. As for Rosselli, he continued to act as a go-between to Dalitz and his other partners in Cleveland.

On April Fool's Day of 1967, Hughes took possession of the Desert Inn. He paid $6.2 million in cash and assumed responsibility for $7 million in liabilities, for a total price of $13.2 million. He did not actually purchase the property but obtained a lease to operate the hotel-casino until the year 2022. The property continued to be owned by New York real estate mogul Harry Helmsley. Dalitz paid Ed Morgan a $150,000 finder's fee, an amount that would be close to a half-million dollars at today's prices. Morgan, in turn, gave $50,000 to Rosselli and $25,000 to Greenspun. Everyone was happy.

Owning a casino is one thing; operating a casino is quite another—and no one in the Hughes organization knew anything about running a casino. "None of us knew snakes eyes from box cars," admitted Raymond Holliday, the executive vice-president of Hughes Tool Company in Houston, the number two man in Hughes's empire next to Maheu. "We didn't know a thing about it [gambling] and nobody here was interested in learning."

Holliday sent Calvin Collier, treasurer of Hughes Tool, to Las Vegas to assist Richard Gray and Maheu. "That was my first good baptism to all of that gambling," Collier said. "I don't think Dick Gray had been exposed to that type of operation or had any experience in it. Mr. Maheu indicated that he had no expertise in it. The fact of the matter is, we were all looking for somebody to run the place." They found someone. After three months of disarray at the Desert Inn, Moe Dalitz agreed to serve as an unpaid consultant for Hughes on casino operations. Dalitz later said he took on the adviser's role only out of the goodness of his heart.

The next casino that Hughes bought was the Sands, paying a price of $14.6 million. The same cast of characters—Morgan, Rosselli, Thomas, and Greenspun—collected fees after the sale. As with the Desert Inn, the middle management at the Sands remained essentially the same. Frank Sinatra might have left the Copa Room because Hughes cut off his credit, but casino manager Carl Cohen and entertainment director Jack Entratter, for example, stayed on the job.

Sinatra's departure resulted in a piquant scene enshrined in Vegas lore. Sinatra, who had once owned 9 percent of the Sands, was forced to sell his interest because he associated with a well-known mobster. But he continued to perform at the Sands. When Hughes bought the Sands, Sinatra knew his days were numbered. In his younger years, when Sinatra was courting Ava Gardner, Hughes had tried to talk her out of marrying Sinatra by enticing Gardner to go on a private cruise on Lake Tahoe, where he made his case. Hughes wanted Ava for himself; but Ava, whose interest in men ran toward matadors, crooners, and short comedians, rebuffed Hughes. (Gardner was in select company. Only a few screen stars ever rejected Hughes, including Jean Simmons and Elizabeth Taylor. "His socks stunk," Taylor said of the rich Romeo.) Sinatra never forgave Hughes for trying to steal Gardner away; and for his part, Hughes's ego was bruised by the thought of losing out to a man he considered a pipsqueak. During his last days at the Sands, Sinatra would lament, "You're wondering why I don't have a drink in my hand? Howard Hughes bought it." The new ownership suddenly discontinued the practice of allowing Sinatra to sign markers and draw money from the casino cage. Sinatra flew into a rage at this insult. He yelled and cursed throughout the casino, destroying anything in his path. When the singer would not pipe down in the presence of casino manager Carl Cohen, the burly former truck driver walloped Sinatra with a right cross to the mouth, knocking out two of Sinatra's front teeth. Sinatra signed on with Caesars Palace.

The third casino acquired by Hughes was the Frontier, a seven-hundred-room property that had been recently remodeled into the "New" Frontier. All the same, the property was going under financially, mainly because of poor management. Two of its owners had been convicted of cheating in a card game at the Friar's Club in Los Angeles. Another partner had been caught entertaining associates of the Zerilli mob family of Detroit. The Frontier's new marquee was a tall affair, and when Hughes read about it in the papers he expressed concern that high winds might topple the sign and make it crash into the Desert Inn across the street. Maheu made inquiries at the Frontier and discovered its dire financial difficulties. Hughes paid $14 million for the property, and shortly thereafter he paid another million to operate the casino.

The other casinos acquired by Hughes were smaller, marginal properties. Hughes did not buy these casinos in order to make money from them; he bought them for strategic reasons. He bought the Castaways (for $3 million), for example, because of the land underneath it. This land—across the Strip from the Sands—stretched from the northern edge of Caesars Palace clear to the end of a very long block. In one of his many grandiose but unkept promises, Hughes proposed to build on this site a vast resort, a city within a city, with the working title of Sands West. This parcel is now occupied by the Mirage and Treasure Island.

His casino purchases exemplify how Hughes's mind worked in matters of real estate. He thought in territorial terms, like a military strategist. He bought the Frontier after purchasing the empty land south of it (now occupied by Fashion Show Mall). Then he bought the Silver Slipper (for $5.36 million), which was right next to the Frontier to the south. Next to the Silver Slipper was the Stardust. He wanted to buy the Stardust for $30.5 million so he would own the entire row of land in front of his headquarters—a Maginot Line of Hughes casinos. Although the Stardust deal did not go through, Washington super-lawyer Ed Morgan received $500,000 in legal fees for the job, of which he passed $150,000 to Maheu.

Hughes bought the ailing Landmark, the tallest building in the state, as a flanking maneuver, solely to install his presence across the street from the huge International Hotel (now the Las Vegas Hilton), which his casino rival Kirk Kerkorian was building. The Landmark was the most inflated purchase Hughes made in Vegas. The property was grossly indebted. Hughes assumed almost $9 million in Teamsters Union loans and about $5.6 million in other debts, and he paid the owners almost $2.5 million.

Hughes bought Harold's Club in Reno for $10.5 million to establish a beachhead in northern Nevada, where he had designs on Bill Harrah's resort.

Besides their strategic locations, the Silver Slipper and the Frontier were useful to Hughes as clearinghouses for political contributions. Cash payments to national politicians, such as Hubert Humphrey and Richard Nixon, were taken mainly from the Frontier's vault. Payments made to Nevada politicians came from the cashier's cage at the Silver Slipper, where $885,500 in political contributions were distributed while Hughes was in Vegas. The Silver Slipper was like a state treasury. Politicians from both parties would send their representatives, or go themselves, to see lawyer Tom Bell at the Silver Slipper. The politicians never signed a receipt. All the payments were made in cash. Maheu would later testify under oath that he passed $50,000 to Senator Alan Bible in 1968 and $70,000 to Senator Howard Cannon in 1970. Governor Laxalt was a major recipient of Hughes's largesse. "From time to time during Paul Laxalt's administration, he asked me to convey to Mr. Hughes the desirability of making political contributions to support particular Republican candidates," Bell later said in a sworn deposition as part of the legal battles, between Hughes's Nevada company and Maheu, that followed Hughes's departure from Las Vegas.

Hughes's casino purchases were overwhelmingly welcomed by state gaming authorities, who rushed his gaming license applications through. The DI, the Sands, the Frontier were all known as mob joints. Hughes was doing the state a service by purchasing these casinos, so the thinking went. In reality, however, it seems that the mob went about its business as usual even after Hughes purchased the casinos.

In his memoirs, Bob Maheu recalled a meeting with Rosselli after the Desert Inn takeover: "We ended up at a lounge at the Desert Inn. I was seeing a side of Johnny I'd never seen before. He looked me right in the eye and said, 'Now, I want to tell you who the casino manager is going to be here, and who your entertainment director is going to be.'"

Maheu told Rosselli to go to hell.

"Johnny said I was making a big mistake. I told him I didn't care—case closed. And I'll tell you, it was the smartest decision I ever made on the spot. If I had let Johnny order me around then, it would have never stopped."

What Maheu did not know was that *it* probably never did stop. During the Hughes years, the Desert Inn and the Sands probably were plundered. Overnight, they went from being two of the Strip's money-making jewels to fading has-beens. The two properties lost money every year that Hughes was in town. Mismanagement and padded payrolls accounted for some of the losses, but not all. What could have brought on this sudden about-face?

The most profitable casino in Nevada in 1967 was Harrah's Lake Tahoe, which made $20 million. How could this smaller, out-of-the-way casino outearn the more popular and more ideally situated Desert Inn (even without its Easter egg hunt and its Tournament of Champions golf tournament) and Sands (even sans Sinatra) combined? The DI and Sands should have at the very least matched the profits of Harrah's. Although there is no hard proof, the only explanation that makes sense is the strong possibility of casino skim operations inside Hughes's three big properties.

While the inexperienced Hughes executives wallowed in their big offices, the casino employees who had been there from the early days may have helped themselves to what they could. It must have been a free-for-all. Casino associates working in league with Rosselli were very likely skimming funds. But it may have not stopped there. Since the mob no longer had a hidden ownership interest in the properties, it did not really matter who else, among the other working stiffs in the casino, stole money. It may have been an unsupervised skim, existing on several levels of freelancing.

"I would get these strange phone calls," Maheu said in his memoirs. "The voice would tell me to watch what was happening in this particular craps game or at a card table on a certain shift. I asked who was calling, but never got an answer. So I would have someone watch the game to find out if anything was wrong. Sometimes we would catch a bad dealer, or somebody was getting signals. Or somebody paying $100 at the craps table and getting $500 in chips. I never knew who was tipping me off."

What a remarkable admission. Maheu did not think to look into the matter more deeply than he did because he did not directly concern himself with casino operations. Maheu's main job was to please Hughes, and that left him little time to do much else.

At the same time, Maheu had established quite a bailiwick for himself in Vegas. "*Bonjour, mon ami,*" Maheu, who had learned French in his native Maine, was fond of saying when he greeted visitors. He received a salary of a half-million dollars a year, far higher than any other Hughes executive; and he was the beneficiary of a virtually unlimited expense account. Since he worked on a consulting basis, he did not occupy a formal position in any of Hughes's companies. His huge office in the Frontier had walls decorated with cowhide pelts. Maheu had use of a Hughes airplane and a Hughes yacht. Hughes built him a palatial home, dubbed Little Caesars Palace, at the Desert Inn golf course. He was a regular tennis partner of Governor Laxalt's. He also had a cabin on Mount Charleston with a helicopter landing pad on the patio. A gregarious, if vainglorious, man, Maheu played his role to the hilt as Hughes's alter-ego and his representative in the world of mortals. Maheu strutted about the stage of life like a pasha. The billionaire had taken a shine to Maheu, a man he had never met, because Maheu was a good troubleshooter, someone who could accomplish sensitive missions.

But all was not right in their marriage. Hughes made horrendous demands on Maheu's time and attention, often complaining in the manner of a lover. "Bob, I am afraid I have lost the magic touch with which we used to find accord and harmony in almost everything we did," Hughes wrote. "Somehow I cannot seem to reach you the way I used to. When I say I cannot seem to establish the relationship we used to have, you say I am imagining things." Hughes would write memos to him or call him every day. He once held Maheu on the telephone for sixteen hours straight. Even on vacation, Maheu would get no rest from his maniacal boss. Sentimentality and family ties held little meaning to Hughes. Maheu, who often felt like quitting and who also began to drink too much alcohol, remained with Hughes, however, because as he said in his memoirs, he was seduced by the trappings of power and wealth.

Then too, Hughes assigned Maheu to stranger and weirder missions, such as the time he told Maheu to bribe President Lyndon Johnson with a million dollars if the president would only stop the underground nuclear testing one hundred miles from Las Vegas. Maheu went to see Johnson but could not bring himself to offer the outright bribe. On other occasions, however, Maheu did deliver money to national politicians in a vain attempt to stop the underground nuclear testing program at the height of the Cold War. When Hubert Humphrey was running for president, Maheu once placed a suitcase, holding $50,000 in cash, on Humphrey's lap in a limousine. Maheu also once delivered $50,000 to Florida businessman Bebe Rebozo to give to his pal, President Richard Nixon.

It was Maheu who went to Larry O'Brien and persuaded the former John Kennedy campaign manager to work for Howard Hughes. Even after O'Brien was selected chairman of the national Democratic Party, he received a monthly retainer from Hughes for unspecified services. The seeds of the Watergate scandal were planted by Hughes when he was in Las Vegas. Why would Nixon condone a break-in of Democratic national headquarters at the Watergate Hotel in Washington, D.C.? What information did Nixon want from Larry O'Brien's files? The most plausible answer is that Nixon wanted to make sure O'Brien did not have any documents that revealed Hughes's cash gifts to Nixon and that could be used against Nixon in his reelection campaign. Nixon attributed his earlier defeat by John Kennedy to the revelation made during the campaign that Nixon had accepted a $205,000 loan from Hughes through Nixon's brother, Donald.

Maheu had gotten a little too full of himself in Las Vegas. Out of his huge office in the Frontier, Maheu nominated himself chief of what he called Hughes Nevada Operations, a company that existed only on paper. Maheu's son Peter became his administrative assistant, paid out of his father's personal salary. The rest of the company was staffed by Maheu's friends, who drew their salaries from the Hughes organization. Maheu's old Holy Cross classmate, Major General Edward Nigro, who had served in the Pentagon, became deputy chief executive officer of Hughes Nevada Operations and president of the Sands. The former head of the FBI office in Nevada, Dean Elson, handled special assignments for Maheu. A former FBI agent and friend of Maheu, Richard Danner, who had introduced Bebe Rebozo to Richard Nixon, was named managing director of the Frontier Hotel.

By 1970 Maheu's privileged position had become the source of envy and antagonism among the three next-highest executives in the Hughes empire: Raymond Holliday, who ran Hughes Tool; Bill Gay, who ran Hughes's Hollywood office and was the Mormon responsible for hiring the Mormon male nurses in Hughes's entourage; and Chester Davis, the attorney who handled Hughes's protracted TWA legal case.

The three formed a cabal to depose Maheu. They gathered evidence showing that Maheu's buddy Nigro had signed a note taking responsibility for several million dollars in debts owed by Los Angeles Airways, a helicopter service that Maheu wanted Hughes to buy. Nigro had no authority from Hughes to make such a guarantee. The group also discovered that Maheu had instructed Hughes Tool Company to make a $4 million loan to gambler Sid Wyman, a part owner of the Dunes. Maheu's justification for the loan was that he had promised Wyman the money to secure his support for the proposed sale of the Dunes to Hughes. But Hughes had never approved such a loan and knew nothing about it. The cabal also insinuated that Maheu had drawn money from the casinos to make political contributions that never reached their recipients.

For the first time in their relationship, Maheu found it difficult to communicate with Hughes. Maheu's messages to Hughes were intercepted by the tycoon's stewards, who reported their contents to Gay instead. Maheu now was fighting for his life. He tried to fire Davis, but the attorney told him to buzz off. The coup de grace was delivered in the summer of 1970 when Hughes received a financial report from Holliday. Hughes had invested $150 million in Nevada since 1967, and what he was about to read was most depressing. The report showed that Hughes's Nevada properties lost $3.2 million in 1968 and $8.4 million in 1969. For the first six months of 1970, the losses amounted to $6.8 million, with a projected year-end loss of $13 million to $14 million.

Hughes blew his top.

The losses can only be explained by skimming operations at Hughes's casinos. Although Maheu had clearly feathered his nest, he was no thief who had stashed away millions. In fact, after Hughes abandoned him, Maheu was reduced to a near-penniless state.

Hughes seems to have been upset not so much over the losses—throughout his career he had shown a cavalier disregard for profits—as he was over the imagined treachery of his trusted right-hand man. Paranoia played a greater role in Hughes's distress than actual loss of money.

Hughes faced the unpleasant task of firing Maheu, but he did not want to be in town when Maheu got the news. In his memos, Hughes often chided Maheu for being overly excitable. Maheu had the elevator key to Hughes's ninth-floor penthouse, but he had never walked past the security desk when delivering his messages to Hughes. The boss knew Maheu's temper could get the best of him, and what Hughes feared was that an irate Maheu might barge into his bedroom to discuss his firing.

Hughes was not quite up to that. He treated Maheu as he did all his other executives: with scorn and suspicion. Hughes played one executive against the other, keeping them all off balance. He had once abruptly severed his friendship with Noah Dietrich, the superb money manager who had nurtured the Hughes fortune while Hughes was in California. Dietrich had been his chief counselor and a personal friend, a man Hughes had known for thirty years. Hughes had the locks changed in Dietrich's office one day and never saw him or spoke to him again. The same thing was about to happen to Maheu. Several weeks before leaving Las Vegas, Hughes signed over his power of attorney to the clique of Gay, Holliday, and Davis. Maheu was not informed.

By the end of 1970 Hughes had suffered one calamity after another, and he was in a mood to move.

First of all, he was not feeling well, and he reluctantly allowed his doctor to examine him. The doctor had strict instructions not to poke into Hughes's rectum in the course of his examination nor to conduct tests of any kind. Nonetheless, the doctor discovered that Hughes had contracted pneumonia. The doctor gave him pills and shots. Hughes also prescribed his own remedy. He told the doctor to give him a total blood transfusion, the blood to be supplied by clean-living Mormons whose background had been investigated. So it was said, so it was done.

On the domestic front, Hughes had bought two properties— the Vera Krupp ranch outside Vegas and the Major Riddle mansion in Rancho Circle—for his wife. Jean Peters told him she would move to Vegas only if Hughes shared the same house with her. He would not do it. He refused to see her at all and ignored her pleas to lead a more normal life. She finally sued for divorce.

On the national front, Hughes had soured on his tender offer to purchase a majority of the stock of the ABC television network. Although ABC management had rejected the offer, Hughes was prepared to buy shares in the open market. At the last moment, he changed his mind. He happened to watch an episode of the *Dating Game*, a program distributed by ABC. Hughes considered the show offensive because he had seen a black man win a date with a white woman. He called off the purchase of ABC, even though it was pointed out to him that the woman on the show was actually a light-colored black woman.

While in Vegas, Hughes had decided to get back in the airline business. He purchased Air West, a regional carrier, for $41 million. This deal quickly got Hughes in trouble when it was charged that he had manipulated the airline's stock prices and forced them to plunge in order to purchase the stock at a low price. The Civil Aeronautics Board and the Securities and Exchange Commission were clamoring to see Hughes in court and in person.

The airline business pestered Hughes from another direction as well. The mismanagement lawsuit filed against him after he sold his shares of TWA had been ruled in the stockholders' favor. Hughes was ordered to pay $145.4 million in damages. Throughout his Vegas years, Hughes worried about the outcome of his suit, which he kept losing at every appellate level. When interest was added to the original damage award, Hughes owed nearly $150 million as he neared the end of his Vegas holiday. To make the TWA payment, Hughes later sold his patrimony, the Hughes Tool Company, manufacturer of the oil drilling bit that had initiated the Hughes fortune. The sale turned out to be unnecessary. After he sold the company, the U.S. Supreme

Court surprisingly decided to hear the TWA case and reversed the decision against Hughes on a legal technicality. The legendary Hughes luck had struck again.

On the nuclear front, Nevada had become an unfit place to live, according to Hughes. Despite Hughes's constant complaints, President Nixon had not been willing to halt the underground nuclear testing at the Nevada Test Site. The shock waves from the explosions sent tremors through the bedroom, and rattled the uneasy mind, of Howard Hughes. The tycoon was afraid that radiation might leak out of the ground. He lived in a private hell of fear.

His paranoia, over things imagined and real, intensified when John Meier, the man Hughes had hired to buy mining claims in Nevada, was discovered to be a crook who received kickbacks from the people who sold him worthless mining rights. Then came the revelation that Hughes's casinos were losing money. Amid this avalanche of bad news, not to mention that Hughes had seen every movie on TV and was bored, the last thing in the world that Hughes's delicate nervous system could withstand was a messy, face-to-face confrontation with the hot-tempered Maheu.

Stretcher bearers hoisted Hughes's frail body down the Desert Inn's interior fire escape. A station wagon ferried him to Nellis Air Force Base, and from there a private jet flew him to the Bahamas. He wore his lucky hat, a snap-brim Stetson fedora. The hat, cocked at a slant in a devil-may-care attitude, reminded invalid Hughes of his aviator days, when he set a world speed record for flying solo around the world and was given a hero's welcome with a ticker-tape parade down Broadway.

Even from the tropics, Hughes thought about his desert "home."

"Last night HRH suggested that, in his opinion, we should consider the following for the Desert Inn," a Hughes aide reported to the Las Vegas office. "Build a foundation that would support a 65-story building. . . . The building should be either square or rectangular in shape and constructed with a steel framework. Between the steel network, glass could be used for the outside walls. If it is necessary to use opaque material in the outside walls, it should be used along the edges so we could have a ribbon of glass extending into the sky."

After Hughes disappeared from Vegas without saying good-bye, Maheu sent his son Peter and several other men to look for him.

Maheu believed that the "Mormon Mafia" around Hughes had kidnapped the tycoon. Maheu's men were on a mission to liberate Hughes and bring him back to Vegas. Instead, the men were caught on the roof of the hotel where Hughes was staying in Nassau.

Maheu later sued Hughes for slander. During a telephone press conference held to denounce the Hughes book, a hoax written by Clifford Irving, Hughes was asked why he had dismissed Maheu in Nevada. "Because he's [a] no good, dishonest son of a bitch, and he stole me blind," Hughes told reporters. Maheu won his lawsuit and was awarded nearly $3 million. But the decision was overturned.

Hughes hopscotched from the Bahamas, to Vancouver, to London, to Nicaragua, and to Mexico, staying clear of the United States altogether for tax purposes. He died in 1976 of kidney failure.

Hughes's holdings passed into the hands of Summa Corporation. The company had been established before Hughes died, and he was never happy with its name. "What the hell does that mean? How do you pronounce it? I don't even know how to pronounce it, or what it is," Hughes exclaimed when he first heard the name. The investments that Hughes made in Las Vegas paid off after Summa sold its casino holdings, reaping a windfall for all of Hughes's distant cousins who inherited his estate by default, since he left no will. The company's other real estate holdings, including its Summerlin housing site, were acquired in 1996 by the Rouse Company, a large East Coast developer based in Columbia, Maryland.

Hughes's death deprived Las Vegas of its benefactor. Everyone involved in any of the Hughes deals in Las Vegas had profited from the experience, except Hughes himself. His money made waves. The waves stirred things up, and this generated the "juice" to keep things moving forward in Las Vegas.

Although he did not keep many of his promises and did not build a thing in Las Vegas, Hughes nonetheless occupies a legendary place in the city's unfolding . . . as well he should, if for no other reason than he was lady luck's wanton gift to the gaming capital of the world.

For more information on Howard Hughes, see:

1. Drosnin, Michael. *Citizen Hughes.* New York: Holt, Rinehart, Winston, 1985.

2. Garrison, Omar V. *Howard Hughes in Las Vegas.* New York: L. Stuart, 1970.

3. Phelan, James. *Howard Hughes: The Hidden Years.* New York: Random House, 1976.

4. Barlett, Donald L. *Empire: The Life, Legend, and Madness of Howard Hughes.* New York: Norton, 1979.

5. Higham, Charles. *Howard Hughes: The Secret Life.* New York: Putnam, 1993.

6. Davenport, Elaine, and Paul Eddy, with Mark Hurwitz. *The Hughes Papers.* New York: Ballantine Books, 1976.

7. Dietrich, Noah, and Bob Thomas. *Howard: The Amazing Mr. Hughes.* New York: Fawcett, 1972.

8. Maheu, Robert. *Next to Hughes.* New York: Harper Collins, 1992.

9. Lacey, Robert. *Little Man: Meyer Lansky and the Gangster Life.* New York: Little, Brown, 1991.

10. Demaris, Ovid. *The Last Mafioso: The Treacherous World of Jimmy Fratianno.* New York: Bantam Books, 1981.

Kirk Kerkorian:
The Reticent Billionaire

Dave Palermo

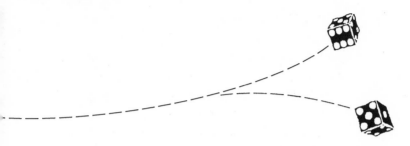

Billionaire financier. Philanthropist. Pioneer aviator. Gambler. Amateur boxer. The son of an Armenian immigrant farmer and raised on the mean streets of South Los Angeles, Kirk Kerkorian has played a major role in shaping Nevada's gambling industry. Along with the late billionaire recluse and fellow aviator Howard Hughes, with whom he has often been compared, Kerkorian in the late 1960s ushered in the era of corporate ownership of Nevada's resort casinos.

Kerkorian in 1969 parlayed the sale of Transamerica Airlines and his share of Caesars Palace to build the $80-million, 1,512-room International Hotel (now the Las Vegas Hilton), a stylish high-rise that dramatically altered the Las Vegas landscape. The International was followed in 1973 by the $106-million, 2,000-room MGM Grand Hotel (now Bally's Las Vegas), considered when it opened to be one of the world's most luxurious hotels. The lion roared again twenty years later with the opening of the second MGM Grand, a cavernous hotel and theme park modeled after the movie *The Wizard of Oz*. The Strip hotel's grand opening in December 1993 marked the third time Kerkorian had built the world's largest hotel in Las Vegas. All three hotels were pioneer landmarks, dramatically expanding the Las Vegas market beyond the dwindling pool of domestic high rollers. The nation's news media heralded the opening of the second MGM Grand, the pyramid-shaped Luxor, and Steve Wynn's Treasure Island as launching the era of Las Vegas as a family-friendly destination resort. But biographer Dial Torgerson, in *Kerkorian: An American Success Story*, noted that the International, the first gambling resort with child-care facilities, "was also aimed at the family and convention trade, which was expected to become increasingly important in the Las Vegas of the 1970s."

Most regard Kerkorian as a gentleman. A few suggest he is cold and flinty. Torgerson said one associate described Kerkorian as having "balls of steel." All agree he is an *intensely* private person. An extremely rare, hour-long interview for this book did little to penetrate Kerkorian's reticence. Dressed casually in a shirt, slacks, and leather jacket and looking tan and fit for his seventy-seven years, Kerkorian talked easily of the late 1940s and 1950s, when he flew charters from Los Angeles to Las Vegas, his often celebrated passengers eager to either get rich or get married. "We were just trying to eat in those days," he said, "and parlay what we did have into something better." Passengers on Kerkorian's Los Angeles Air Service included gambler Nick "the Greek" Dandolas and the notorious Benjamin "Bugsy" Siegel. "Siegel played big in those years," said Kerkorian, recalling 2 A.M. flights with Siegel on Kerkorian's twin-engine "bamboo bomber." He spoke fondly of fellow aviator Howard Hughes, despite the reclusive billionaire's efforts to keep Kerkorian from building the International.

"I met him on four different occasions," Kerkorian said of Hughes, who even before his shut-in period preferred the telephone to face-to-face conversations because of his deafness. "I liked him. He was a helluva guy. If you take him early in his career, he didn't get the credit he deserves." But Kerkorian volunteered little insight into his motivations behind building the three Las Vegas hotels, all of which flew in the face of skeptics who said they were too big or, in the case of the International, too far off the Strip. He declined to discuss the conceptual seeds that gave root to the International and the two MGM Grands.

The interview served largely to confirm just how strongly Kerkorian prefers to remain out of the public spotlight. "I think it's better to keep your business private," he said. "He is perhaps America's most famous and misunderstood Armenian, certainly its most enigmatic," said writer Mark Arax, who profiled Kerkorian in *Armenian International* magazine. "He exists in the public mind largely as a caricature, an accumulation of misleading and conflicting images."

"To my knowledge, Kirk Kerkorian has never said he's going to do something that he hasn't done," Bob Maxey, president of MGM

Grand Inc., said at the October 1991 groundbreaking of Kerkorian's $1-billion, 5,005-room MGM Grand Hotel and Theme Park. "Kirk is a great, instinctive person. He makes the right decisions," Maxey said. "His instincts in developing things, in creating things, even selling things, are without parallel. This guy doesn't make mistakes. But he does it by instinct."

"Kirk? I played tennis with Kirk just yesterday," Burt Cohen, president of the Desert Inn, said of his boss in 1991, when Kerkorian's Tracinda Corporation owned the Strip hotel. "He has a wicked forehand." Pressed to elaborate on his impressions of Kerkorian, Cohen replied: "He has no entourage. He carries his own baggage. He drives his own car. He has no pretensions. None whatsoever. And he is very much the gentleman."

The meeting took place in the fall of 1989. Armenia was a crippled region, suffering from the Azeri blockade and the devastating 1988 earthquake. Dozens of its more isolated villages had not yet received any humanitarian aid. They were faced with the prospects of a winter without medical supplies and heating oil. Armenian Harut Sassounian, publisher of the *California Courier,* believed there was one man who could deliver supplies to the beleaguered Diaspora. He arranged for a meeting with billionaire financier Kirk Kerkorian, a man known for his quiet philanthropy and skills as an aviator. "He asked me more than a hundred very precise, specific questions that needed 'yes' or 'no' or very short answers," Sassounian said of the meeting, recounted by writer Arax in *Armenian International.* "What kind of planes? What kind of trucks? What kind of runways and overland routes? He was no-nonsense. He wanted to see if I had done my homework, and he wanted to see if this was doable."

"Once he was satisfied that it could be done, he wasted no time saying yes," Sassounian recalled. "So a crazy idea—a dream, a fantasy—immediately became a reality with the nod of his head." The meeting led to the airlifting, in December 1989, of forty tons of supplies. There have been dozens of other flights since then, including the shipment in the winter of 1993 of 200,000 tons of heating fuel purchased by the United Armenian Fund, an umbrella organization for Armenian church and civic organizations and Kerkorian's Lincy Foundation, named after his daughters, Linda and Tracy. Operation Winter Fuel was a $21-million project, $14 million of which came from the pockets of Kerkorian. "Contrary to what some people might believe, Mr. Kerkorian has never forgotten his roots," said Hirair Hovnanian, chairmen of the Armenian Assembly, based in Washington, D.C. "He has given without expecting one thing in return. He doesn't seek any recognition. He doesn't want any monuments in his name. I am hoping one day very soon he will visit Armenia and the people there will get to meet this giant of a man. . . . He is a hero."

"I never had a master plan for my life," Kerkorian said. "I've just been tremendously fortunate."

Kerkor (Kirk) Kerkorian was born June 6, 1917, the youngest of four children. His father, Ahron, amassed a small fortune farming watermelons, grapes, and almonds on several ranches in the San Joaquin Valley, property he lost in the Great Depression. A strong man with a fiery temper, Ahron Kerkorian, with his handlebar mustache and resemblance to the Mexican bandit Pancho Villa, earned the nickname Villa. Torgerson wrote that the elder Kerkorian once halted an auction of his farm in Weedpath by leaping onto his horse and driving the auctioneer and prospective buyers off with a Colt pistol. When one of those in the crowd turned and threatened Kerkorian, he chopped off the man's ear with a hoe.

The family settled in Los Angeles, where Kirk Kerkorian hawked papers and ran with a gang called the League of Nations. He wound up in reform school and never graduated high school. Instead, he helped with the family business, trucking produce from the San Joaquin Valley to Los Angeles. Kerkorian grew up tough, hard, and lean, serving a grueling stint with the Civilian Conservation Corps, clearing roads and logging trails through the Sequoia National Park. He steam-cleaned engines and later followed the lead of his older brother, Nish, a professional boxer. Kerkorian joined the amateur ranks during an era when main events drew thousands of spectators. He won twenty-nine of thirty-three fights, his deadly right cross earning him the moniker Rifle Right Kerkorian.

"My first love," said Kerkorian, "is as a professional pilot." The love affair began the day in 1939 that a friend, Ted O'Flaherty, took him on a flight from Alhambra Airport in a Piper J-3 Cub. Kerkorian got a commercial license in 1941, taught Army pilots how to fly, and joined the Royal Air Force, ferrying Canadian-built mosquito bombers across the North Atlantic Ocean from Labrador to Scotland. The missions were risky. The wooden planes were light and swift, equipped with Rolls-Royce engines, but they did not fly well in cold weather. One of every four planes wound up smashed to bits on the coast or ocean floor. An attempt to break a transatlantic speed record, ruined by an insufficient tail-wind, almost proved fatal when Kerkorkian landed at Prestwick, Scotland, his plane choking from the lack of fuel. A second close call occurred in the winter of 1943, when a down draft caught Kerkorian's c-47 on takeoff from Gander, Newfoundland, and almost sent it crashing into the forest below. Once out of the service, Kerkorian bought a twin-engine Cessna and began flying air charters. In 1947 he bought Los Angeles Air Service, which consisted of a DC-3, a twin-engine Cessna and a single-engine Beechcraft. When the Civil Aeronautics Board began tightening up regulations on charter airlines, Kerkorian moved out of that business and became a nationally prominent airplane dealer. He bought a Douglas c-54—smelly from hauling livestock to Guatemala and its fuselage rotting from cattle urine—refurbished it and sold it to Northeast Airlines two years later for $340,000. He bought two DC-6 projets and began flying military personnel from Scott Air Force Base (Illinois) to North Africa. Los Angeles Air Service was renamed Trans International Airlines Inc. and reentered the passenger business in 1959. TIA became one of the first supplemental airlines with jet aircraft in 1962, when Kerkorian bought a DC-8 Jet Trader and began flying high-priority government loads from Travis Air Force Base, near San Francisco, to Guam. The business thrived. After six years of ownership swaps—including the sale and repurchase of the company from Studebaker Inc.—Kerkorian in 1968 sold his controlling interest in the airline to Transamerica Corporation for $104 million in stock. He then turned his attention to building the first of his three magnificent hotels.

"We always felt that Las Vegas had a great future," Kerkorian said of Las Vegas in the 1950s and 1960s. "People [lending institutions] didn't want to push it because it was gambling."

A gambler from the years of flying charters to Las Vegas (one pit boss referred to him as the Perry Como of the crap table because of his quiet demeanor), Kerkorian first became an investor in 1955 when he bought a $50,000 piece of the Dunes Hotel and Country Club. He lost it all, an experience that soured him on investing in any venture he did not control. "Kerkorian has a deep and abiding distaste for having his money in anything where he does not pull all the strings," said a longtime associate. In 1962 Kerkorian bought eighty acres on the Strip across from the Flamingo Hotel, the site of what in 1966 would become Caesars Palace. Having bought the property for $960,000, Kerkorian leased the land to Caesars for $190,000 and 15 percent of the gross per year. Two years later, after paying some $4 million in rent, Caesars bought Kerkorian out for $5 million. *Fortune* called it "one of the most successful land speculations in Las Vegas history."

Kerkorian bought the Flamingo in 1967 for $12.5 million. That same year he purchased an eighty-two-acre site on Paradise Road for $5 million. He had the Transamerica stock, cash, the Flamingo, and the land on Paradise Road. But the Bank of America, despite a long and profitable association with Kerkorian, refused to lend him the money to build the International. Some say the refusal was because Hughes also banked with the financial institution. Despite Kerkorian's conciliatory attitude toward the eccentric Hughes, the reclusive billionaire considered Kerkorian a rival. Hughes took steps to block the construction of the International, at one point announcing that the Sands would be expanded into the world's largest hotel. He tried to discourage Kerkorian by leaking a fictitious memo that the Atomic Energy Commission intended to step up underground testing in the desert north of Las Vegas. Hughes suggested to his aide Bob Maheu that the company swap the Stardust for Kerkorian's property on Paradise Road.

Kerkorian was not to be deterred. "I wore out two pairs of shoes pounding the pavement, looking for financing," Fred Benninger, Kerkorian's partner in the International venture, told Torgerson. "I don't think too many people in the financial world really believed we were going to do it. They wanted to see something. They asked, 'When is he going to break ground?' It's hard to finance a hotel, wherever it is. And if it's in Las Vegas it's twice as hard. People don't believe that Las Vegas has ever changed from the old days. Most of those Eastern money people have never been to Las Vegas." Kerkorian had no doubts the project would prove successful. "The International looked like a real plus to us," he said. "Most of the hotels in town had 250 rooms and they were growing like Topsy. I had total confidence or I wouldn't have gone into the project. Las Vegas has always been on the plus side for us."

Kerkorian broke ground in 1967 with a $30-million loan from Nevada National Bank of Commerce, less than half the $80 million needed to finish the job. Kerkorian invested $16.6 million of his own money in the project, established Leisure International Corporation, and began selling stock to finance completion of the project. When the International was near completion, the common stock, which opened at $5 a share, was selling for more than $50. The hotel opened in the summer of 1969. The following fall, Kerkorian's $16.6 million was worth $180 million.

Barbra Streisand, who would open the second MGM Grand, was the headline act when the International opened for business. Actor Cary Grant, a close friend of Kerkorian's, also took the stage on opening night. "Kirk," Grant said, "I know you don't like this kind of thing, but I want everybody here to see the guy who made this spectacular hotel possible." Kerkorian stood up for a quick second, then sat back down. "Some claim he was blushing under his desert tan," Torgeson wrote.

A recession forced Kerkorian to sell his interests in the International and Flamingo to Hilton Hotels Corporation in 1970 and 1971 at rock-bottom prices. Within months after the titles changed hands, Kerkorian announced plans to build the first MGM Grand Hotel. The $106-million, twenty-six-story-high-rise resort opened December 5, 1973, with a celebrity gala. It was the type of gathering the shy Kerkorian normally would avoid. It was at the groundbreaking for the MGM that Kerkorian replied to a bystander who had remarked about his wealth: "What good does it do being rich? I can't do what I want to do. I don't like to get dressed up and go to see bankers. I hate that kind of thing. You know, I don't want to be here. I don't want to be here right now."

Kerkorian had turned his attention back to the airline business in 1970, purchasing a controlling interest in Western Airlines. In 1976 he sold off 17 percent of the carrier's stock for $30 million. Buoyed by the success of the MGM Grand in Las Vegas, Kerkorkian expanded his operation to Reno, opening the 2,000-room, $131-million MGM Grand in 1978. He incurred the wrath of Hollywood when he obtained a majority of Metro-Goldwyn-Mayer in 1974 and followed that up in 1981 with the acquisition of United Artists Studios. He sliced MGM/UA budgets, produced only a handful of movies, hired and fired a number of top executives, and auctioned off the studio's memorabilia and several cherished films, including *The Wizard of Oz* and *Gone with the Wind*. He sold the studio in 1990 to Italian financier Giancarlo Parretti's Pathe Communications Corporation for $1.3 billion. Sentimentalists accused Kerkorkian of gutting the film giants; but an investor who held $100 worth of MGM stock in 1975 would have made $2,687 in 1986. It is a pattern of profit that defines Kerkorian throughout his financial career. "Every shareholder who has participated with him has doubled or tripled his money," one stock analyst said. "That's a record few men have."

Kerkorian was in the midst of merging MGM and UA in 1980 when tragedy struck: A devastating fire swept the casino and upper floors of the MGM Grand, killing eighty-seven people and injuring hundreds of others. Fire investigators said inadequate fire alarms and other safety devices contributed to the disaster. Kerkorian is reluctant to discuss the fire. "We had a helluva team there," he said of the company's top executives. "I went along with what the team thought." A member of that team, Alvin Benedict, chairman of MGM Grand Hotels, said Kerkorian met with a group of associates within hours after the fire was extinguished. "Kirk's first question was, 'Where do we start?'" Benedict said. "Most corporations would have abandoned this property. We got into the hotel for the first time three or four days after the fire. I figured there was no way we could come out of this. I think the idea of walking away and forgetting about rebuilding the property was in the back of everybody's mind. That's what most people would have done." The hotel reopened eight months later.

Kerkorian sold the first MGM Grand and the MGM in Reno to Bally Manufacturing Corporation in 1986 for $594 million. He said he was "sad" about the sale. But confidants contend Kerkorian has no strong desire for possessions. "I'm not married to anything," Torgerson quoted Kerkorian in his biography. The author said Kerkorian's absence of sentimentality was the possible result of the constant uprooting during his childhood. "Somehow he apparently missed the hang-up that possessions are permanent," Torgerson wrote.

Loaded with cash from the MGM/UA sale, Kerkorian in 1990 began investing in Chrysler Corporation (soon becoming its biggest stockholder) and turned his attention to building the second and grandest MGM Grand. The project would consist of a 330-acre theme park and a 171,500-square-foot casino, nearly twice the gambling space of the larger Strip hotels. It would provide attractions for children, gaming machines for the five-cent slot player and a gold-and-marble baccarat pit for high rollers laying down $250,000 on the flip of a card. "I like the fact that this property takes care of everybody," said Kerkorkian, who owned 73 percent of the stock of MGM Grand Inc. before the company sold its only nongaming subsidiary, MGM Grand Air, in January 1995. "He doesn't do it for the money," retired Chrysler Corporation chief executive officer Lee Iacocca said of his longtime friend. "He does it because he gets bug-eyed like a little kid when he goes through the place."

Although he maintains a house in Los Angeles, Kerkorian calls Las Vegas home. His Lincy Foundation has contributed millions of dollars to local charities and the University of Nevada, Las Vegas. His daughters (from his second marriage, to Jean Maree Hardy, a one-time dancer at the Thunderbird Hotel) were born here: Tracy in 1959 and Linda in 1965.

Torgerson, in reviewing Kerkorkian's career, said, "He made many moves which seemed inspired by extrasensory perception." Despite what he termed "a few bad breaks," Kerkorian in the interview for this book acknowledged having been fortunate. But he told one interviewer: "Some people say that things turn out for me accidentally. They don't. Nothing has ever happened to me by accident."

Kerkorian shows no signs of slowing down. But he does maintain a measure of nostalgia for the old days, recalling past friendships ("I have nothing but fond memories of old friends like Wilbur Clark, Sam Boyd, and Moe Dalitz"), midnight charter flights over the desert landscape, and turning deals that changed the face of the Las Vegas Strip. "The first fruits are the most fun, I have to admit," he said.

Steve Wynn: King of Wow!
Mark Seal

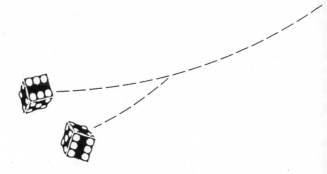

The Las Vegas Strip is on fire. Fireworks, then fireballs, then an explosion that will be seen around the world. But first comes ceremony. While the kings of corporate Las Vegas watch from their penthouses, a dust-covered crowd of two hundred thousand bellows in the street, *"Blow it up! Blow it up! Blow it up!"*

A block away, Steve Wynn, with his dark suit and even darker pompadour, stands on the pirate-ship deck of his newest mega-hotel, Treasure Island, a thirty-two-story, $430-million casino/hotel, whose front is called Buccaneer Bay, a fantastic pirate-ship lagoon where a sea battle erupts every fifteen minutes. Surrounded by politicians, celebrities, and high rollers from across the planet, Wynn is, as always, calling the shots. Last night, he christened Treasure Island in a ceremony worthy of prime-time TV. Now, he is giving the order to fire a "ceremonial" cannon that will blow up a piece of Las Vegas's past: the legendary Dunes Hotel, which Wynn's Mirage Resorts Inc. bought for $70 million and will transform, by 1998, into the Bellagio—a resort that Wynn predicts will be "the single most extravagant hotel ever built on earth," set around its own fourteen-acre lake.

"Ready, " Wynn shouts, "aim, *fire!*"

A curtain of flames rises up the hotel's walls. The neon sign that beckoned gamblers for almost a decade crashes to the ground. Black smoke darkens the desert sky, and the twenty-three-story Dunes comes down in an implosion of smoke and rubble and street-corner *wow!*s.

The message is as loud as the blast: The old Las Vegas is falling and a new Vegas is being born, a Vegas where the grizzled gambler has given way to the all-American tourist, where the old nickname, Glitter Gulch, has been unofficially changed to Destination Resort, a getaway with something for everybody. Tonight's spectacle is so ready-for-prime-time it will air in a made-for-TV movie about pirates in modern-day Vegas on NBC. *Treasure Island: The Adventure Begins* was written by *Hook* screenwriter James V. Hart and features the star of *The Young Indiana Jones Chronicles.* As executive producer, Wynn financed the production budget and bought the air time (for $1.7 million) to show the movie. The movie's climax will, of course, be the implosion.

Steve Wynn's battle is not against pirates but, as always, against Numbers. Can Wynn keep on winning? Since he opened the Mirage in 1989, Wynn has been a human bellwether for the Las Vegas business climate. "A visionary" is the phrase most often used to describe this son of a small-time bingo operator who supposedly sees the future and bends it to his dreams. "Now, you have spectacular grand theme resorts in Las Vegas, but before he built the Mirage you had none of those," says Tom Hantges, a USA Capital Management Group analyst.

So what does Wynn see now? To find out, you have to wait for the smoke to clear and the crowds to depart. Then an even bigger show takes the stage: Steve Wynn presenting his vision of Las Vegas's future.

"Hey, what are you doing in your room?"

The voice of the impresario of the New Las Vegas blares out of the TV into my sunny Mirage bedroom, summoning me from room to casino like the horns of reveille.

"Hi, I'm Steve Wynn," the video continues. "In the next few minutes I'm gonna show you around." Wynn's video tour, in which he is heard but not seen, plays continuously in the 3,044 guest rooms and suites in his Mirage hotel and is designed as a promotion for hotel guests. But today it is a wake-up call for me: Come and meet the wizard, it seems to be saying, the wizard of the Mirage.

Past the fiery volcano spewing flames, smoke, and a chorus of tourist *wow!*s on the quarter hour, past the sharks in the twenty-thousand-gallon registration desk aquarium and the Royal White Tigers prowling in the tropical rain forest of a lobby, past the steely screams of a thousand slot machines and a million broken dreams, *he* is waiting and, it seems, watching; for Steve Wynn's voice is everywhere, personally guiding 2 million guests a year through his pleasure dome. It bleeds out of hidden speakers on the raised moving sidewalks leading into his hotel from the Strip and from countless corners in his concrete creation.

Meeting the man in charge is a bit like walking through the curtain behind the façade that hid the Wizard of Oz. This Wiz, however, is all business—listed as the highest-paid executive in America with an annual salary of $34.2 million—and he does not hide behind a curtain. Wynn is perpetually on the podium, touting the New Vegas, the town of Disney-style theme parks and family entertainment.

When he opened the Mirage in 1989, even Las Vegas locals laughed at his audacity: *$1 million a day!* That was what Wynn needed to win in the Mirage casino to cover his overhead. One hundred thousand people were expected on opening day; *two hundred thousand* showed up. The casino won $40 million the first month and posted $44 million in first-quarter profits (while next-door Caesars Palace's earnings dropped 43 percent), and fifty-six-year-old Steve Wynn has become, according to a 1994 *Time* article, "the new face of gambling in America, ingratiating and scrubbed . . . [softening] resistance to what once was considered a slightly sinful indulgence."

Now, with the opening of Treasure Island, the numbers to cover his overhead are much less than the Mirage's million. But the game's the same: luring business from the increasingly heated competition.

I am led by a publicist through rooms that seem to grow increasingly brighter in color, from a merely bright magenta waiting room into Wynn's absolutely electrifying office. The carpet is streaked with rivulets of primary colors. The chairs are such a bright shade of magenta they seem to be floating. And leaning back in a white leather chair with armrests big as hotel pillows, his white tennis shoes kicked up on his desk, wearing blue jeans and a black Donald Duck T-shirt, is Steve Wynn. His white teeth glisten. He simultaneously eats a malt-nut Power Bar, talks on the telephone, plays with his two dogs, and grins and waves a welcome.

A framed credo from Jonathan Swift sits on Wynn's desk: "Vision is the art of seeing things invisible."

Today, he cannot even see across his office with clarity. At twenty-nine, he was diagnosed with retinitis pigmentosa, an eye disorder in which light causes pain and the field of vision is gradually reduced.

Steve Wynn at a Mirage press conference, 1991. (Courtesy Las Vegas News Bureau)

Wynn could one day be blind. "If you've got a good self-image, you can deal with handicaps," Wynn once said. "If you don't, you can have good vision and be Batman, and you're ready to kill yourself. You say eyes, and it's the most horrible thing to all of us. There's a lot of pity. The most horrible thing about this and the reason I hate to discuss it is someone will say, 'Oh, I heard about your eyes.' I'm about as pathetic or sympathetic a character as Attila the Hun."

Today, however, when asked about the state of his disease, Wynn answers quickly and dismissively. "It's stayed the same," he says. Steve Wynn does not like to talk about weaknesses. But ask him about the future of Vegas, and he straightens in his chair like a yokel who has just hit a jackpot.

"Look at it!" he says, motioning toward his office windows to the Las Vegas beyond. "Just changing itself right before your eyes! It's incredible! Change is running over every city in America. Look at this place! *Wow.* Looks like the Romanian gymnastic team with Nadia Comaneci. The industry is just nimble. The old joints are going into the toilet, but the new ones are all fresh and lively. *Recession?* Money coming by the billion. Two billion is being spent here this year. These [Wynn's] three joints. Two billion! *Wow.*"

Wynn's joints—the Mirage, the Golden Nugget, Treasure Island, and soon Bellagio—are representative of the corporate takeover of

American gambling, the hot resort growth industry for all-American companies like Holiday Inn and Hilton. As gambling is legalized and legitimized (by some estimates in half the states by the turn of the century) Wynn has marshaled his considerable forces for an expansion. So far he has been largely unsuccessful in the heartland: voted down by the state legislature for a hotel/casino in Bridgeport, Connecticut; losing a bid for a riverboat operation in West Dundee, Illinois; thwarted in Kansas City, New Orleans, and Sydney, Australia. But he continues to doggedly push for new locations, envisioning an international collection of hotel/casinos less akin to Bugsy Siegel than Walt Disney, another major Wynn mentor. "We don't build these places for kids," says Wynn. "They couldn't afford it. We build 'em for the child in each of us."

Because everything in Wynn's world is spectacle, the show he presents for me today is the Vegas boss as Regular Guy. Where is the titan who is described by many as impetuous, impatient, and intimidating, possessing a temper as explosive as his volcano? "He's just calm and cool and all of a sudden somebody does or says something and he just explodes," says one competitor. Maybe he has released his frustration through activity. (He's a wind-surfer, jet skier, body builder, and, most avidly, a golfer.) Today Wynn is relaxed, playful, and fun-loving, a regular guy who says he is luckier than smart.

"Oh, Joycceee!" he calls, summoning models and mockups of proposed developments from his secretary in a voice that is as sweet as a schoolboy's. Forget the image of the Vegas kingpin watching every gambler beneath the mirrored ceiling of his casino via closed-circuit TV. Wynn cannot even tune his TV to watch the six Atlantic Bottlenose dolphins in his dolphin domain behind the Mirage without help.

Today, Wynn is no Wizard. But he is a marvelous show. He blasts away at his lesser competitors, while paying homage to the mighty neighbors. He bounds around the office, telling jokes and doing impersonations, from redneck riverboat captain to Yiddish mama to local tourist—the 34.2-million-dollar man as lounge act.

Ask him to elaborate on his resort philosophy, and he offers not merely an answer but a theatrical production in which he plays both the hotel boss and the customer. He leans in so close I can smell the malted scent of the Power Bar on his breath and stare into his ace-of-spades-black irises. For starters, Wynn does not think of himself as being in the gambling business.

"We're in the entertainment and recreational business now," he says. "Although I love casinos! I'm not trying to excuse them or masquerade them. I'm just saying if you go and interview these people [the customers], that's what's going on out there. And if that's what's going on in their minds, I wanna play their game. I wanna come at them in a way they're interested in hearing my spiel, that is."

Now, he shifts into the persona of the tourist, walking in off the desert: "Where's the fun of it? Don't tell me you've got slot machines, Mr. Wynn. I'm not that excited. What is there to *do* besides gaming?" His voice is soft and hypnotic, the Vegas boss as snake charmer. "You say, 'Well, there's Cirque du Soleil.'"

He snaps back into the tourist persona. "You mean that French circus?" he asks.

"*Yeah*. And there's Siegfried and Roy."

"The ones with the tigers?" he grins excitedly.

"*Yeah*. And restaurants. And swimming pools. Volcanoes. Tigers that you can watch."

Now that he has the visitor inside the doors, Wynn is ready to deal the cards. "Now, one of the side effects of this is if you draw this kind of a crowd, that's where the high rollers wanna be, too. So you build beautiful suites and a Salon Privé. Give 'em credit. Buy a Gulfstream jet. Have the right staff. And they'll come and play Baccarat for $100,000 a card. But that's not the mainstream of this place. Although we've got the most of that kind of stuff in the world, there's a much bigger game out there. And that is the resort, the destination for everybody, the mainstream economic recreational fun place to go."

Perhaps the *coup de grace* for the Mirage gamblers—and only the highest of the high rollers qualify—is Wynn's magnificent Shadow Creek, his private golf course built at a cost of more than $40 million and once included in *Golf Digest*'s top ten courses in America. Several Oriental gamblers who wager up to $100,000 a hand at baccarat have switched their allegiance from other top Las Vegas hotels to the Mirage, solely for the privilege of being allowed to stroll the fairways of Shadow Creek.

Wynn's voice lowers to a whisper. "The definition of success in our business is when someone walks through the door and says, 'Oh, boy, *look at this place!*' . . . A theme park is where you go to get a WOW, six wows, eight wows in a day, then you go home. Pay your forty dollars, buy a T-shirt and say, 'Great, see ya in two years.' That's not the business I'm in. I'm in the business of people saying, 'Let's linger. Let's loiter here. I wish I was staying in this place. I wonder what the rooms are like.'"

He leans back and smiles.

"That's the sound of victory."

Steve Wynn has spent his life pursuing the ultimate "Wow!"

An only child until he was ten, Wynn grew up the adored son of Zelma and Mike Wynn. His devotion to his father is displayed on his office wall: a framed portrait of his father at age forty-five, a forever-young image of Wynn's mentor and motivation.

Mike Wynn was the son of a vaudevillian. His father, perpetually on the road, left his two sons and daughter to be raised by foster parents. When Mike was seventeen, he became a manager of bingo games along the East Coast. Later, applying for a job at a Boston soft drink company and hearing that his potential employer was anti-Semitic, he changed his name from Weinberg to Wynn.

When Steve was ten, he followed his inveterate gambler father to fabled Las Vegas to open a bingo parlor above the Silver Slipper casino. They rode horses together, dined at dinner shows, and bathed in neon. The parlor flopped in six weeks, its demise attributable to the entrance of a formidable competitor into the bingo fray. The competitor's name? The Golden Nugget. Father and son headed back east, where Wynn enrolled in Manlius Military Academy, a prep school for West Point.

"[Wynn] and my brother were champion water skiers," says Artie Nathan, now director of human resources at Mirage Resorts Inc. "And they built their own water skis. They would build them shorter and shorter and shorter, and the shorter the ski the more difficult it is. And they were unwilling to accept any level of difficulty as being beyond them. They eventually had shoe-skis, the size of sneakers."

Steve Wynn wanted to be a doctor. But on Sundays away from the University of Pennsylvania, he worked in his father's bingo hall, then located in a suburb of Washington, D.C. Later, Wynn switched his major to English literature and took some classes at Penn's famed Wharton School of Business. Life was looking rosy. But three weeks before receiving his B.A., Wynn's father died on the operating table during open-heart surgery. He was forty-six.

In 1985 Wynn recalled his father's death for *Las Vegan Magazine* writer Scott A. Zamost. He discussed the anguishing three-hour wait in the University of Minnesota hospital and his horror when the surgeon emerged, head bowed, saying, "Sorry."

His father's death affected Wynn so profoundly that he has never been truly afraid since, he told Zamost. "I'd give up everything for fifteen minutes with my father. To have him walk through this hotel and see what happened. Now you're talking about something more than a big number." His voice trailed to a whisper. "I miss the thrill of showing my dad that it worked out OK. He would have been awful proud."

Wynn abandoned his own career plans in order to take over his father's bingo business, turning around the floundering games. His wife, Elaine, who had once been Miss Miami Beach, counted the money; Wynn read the numbers. But it was not just bingo he was selling. "It was making the bingo a social recreational experience." he says. "My bingo players used to wear costumes on Halloween."

In 1967, twenty-five years old and still a bit naïve, he invested $45,000 of his bingo profits for a 3 percent piece of the action of the Frontier Hotel, just opening as a new resort on the Strip. Wynn, his wife, and ten-month-old daughter moved to Las Vegas. He got his gaming license in June 1967 and became the Frontier's slot manager and assistant credit manager. Four months later, Howard Hughes bought the hotel, just after the sheriff and two investigators broke up a meeting between the Frontier's managing director and an alleged Detroit mobster. Eventually, six people, some of them organized-crime figures, were convicted for concealing the Frontier's true ownership.

Wynn was not part of the investigation; he left the Frontier years before the convictions. But the bust taught him an important lesson: Beware of all business associations. He found a supporter in E. Parry Thomas, then chairman of the Bank of Las Vegas. Thomas represented Hughes in the Frontier purchase; soon, he set up Steve Wynn in the wholesale liquor distributing business called Best Brands. Through the liquor business, Wynn discovered Las Vegas's second most important currency: connections. He became acquainted with the city's top hotel executives.

When Wynn sold Best Brands in the summer of 1971, a new opportunity awaited. Wynn's realtor, who also represented the financially ubiquitous Howard Hughes, listened to Wynn's dream of purchasing a sliver of land on the northwest corner of Flamingo Road and Las

Vegas Boulevard, then used as part of the Caesars Palace parking lot. The realtor told him to forget about it; Hughes was buying every possible piece of available Strip property, not selling. But Wynn kept calling. He wanted to build a small casino with a few slot machines—maybe even force Caesars Palace to buy it from him.

When the realtor called Wynn at home on a Sunday with news that Hughes was willing to sell the property, his first Vegas land sale, both Wynn and the realtor were startled. The price: $1.1 million. Wynn jumped at the deal, although he had to give up 33 percent of the deal to a friend, Abraham Rosenberg, founder of J&B Scotch, for signing the bank note. Eleven months later, Wynn sold the 1,300-by-150-foot property, overhung with power lines, to Caesars Palace for $2.25 million. With a net profit of $766,000, Wynn was ready to become a player.

He started buying Golden Nugget stock in 1969, initially purchasing fourteen thousand shares. Having heard that a group from the Dunes proposed a tender offer, he expected to turn a profit. When the offer never came, the stock remained flat. But Wynn kept buying: four thousand shares in 1971, ninety-two thousand more in 1972. By 1973 he owned 5.5 percent of the Golden Nugget's stock—which required him to be licensed by the state Gaming Control Board. Once licensed, Wynn said he was not interested in a takeover or in starting a proxy fight. "I might be a bingo consultant there," Wynn said.

A bar owner who had worked with Wynn in his liquor days and heard of his licensing for the Nugget called him at home one night with some interesting news. A group of dealers, floor men, and shift bosses at the Nugget were stealing Nugget cash each day in early morning meetings at the bar. Wynn wanted to act, but his hands were tied. He was only a stockholder, not a board member, and thus had no power. That was about to change.

E. Parry Thomas pulled strings with Nugget president Buck Blaine, and Wynn became a director and executive vice-president. He then asked Blaine what it would cost for him to resign. The price was $18,000 for three years. To get the man once known as Mr. Nugget on his side, Wynn paid him $30,000 for five years, then within a month made a tender offer for 225,000 more shares. On August 1, 1973, Steve Wynn was elected president and chairman of the Golden Nugget at a special board of directors meeting.

He walked in and cleaned up. When the bust was over, 160 casino operators had been fired. Even parking attendants were stealing cash from parking tickets. At age thirty-one, the largest Nugget share-holder with 13 percent of the company, Wynn had learned another lesson: Employee loyalty is king. Who could be more loyal than his own brother? Wynn hired Kenneth Wynn, then twenty-one and working in a men's store at the Las Vegas Hilton, as a director. The brothers had their work cut out for them; the Nugget had a weary casino, no hotel rooms, and 850 employees. Within months, they remodeled the casino, quadrupled pretax profits, from $1.1 million to $4 million, and announced plans for a new high-rise. Within a year, the 579-room Golden Nugget Gambling Hall and Rooming House opened. Pretax profits jumped to $7.7 million.

But Wynn still was not satisfied. He knew there had to be more. He went to Atlantic City, where the new Resorts International was the harbinger of the new age gambling palace, overrun with crossover crowds in palatial surroundings. If this was the future, Wynn wanted into the game. Dressed in blue jeans and a Willie Nelson T-shirt, he walked into the decrepit Strand Motel, introduced himself to the owner, and offered $8 million for the property. He bought it for $8.5 million, borrowing most of the money.

Opening in December 1980 as the Atlantic City Golden Nugget, the 522-room hotel hit big. It generated operating revenues in its first year of $183.2 million, accounting for 77 percent of the company's total revenues. In terms of gaming revenues, the Nugget obliterated all its competitors.

Buy Wynn did not want just the gamblers; he wanted the stars. He stole Frank Sinatra away from Resorts in 1982, signing a three-year contract for the services of Ol' Blue Eyes. By 1983 Wynn was ready to return Frank west to Vegas. He had plans for a new Golden Nugget tower: not the same string of suites, but something that could take on Caesars Palace's high-roller luster. Something that would truly be a "Wow!"

It was not the ideal time to think big. None of the Strip hotels were booming in the early 1980s, and nobody wanted to go downtown—except Frank Sinatra. He signed a deal for forty performances at both the eastern and western Nuggets. And to prove his confidence in Wynn's "Wow!" Frank even went on television commercials and the party circuit with his new employer.

The new Nugget opened in 1985 with a celebration worthy of a sultan's court. High rollers flocked. Helium balloons filled the desert sky. And the eighteen-story, four-star hotel tower was booked solid.

The new age of Las Vegas gambling had arrived and with it, Steve Wynn.

Deal after deal, he upped the ante on the "Wow!" He built a new Nugget in nearby Laughlin, Nevada, after selling his Atlantic City Golden Nugget to Bally's for a $260-million profit. He took on a $1-billion debt (much of it in Michael Milken junk bonds) to build the Mirage. And always he kept his antenna out for the next best thing. Because vision, as Swift and Wynn obviously agree, is the art of seeing things invisible.

By the late 1980s Wynn knew there was a market for something new, something even bigger. "It was my growing feeling that Las Vegas had a terrible kind of sameness to it," he says in his office. "Boxes of rooms on top of rooms filled with slot machines." He pauses. "I'm not a gambler. I wouldn't go across the street to shoot dice except as a lark maybe twice a year. But I'd go regularly to see a wonderment or a new attraction. So would you."

The concept for Treasure Island came not from his high-powered Los Angeles architects nor from his multimillion-dollar executive brain trust. The concept, he says, was delivered by the pizza guys. Wynn had been toying with a Casablanca theme, "you know, Marrakech and Rick's Cafe, that whole Beau Geste kind of look," he says. But then the owner of the PepsiCo-owned California Pizza Kitchen chain, which has a branch in the middle of the Mirage's casino, uttered a simple, magical suggestion. "He said, 'We got another idea. Listen to this.'" Here, Wynn deepens his radio-ready baritone and belts out the name like two snaps of his fingers. "*Treasure Island*. Think of the fun." Wynn cocks his head for emphasis, as if he's been hit by lightning. "And I thought, 'Boy, that would be fun!'"

The old Las Vegas may have been about gambling action, but the new Las Vegas is all about attractions—Disney-style themes and rides and spectacle—and Wynn knew he needed something stupendous for the winter of 1993. After the Mirage opened in 1989, Las Vegas had undergone unprecedented change, with new hotel/casino-*cum*—theme parks designed to snag families, people who do not think of themselves as gamblers but eventually end up at the tables.

The middle-American market was the target. Circus Circus Inc. was creating the recently opened Luxor, a Hanging Gardens of Babylon theme hotel extravaganza and casino, and was building a five-acre Grand Slam Canyon adventure- and water-park dome with the world's largest indoor roller coaster, which debuted in 1995. MGM Grand was hoisting a gargantuan 5,000-room hotel complete with a thirty-three-acre Wizard of Oz theme park to open in late 1993. Thus Wynn, whose no-neon Mirage had become the most successful hotel in the hospitality industry, truly needed a "WOW."

After hearing the Treasure Island idea, Wynn called his architect, Los Angeles–based John Jerde, creator of New Age shopping centers, resorts, and developments around the world, who was working on the Casablanca plans. "I said, 'Stop! Listen to me! *Treasure Island.* But more. Imagine if there was a bay. And we had a pirate ship parked there as part of the front. And then every hour on the hour a British ship comes around the corner and they yell, 'Lay down your arms!' And they have a fight.'"

He leans in conspiratorially, addressing his competition. "Before those guys have an awards banquet about how clever they are, they're going to have to deal with Treasure Island," he says. "It's a piece of work."

"Those guys," of course, have plenty to say about Steve Wynn. His competitors say Wynn pushes himself too much, that the place for the Vegas CEO is in the boardroom, not America's living room. They remember his TV ads when he opened the Golden Nugget: Steve Wynn and Frank Sinatra in a suite with Sinatra pinching "the kid's" cheek and asking for fresh towels. Wynn even once wrote a ballad for the Nevada Dance Theater with a theme close to his heart: the history of Las Vegas.

"I try to get him to cool it," says former Circus Circus CEO Bill Bennett. "He has a tendency to get himself in trouble from time to time. . . . He's been out on a road-show selling the Treasure Island thing and talking to analysts and big-group buyers and somebody started hitting him with questions, 'You do a lot of business and you make a lot of noise but the net profit's not there.' Which is true.

"I just kid him about that, 'If you'd put as much effort into pushing your properties as you do in pushing yourself, they would really be the most profitable properties in the state.'"

Replies Wynn: "Operating profits for the Mirage were $189,000 to every million the first year, a little more the second year. Last year, it was $170,000. It went down because of the Japanese component [fewer tourists arriving from Japan]. Plus this last summer we have been carrying about $400,000 a month on payroll on this new hotel."

And Treasure Island? "I haven't been inside but I'm not very impressed with the outside," says Bennett, whose former holdings, Excalibur and Luxor, compete with Wynn's resorts. "I don't think Steve's impressed with the outside. He keeps changing colors. . . . He's trying to get a look of a South Pacific hut on a skyscraper and that's pretty difficult to do. Steve is pretty clever on those things. I don't think what you're looking at on the outside is the final thing. Steve'll keep banging away at it until he gets a look that he likes."

But, Bennett adds, "I don't see any way that he'll lose any money. He'll make money. It's going to be a good property."

Now, with his Vegas future secure, Wynn has his eyes on the heartland. He will not say how much he has budgeted for expansion. But Wynn has built a human resources department that can marshal a staff within days, and he is looking at every location where legislatures make gaming legal.

"In the next sixteen months there will be twice as many jurisdictions as there are today," he says. "And in the sixteen months following that there will be four times as many. Or eight times as many. We'll be trying to measure all those business opportunities and make an intelligent decision on one or two of 'em. We can't be everywhere. That's not the kind of company we are. . . . The tax rate's gotta be right. The regulatory climate's gotta be right. Our location's gotta be right. We can get the money. Money's usually the least problem. 'Cause there's plenty of it around. We did a [public financing of] a hundred million yesterday. At nine and a quarter percent."

But while the money may be easy, what is tough in expanding out of Vegas is convincing communities and legislatures of Wynn's devotion to the local economies. That takes more than money. That takes Steve Wynn's considerable gift of persuasion and corporate resources.

To this end, Mirage Resorts human resources director Artie Nathan travels across America, redefining the image of the Las Vegas casino. "We're out to show that we're not a bunch of sharpies [promising everything, delivering nothing] from the desert," says Nathan. "We're a bunch of businessmen and women who run a business as well as anybody in America."

Nathan regularly takes forty uniformed Mirage employees before audiences of fifteen thousand in wintry places like Bridgeport and Hartford in Meet the Mirage nights. "What they really want to know is our corporate values," says Nathan, who will rattle off a litany of commitments to answer their questions: Charity? Mirage Resorts Inc. is the largest single United Way pledge company in the history of Nevada. Voter registration? All of its employees are registered to vote and 90 percent voted in the last election. Community service? The employees of the Mirage donated fourteen thousand volunteer hours last year. With gambling proliferating, Nathan, the largest college recruiter in the hotel industry, says he can marshal a staff of six thousand in three months.

But in Wynn's office, the expansion dreams and schemes are far away. As the skies outside his windows darken, an assistant enters. The working day is done, at least for Wynn's "mutts," Cleo and Toasty. Time for the ten-minute drive for dinner at home, where Wynn's wife and two daughters are waiting. He and his wife divorced but re-married. They laugh about it now, saying they are back together be-cause "the divorce just didn't work out."

Any strained family bonds certainly were strengthened as a result of a traumatic event: daughter Kevin's kidnapping in the summer of 1993. The Wynn family's composure was remarkable during the or-deal, which ended without any physical harm to the young woman and the indictment and conviction of three co-conspirators.

Wynn's fortitude was certainly never more tested than during the stressful hours immediately following the crime, but everyone from law enforcement to the general public lauded him for his composure and resolve under such tremendous stress.

Now, he gets down on all fours on his technicolor carpets and wrestles with his dogs. The mutts seem reluctant to leave the Mirage, which Wynn, naturally, finds endearing.

"They'd rather hang out here because there's more excitement," he says as his assistant and secretary erupt in a chorus of grins and whistles. "Gimme that dog! Come here! Come here, Munchkin."

"But look," Wynn says, rising. "Being a visionary has to do with knowing where the market wants to go, maybe about five minutes ahead of the other guys."

It also means knowing not to sweat the small stuff.

"Some analyst asked me once, 'Aren't you concerned about these riverboats [on which gambling has been legalized in some states] and Indians [tribes recognized as sovereign states, able to set their own laws on gambling]?'" he says, in my face for a final curtain call.

His elastic voice soars into the high range, a comedian's cackle from a Vegas showroom. "Riverboats and Indians!" he exclaims. "What would I be afraid of them for? . . . You wanna know what to be afraid of? I'm afraid of Caesars Palace! They're right there! Those are tough guys! I'm afraid of Circus Circus! Whadda I gotta be afraid of [Indian bingo parlors and casinos] for? I'm afraid of Circus. The guy's got a seven-hundred-million-dollar credit line and imaginative designers! That's a guy to be afraid of! Here is a dangerous guy!"

Suddenly, he turns solemn, as if reciting a benediction. "We're in the entertainment and leisure recreational business: Give the people what they want, and even if there's a casino on both sides of you, they'll come to your place. Trust a slot machine," he says, slapping his hands together hard, "and you're [screwed] if there's another slot machine. If you're the only guy [gambling operator] in town, you're gonna look like a rocket scientist. Like those riverboats you been reading about. Can't get near 'em! Dumps in [the] Mississippi! Filthy shacks. [He lowers his voice, imitating a hayseed operator.] 'Gonna win a hundred million!' [Then back to reality.] Investment of eleven million. The guy's gonna make his investment back in four months. [Voice now like a Yiddish mama.] BIG DEAL! [Now almost singing.] Wait until somebody comes next door. He'll die as quick as he lived. Like a young gunfighter."

Leaving Wynn's office, I join a crowd mobbing an elaborate miniature mock-up of Treasure Island. From hidden speakers, Wynn's voice booms like a pirate's cry, giving the multitudes a preview of his latest mousetrap: "Cannons thunder and pirates plunder. . . . Treasure Island at the Mirage. . . . You can travel the seven seas and never see anything like it again."

When the tape is over and it begins cueing up again, a little boy lingers beside his mother, his mouth open wide. "Mama," he asks, "are the pirates good?"

The mother smiles. "Only in Las Vegas," she says.

Cowboys, Crooks, & Corporations: How Popular Literature Has Treated Las Vegas

John H. Irsfeld

From cowboys to crooks to corporations—that is the sequence of dynasties in the popular literature of Las Vegas since the gold-rush days of the nineteenth century.

The Years of the Cowboy—and the prospector, the itinerant salesman, and the restless ordinary citizen drawn by the path of the sun—cover the period from territorial days through World War II. This dynasty has not completely died out in Nevada, of course, and is especially well represented in Washoe County and the rurals, most notably Elko. There one will see gambling halls pretending it is a hundred years ago, and patrons buying into the pretense: big hats, handlebar mustaches, Levis, and cowboy boots. You would think you were back in Texas.

Even as late as 1939, the Las Vegas Chamber of Commerce published a tourism brochure complete with a cartoon map of the area. The legend at the top of the map read, "Las Vegas, Nevada. Still a Frontier Town." In the lower right-hand corner was written, "This map is dedicated to the prospector . . . ageless symbol of courage who has built the West. . . . Alone . . . with only his burro . . . he travels far in his quest of bidden treasures. . . . He is the spirit of adventure, the conqueror of the unknown, the founder of empire." The brochure was motivated by the heavy visitor attendance at what was popularly referred to at the time as the Eighth Wonder of the World: Hoover Dam. The biggest urban attractions in the drawing are the Club Apache, a stage with dancing girls on it, and the county courthouse, in front of which an official is snipping with giant scissors the ties of matrimony between a man and a woman. Dominating the picture, however, are the rural attractions, including a wagon train, horseback riding, hunting, boating, and a rodeo.

In short, the Las Vegas Chamber of Commerce was still big on country when country was only a decade or so away from being largely replaced in Clark County by something new and far less—by most accounts—wholesome. There are no big-time cowboy places in Las Vegas anymore. Sam's Town hints at it; and surely the Horseshoe, with its no-limits gambling, has a claim, though it is really more urban 1940s than it is country. There did remain on the Strip, even into the early 1970s, a place called the Bonanza, which used to sit right where Bally's is now and that had wooden floors and sold nickel beer and called itself just a plain old cowboy joint. It even featured Lorne Greene as its opening attraction in July 1967. Gone. If you want the West, go north to Reno, or go east: Arizona is big on the West.

The gambling done in the Cowboy Years is probably represented better in old cowboy movies than in popular literature, since gambling does not do so well in narrative dress as it does in cowboy outfits up on the silver screen. Still, that picture lasted a long time, through the more than twenty years of gambling drought in this century and into the early days of the rise of the Strip, when the El Rancho Vegas, which opened in April 1941, and the Last Frontier, which opened a year and a half later, sat out on Las Vegas Boulevard South and watched the new lady called the Flamingo prance haltingly into town. She was, as everyone now knows, only one in a long line of younger, flashier, sometimes even more beautiful ladies out on the Los Angeles highway with her skirt up high on her thigh, just in case.

One transitional and oblique reference to the rural past of gambling was embedded in the mass consciousness in Tom Wolfe's essay "Las Vegas (What?) Las Vegas (Can't hear you! Too noisy) Las Vegas!!!" in his best-selling book *The Kandy-Kolored Tangerine-Flake Streamline Baby*. The picture he paints of the "Western sports, fifty-eight-year-old men who wear Texas string ties," and "the old babes at the slot machines" with a "Dixie Cup full of nickels or dimes in the left hand and an Iron Boy work glove on the right hand to keep the calluses from getting sore," shows both where Las Vegas was and where, in this second configuration, it is going.

The notorious Benjamin Siegel is often called the father of modern-day Las Vegas. Partly what people mean when they extend him this doubly dubious honor is that he changed the dress code. He took away the cowboy outfits—now that Benny Binion and Sam Boyd are gone, cowboy outfits show up in Clark County only at Helldorado and the National Finals Rodeo—and substituted the tuxedo and the cocktail dress, among other things. Of course, as even the most casual observer knows, the tuxedo in Vegas is now just the work suit of the *maître d'*, the baccarat dealer, and the half dozen or so musicians employed in the few show rooms in town that still feature live music.

Siegel also substituted for boots and spurs the snap-brim hat and the draped suit with the bulge under the coat. In other words, the cowboy gave way to the men with dubious connections and bad rap sheets. Gambling may not have been legal back east or in Los Angeles, but it was in Nevada, a parlay that caused many men to give up lives of crime by changing nothing more than their addresses. A few of the cowboys hung on, but mostly they disappeared, surrendering to Dynaflo automatic-drive Buicks and Prell shampoo.

Benny Binion was a transitional figure in these times, a cowboy moving into the modern world. Two good stories about Benny Binion come from Gary Cartwright's "Benny and the Boys," which appeared in the October 1991 issue of *Texas Monthly*.

Benny was a product of turn-of-the-century Texas, when gambling was an accepted occupation and killing was a proper way of settling things, Old West style. It was an era that placed enormous value on individual initiative. The moral collapse that started with Prohibition and accelerated into the Great Depression made criminals out of people who were not otherwise inclined, fostering a disdain for the law, an obsession with betrayal, a willingness to do almost anything to get by. The mindset of the times was compressed in a saying that Benny repeated all of his life: "Never holler whoa or look back in a bad place." When Benny thought of the Depression, he thought of what his pal Red Nose Kelly said one Thanksgiving Day when the bartender at the C&W poolroom asked him what he was thankful for. "Chili's a dime and I still like it," Red Nose replied straight off.

The second story is shorter and sweeter and attributed to Benny Binion's later years, after he had served forty-two months in prison for federal income tax evasion and for operating an illegal policy wheel back in Texas. According to Cartwright, Benny Binion got religion in prison, from a Catholic priest. "Religion is too strong a mystery to doubt," Cartwright quotes him as saying. "When a preacher from North Carolina lost $1,000 of his congregation's money shooting craps at the Horseshoe, Benny gave the money back. 'God may forgive you, preacher,' he said, 'but your congregation won't.'"

Accounts of the move into Las Vegas during the 1940s and 1950s by these questionable outside interests can be found in any number of popular biographies and novels, including, for example, George Carpozi Jr.'s *Bugsy: The Bloodthirsty, Lusty Life of Benjamin "Bugsy" Siegel.* (While Siegel's Las Vegas career is dealt with elsewhere in this present book, it is necessary to bring him up now since he must bear the lion's share of credit or blame for serving as the catalyst that shifted Las Vegas away from its cowboy emphasis.) Carpozi writes that after being busted for gambling in the summer of 1944, "Bugsy began to look for less troublesome ways to earn a crooked dollar. His attention was drawn to the free-wheeling oasis town of Las Vegas, Nevada, a mere three hundred miles from Los Angeles, as a logical layout for conquests. An assortment of Los Angeles gamblers had already emigrated to the desert spa, where gambling was legal, and had planted impressive roots in that fertile territory." Carpozi's book, ill-written though it is (Siegel was a man "who had lived by the gun—and who died by the gun") and poorly researched (other, more reliable sources, place Siegel in Las Vegas running a racing wire as early as 1941, although it was still after the El Rancho Vegas had opened), is nonetheless a model of its kind. There are a great many bad books about Las Vegas.

The dress code nowadays in Las Vegas is for the most part appropriate for a place that many, thinking themselves original, call a Disneyland for Adults, which is to say, shorts and T-shirts in warm weather, khakis, blue jeans, and warm-up suits when it is cool. You cannot blame this all on the tourists, either; these are the clothes Las Vegans also wear. Still, that is probably more a comment on the times than the place. I have read that even in New York people no longer dress any differently for the theater than they do for the subway.

Indeed, as *Time* reported in its January 10, 1994, issue, "Booming with three new mega-hotel-casinos, the city now seems mainstream. But that's only because the rest of America has become more like Vegas." I fear it is true because I know that drivers in Washington, D.C., Kansas City, Dallas–Fort Worth, and even Reno drive just like we drive here. I fear it is true because the kids on every college campus in the country I visit nowadays look just like ours do here at home: earrings, grunge—which will never be out of fashion for students—baseball caps on backward, and Walkman earphones passing on to them their secret tribal instructions. I fear it is true because the editorials I read in all the many Sunday papers I go through every week are equally uncivilized, even—the irony apparently lost on them—when they are viciously attacking barbarism. I fear it is true because gambling is now legal in one form or another in all but two of the forty-nine other states, and most of the big operators in Las Vegas continue to scour this country and others looking for other likely new venues in which to expand their particular brand of entertainment.

But how could it be true? If the Cowboy Years had lasted in Las Vegas, this shift of values in the rest of the states could perhaps be chalked up to a desire on their part to Return to the Good Old Days that we continually celebrate; but alas, those years did not last, any more than the Criminal Years lasted, any more than either one of those illusions in fact ever constituted the whole truth about this peculiarly peculiar place.

But you would not know it by reading the popular literature of the town since World War II, which has painted a picture of a place that let the worst of the cowboys combine with the worst of the crooks to create a rotten borough, as it has been called. The picture of Las Vegas painted in that literature has been, for the most part, one of organized crime, venal locals, and middle-class sleaze on vacation and out of control, sliding down a razor blade to hell on the roll of the dice, the spin of the wheel, the cut of the deck, and the deal—in every sense of that word—all mixed up with heavy doses of drugs, sex, and rock and roll. Nobody's perfect.

In short, the picture has not always been pretty, even when painted by writers whose credentials would argue that at least they would be honest. What it has been, however—with notable exceptions—is pretty consistent.

Perhaps the most commonly referenced book in stories about the Las Vegas years dominated by people outside the law is *The Green Felt Jungle*, by Ed Reid and Ovid Demaris, both former Las Vegas newspapermen. Depending on your point of view, it is either a hard-hitting exposé or poorly documented and sloppily written sensationalism. Here's a sample from chapter 2, "Dawn of a Golden Age," about a famous meeting right after World War II between Benjamin "Bugsy" Siegel and Lucky Luciano: "They met formally in Luciano's suite of rooms in one of Havana's finest luxury hotels. Lucky smiled and shook hands, but there was a hard, fixed look in his dark, opaque eyes. The thick eyelids drooped almost closed." And so on. When faced with prose such as this, careful readers ask themselves such questions as why the techniques of fiction are used in a book that purports to be factual.

One of the best of the popular biographies is Robert Lacey's *Little Man: Meyer Lansky and the Gangster Life* (New York: Little, Brown, 1991). Lacey does not spend a lot of time on Las Vegas, but he does document scrupulously—and write well—and leaves the reader with the sense that he has been dealt a straight hand. It is Lacey's contention that "Lansky was the key man in 1946 and 1947, providing some of the financing to help Bugsy Siegel get started in Las Vegas, the most profitable piece of business diversification that the Mob ever did." According to Lacey, "Las Vegas offered Meyer Lansky the second great chance in his life to go legit, but he made no special effort to take it. Several dozen former bootleggers, bookies, and carpetjoint operators flooded into Las Vegas from different corners of America in the late 1940s, seizing the opportunity to sidestep their pasts—and most of Ben Siegel's coinvestors in the El Cortez [which he invested in prior to the Flamingo hotel project] fell into this category." According to Lacey, Siegel had seen and admired the success of both the El Rancho Vegas and the Last Frontier and had tried to buy the former. It was not for sale. The El Cortez was, however, and so Siegel and several others bought it. Lansky, says Lacey, "was content to be little more than a sleeping partner in the El Cortez project, investing $60,000, a 10 percent stake, and trusting Siegel to handle it." He did. In six months, Siegel and his group sold the El Cortez for a profit of $166,000, and decided to reinvest the whole nut, which was well over $600,000, in the Flamingo. Lansky let his 10 points ride.

According to Lacey,

> The Flamingo Hotel Casino was the brainchild of Billy Wilkerson, the suave, waxed-mustached founder of the *Hollywood Reporter*, who also created the Café Trocadero, Ciro's, and La Rue's, a trio of successful Hollywood nightspots which between [sic] them formed the beginning of Sunset Strip.
>
> It was Wilkerson's idea to transport the sophistication of these nightspots to Las Vegas, for though El Rancho and the Last Frontier had their luxury, their atmosphere remained in the

"Howdy, pardner" dude ranch tradition. Wilkerson envisioned something more glitzy, a refuge from the desert and sagebrush— a showroom that featured major stars, and a casino ambiance that was Beverly Hills, rather than Nevada.

It is Lacey's further contention that the murder of Ben Siegel "roused people's curiosity about the play city on the other side of the country, and if they had to name one hotel that summed that place up, then that hotel was Bugsy's palace in the desert. The Flamingo came to represent the new, wickedly enticing Las Vegas.

"Ben Siegel did not invent the luxury resort hotel-casino. He did not found the Las Vegas Strip. He did not buy the land or first conceive the project that became the Flamingo. But by his death he made them famous."

Of the three dozen or more books either centrally or tangentially about Las Vegas that I read or reread in the course of several months, Lacey's book is one of the most valuable, and certainly one of the most trustworthy.

In *The Godfather*, Mario Puzo's wonderful book about mob life, the narrator says of a meeting among the ruling crime families in America, "It was agreed that Las Vegas and Miami were to be open cities where any of the Families could operate. They all recognized that these were the cities of the future. It was also agreed that no violence would be permitted in these cities and that petty criminals of all types were to be discouraged."

Not much later, the scion of the Corleone Family, Michael, announces to a group of intimates at supper that "the Corleone Family is thinking of moving out here to Vegas. Selling out all our interests in the olive oil business and settling here. The Don and Hagen and myself have talked it over and we think here is where the future is for the Family."

The trouble is, the Corleones want to buy a hotel that belongs to a Moe Greene, who does not want to sell. Michael says, in the way of his father the Don, "I'll make him an offer he can't refuse," a line that has since entered the national vocabulary.

"Moe Greene was a handsome hood who had made his rep as a Murder Incorporated executioner in Brooklyn. He had branched out into gambling and gone west to seek his fortune, had been the first person to see the possibilities of Las Vegas and built one of the first hotel casinos on the Strip. He still had murderous tantrums and was feared by everyone in the hotel." Sound familiar?

Moe refuses to sell. Michael Corleone has him killed, "shot to death in the Hollywood home of his movie-star mistress." Sound even more familiar?

Probably the best writing about gambling in Las Vegas in modern times is that done by Mario Puzo, especially in *Fools Die* but also in the text he provided for the lava lamp coffee-table book *Inside Las Vegas*. By way of comparison, *Mustang Sally*, a 1992 novel by Edward Allen, demonstrates a good understanding of the various table games, but it all comes off as expertise looking at itself in a mirror. That is to say, the narrator— and thus the author—clearly knows what he is talking about technically when he writes:

> The last person rolling the dice has just "sevened out," that is, rolled a seven before he managed to roll his point number, so all the bets on the table have been taken away, the dice are about to be passed to the next player, the twin pucks that indicate what the point is have been moved to the side and flipped to the "off" side, and all the boxes and bars and diagrams on the table are empty except for the new pass-line bets that everybody is putting down. I put a hundred-dollar bill on the table in front of the dealer opposite me and say, "Change, please," taking my hand away, because dealers are forbidden to take money directly from a customer's hand.

This is textbook stuff; this is teaching school.

Compare it with this:

> Jordan unripped the outside pocket of his Vegas Winner sports jacket and heaped black hundred-dollar chips into his table rack. He bet two hundred on the line, backed up his number and then bought all the numbers for five hundred dollars each. He held the dice for almost an hour. After the first fifteen minutes the electricity of his hot hand ran through the casino and the table jammed full. He pressed his bets to the limit of five hundred, and the magical numbers kept rolling out of his hand. In his mind he banished the fatal seven to hell. He forbade it to appear. His table rack filled to overflowing with black chips.

I do not know anything much about Edward Allen except that the dust jacket of his book says he is a creative writing teacher at a university in Oklahoma. I know little more about Mario Puzo, except that he clearly loves gambling, loves it so much that he gave it up, he says in *Inside Las Vegas*, when he realized, first, he could not write if he continued to gamble, and second, once he was rich, he could not "afford, economically, to gamble. The simple reason being that to gamble is to risk, that is, to approach the 'ruin factor.' When I was poor the ruin factor was not important. Hell, I was ruined anyway. But now I have too much to lose and the 'ruin factor' is decisive. Of course I had to lose a great deal of money and come near to 'ruin' before I could figure this out. Gambling education is not cheap." By way of advice, he adds that a gambler will always be all right if he never writes a check or signs a chit while he is gambling in Las Vegas; that is, if he plays only with the gambling money he brings with him soberly, before the fact, when he comes to town.

Puzo, as I have said before in another venue, has a big heart, and that shows in his work. He is an honest writer in the sense that he never appears to be letting himself off the hook, as many writers do. He reveals this by being just as hard on himself or the character clearly identifiable with him as he is on his other characters, a rare quality among writers.

Wolfe's essay "Las Vegas (What?)" appeared in *The Kandy-Kolored Tangerine-Flake Streamline Baby* in 1965 but had been published in *Esquire* several months earlier. In the book's introduction, Wolfe touches on the cultural impact of Las Vegas on the rest of the country in a sense wider than the subsequent nationwide proliferation of gambling. He asserts that what he calls the "super-hyper-version" of "a whole new style of life in America" is to be found in Las Vegas. It is, he says,

> the Versailles of America. . . . Las Vegas happened to be created after the war, with war money, by gangsters. Gangsters happened to be the first uneducated . . . but more to the point, unaristocratic, *outside* of the aristocratic tradition . . . the first uneducated, prole-petty-burgher Americans to have enough money to build a monument to their style of life. They built it in an isolated spot, Las Vegas, out in the desert, just like Louis XIV, the Sun King, who purposely went outside of Paris, into the countryside, to create a fantastic baroque environment to celebrate his rule. It is no accident that Las Vegas and Versailles are the only two architecturally uniform cities in Western history.

The important thing about the building of Las Vegas is not that the builders were gangsters but that they were proles. They celebrated, very early, the new style of life in America—using the money pumped in by the war to show a prole vision . . . *Glamor!* . . . of style. The usual thing has happened, of course. Because it is prole, it gets ignored, except on the most sensational level. Yet long after Las Vegas' influence as a gambling heaven has gone, Las Vegas' forms and symbols will be influencing American life.

Aside from these more serious considerations, Wolfe's essay paints one of the most accurate pictures of life as it goes on daily, essentially, inside a Las Vegas casino, not just in the 1960s, but in our time as well.

Outside of the business sections of newspapers and news magazines, there is very little popular literature revealing the new corporate breed of operators in the Las Vegas gambling world, or much else about that world. Nonetheless, corporations in the 1960s began to take over the world of gaming in Las Vegas, supplanting the crooks that came before them just as they had, in their time, supplanted the cowboys.

Parry Thomas, the former head of Valley Bank of Nevada, now Bank of America, Nevada, is generally acknowledged as the first man responsible for honestly brokering and/or providing legitimate loans to legitimate operators to build or renovate their properties, thus obviating their need to depend on illegitimate sources. Steve Wynn, chairman of the board of Mirage Resorts Inc., has long acknowledged his indebtedness to Thomas for his early help in Wynn's rise to prominence, not only in Las Vegas gaming but in gaming across the nation.

Both a step ahead of Thomas and a step behind him came the fabulous Howard Hughes, who had been a frequent visitor to Las Vegas during its tarnished years. In the 1940s Hughes bought more than forty thousand acres of land south and west of Las Vegas, which he held for futures. He was a step behind Thomas in that he began to buy Las Vegas casino properties two decades later, but still within weeks of his arrival back in town on Thanksgiving of 1966. By the spring of 1967 he had bought the Desert Inn Hotel and Casino, the Sands, the Frontier, the Castaways, and the Silver Slipper. He eventually bought the Landmark also, as well as Harold's Club in Reno.

Hughes's ownership of these—and many other properties in Las Vegas—and Thomas's demonstration of the faith the legitimate business community had in gambling and its importance to the city combined to pave the way for the corporate takeovers to come. Many argue that Hughes was the first to demand that every constituent part of a property be self-supporting. Others claim this to be a myth, that such a change did not occur until after Hughes, as gaming properties positioned themselves toward public ownership. In any event, in the old days, the casino carried the rest of the operation, no matter how badly the rest fared. After the old way was abandoned, restaurants had to be self-supporting, as did gift shops, the hotel, and all the rest. Surely this made better business sense, but the change was another in the modernization, impersonalization, and—for want of a better word—Americanization of Las Vegas. Surely the change was for the better, and yet . . .

Only one little piece was missing, according to Donn Knepp's book *Las Vegas: The Entertainment Capital,* and that "was assured in 1967, when Nevada lawmakers passed legislation that made the city attractive to corporate interests. The new law stated that only major stockholders, officers, and directors of the corporation would need licensing approval, and its effect was felt immediately. The advent of public corporations into the gaming industry lessened scrutiny by the government, with the exception of the Internal Revenue Service. The orderly structure of the corporation was on the Las Vegas scene to stay—as long as the bottom line was written in black."

Some argue that the corporate presence in Las Vegas casinos has dimmed the luster of the stars who used to own the joints in olden times. Those who make such arguments clearly forget—or undervalue—the many luminaries who still shine on the scene, including Bill Boyd, Frank Fertitta, Kirk Kerkorian, Claudine Williams, and that luminary of luminaries, Steve Wynn. In the wake of his great successes with the Golden Nugget, the Mirage, and Treasure Island, Wynn seems to have emerged as a worthy heir to the mantle of stardom worn in earlier times by some of the most notorious of the cowboys and the criminals. It is his name and face that grace the media these days, along with price quotes, from the various stock exchanges, on Mirage properties' stock. These men have not made it into the novels and stories yet, but they will as soon as the great Las Vegas novel appears (Mario Puzo's good, yet failed, shot at it in *Fools Die* notwithstanding).

Still, the picture of Las Vegas in popular literature has not varied much through the years. Its reputation as a sin city has stuck, and even the corporate presence in the industry cannot—dare not—erase it. Locals complain when a program such as Dan Rather's *48 Hours* comes to town and purports to substantiate the truth of all the hype we have been selling about ourselves for years; but even a cursory glance at the back pages of the *Los Angeles Times* Calendar section clearly reveals what it is we *are* selling, first and foremost, before the theme parks and the family fun, before the golf courses, the shows, the food, the sun—we are selling sin: sex, drugs, and rock and roll, to put it lightly, as well as, I should add, metaphorically. We sanitized sin long before safe sex appeared in the wider world. We sell an illusion of evil that is prophylactically sealed, for the most part, because really—as you know—really we are truly just a city of churches.

Edward Allen's narrator says in *Mustang Sally,* "Trouble makes everything go boom, boom, boom, as if I have stepped out of my hotel on the Las Vegas Strip and it's the middle of summer with the wind blowing and the fire is whooshing out of the Mirage volcano and painting everybody's face yellow, and I have a little handout magazine in my pocket that some scroungy old guy gave me—on the inside flap: 'Wild Girls, Direct to your Room, Totally Nude,'" which is certainly one of the promises our advertising makes, even if implicitly, obliquely; even if not really, or only rarely; or maybe once. All of this is for the nongambler, of course; the gambler does not have to be sold. He knows what is here, and that is why he comes.

Time is certainly correct in contending that the rest of the country has become more like Las Vegas. Stephen Wright's take on that fact in his excellent and curious novel *Going Native* is, however, even less flattering than *Time*'s. Wylie Jones, Rho Jones's husband, comes home late from work on a Friday afternoon one summer. They are having another couple, Tommy and Gerri Hanna, over for supper. Somewhere in the course of the evening, Wylie goes inside the house from the patio where the party has settled, walks out the front door, and disappears. He is to show up again periodically throughout the remaining seven chapters in the book, sometimes only obliquely identified, but always clearly him, heading west. He travels in a stolen, late-'60s Ford Galaxy, and the farther west he goes, the harsher the civil landscape becomes. Indeed, his version in this book of what we have done to ourselves in this country can be seen as a more recent variation on the same theme in Cormac McCarthy's relentless *Blood Meridian.*

Chapter 6 of Wright's book, "The Queen of Diamonds," is set in Las Vegas, and it is a Las Vegas no one who lives here is going to like. Jessie Horn's latest mate Garrett has split, and she has two kids to care for, one of whom attends Moe Dalitz Elementary School, and a female lover named Nikki to nurture. Jessie grew up in Las Vegas, went to Benny Binion High School, and now works weddings at the Happy Chapel.

At one point, the narrator reminisces about Jessie's past.

> Her first lover was a kid named Dow Webb who'd ridden in on Greyhound from St. Cloud, Minnesota, top of the world, age of twenty-one. His Uncle Early knew a guy who knew a guy. City was his for the asking. So was Jessie. She was impressed by his smile, his confidence, his chest. She was seventeen, running the streets at night with a pack of girls in an adults' play town with too little to occupy the restless and the underaged. They met one hot dangerous 3 a.m. out at the neon graveyard on Cameron Street, where Jessie and Luane and Suze (the Three Mousseketeers) and Dow and a pair of wire cutters were all attempting to breach the fence in quest of valuable sign junk.

Right away you can see that while this has some familiar elements, it has something new, too.

Six weeks later Jessie and Dow are living together in that ubiquitous Las Vegas trailer court, eating macaroni and screwing their brains out. Jessie skips from job to job, while Dow tries to perfect the gambling system that he has been working on since he was a little kid. His destiny "was to win, whether by cheating ten-year-olds out of their lunch money or lying to his parents, what did it matter as long as debits were avoided. He was different, he experienced defeat physically, loss equivalent to a bullet in the chest, so when at last he achieved his boyhood dream of getting to Vegas and the city responded by employing his body for target practice, he died into rages only time and convalescence from the gaming tables could cure." Strong stuff, with—again—elements of the familiar as well as the unfamiliar.

The love between Jessie and Dow can last only as long as he wins, which is, of course, not often. "Time ran out on them, Dow at his cluttered table of soiled cards and useless charts, waiting for the Wheel to turn, Jessie at the bedroom window, studying the desert outside for clues. The desert neither waited nor hoped, it endured. The Lizard God remembered when rock flowed like a river, remembered when it would again, the passage between these events no more than the blink of one hooded implacable eye. This town is doomed, she thought, and we, its inhabitants."

An extreme view, perhaps, and certainly one inconsistent with the booster mentality that has both guided and benefited from the town's steady growth and prosperity since World War II.

Jessie's next man—the man she has just split from when the chapter starts—is Garret Pugh, whom she met when she was a dancing slave girl at a joint called Nero's Feast and he was Spartacus. "By day Garrett carried a spear through Nero's Feast; at night he attended classes at Tom and Jerry's Dealers School." By now, the cartoon echoes are abundantly clear: Wylie Jones, Tom and Gerri Hanna, Tom and Jerry's Dealers School, and so on. The references are primarily to the culture and only secondarily to the structure of the text, which is as much a chase story as it is a search-and-destroy story. No further comment about cartoons is necessary beyond taking a quick look at the Excalibur Hotel and Casino. It's a small world.

Garrett and Jessie take up together. She likes the fact that he is handsome and that he wants to be a dealer, rather than a player, like Dow. The first week of dealers school "was devoted to how customers cheat, the remaining five weeks to how to cheat the customers." This isolated utterance is, by the way, the only instance I have found alleging that cheating customers goes on in Las Vegas's gaming stores. The opposite is true. Every other book has accentuated the fact that gaming in Las Vegas is the most honest in the world. In three decades in town, I have heard of such a thing only a few times, and then only to illustrate the awful things that can happen to a dealer who or a joint that breaks the cardinal rule and tries to cheat a customer. The fact is, the percentage is always with the house, so the house does not have to cheat.

Puzo entitles one chapter "The Honesty of Gambling in Vegas" in his book *Inside Las Vegas*. Admitting that he is often asked if gambling in Las Vegas is honest, and that he is a very suspicious gambler himself—he says "paranoid"—he concludes that "after fifteen years of watching and trying to figure out how they cheat, I reluctantly come to the conclusion that Vegas has honest casino gambling and it may be the first time in the history of civilization that gaming houses have been run straight."

First, Puzo argues—as I argue—that the house percentages make cheating unnecessary; second, Nevada has very tough laws, along with good policing, to guard against cheating; and last, the gambling joints in Las Vegas want repeat business. More than 30 million visitors a year come to Las Vegas now. If some of them were not repeat customers, it would not take long to wear out the market.

Historically, the bigger problems, both in the literature and in life, have been customers cheating the house, dealers cheating the house, or the house cheating the IRS. In fact, Puzo goes on to argue, that is why the conglomerates finally got into the biz, because they found out the games were honest and *still* the profits were big. Benny Binion's take on this was typical Benny: "I don't go looking for cheats," he once told Steve Wynn. "I go looking for customers."

It is tempting to return to Jessie and Garrett Pugh, to watch him humiliated by his superiors as he tries to deal; to watch him as he steals, gets caught, and is taken away by casino security; to watch as Wylie Jones—here called Tom—shows up at the Happy Chapel, where he marries a roulette dealer, steals "a half a dozen or so" of the most expensive wedding rings—"the Shower of Gold, the Bird of Paradise, Crystal Blue Ecstasy, the Crown of Fire"—and disappears. I will not do so, but I do encourage anyone with a taste for such works as Spengler's *Decline of the West* to take a look at this very good—and dark—book.

There are two other books that must be accounted for, even though they do not fit neatly into the three historical periods I have marked out. They are John Gregory Dunne's *Vegas: A Memoir of a Dark Season* and Hunter S. Thompson's *Fear and Loathing in Las Vegas*.

Dunne came to Las Vegas even though, as he says, "I did not gamble, cared not at all about the Mob and even less about Howard Hughes. But," he adds, "there were other stories and other people, and there were days when I told myself that through the travail of others I might come to grips with myself, that I might, as it were, find absolution through voyeurism. Those were the good days." His interest settles on "Artha, a student of cosmetology by day, a hooker by night; Buster Mano, a private detective whose specialty is tracking down errant husbands; and Jackie Kasey, a lounge comic who makes $10,000 a week but is only a 'semi-name.'" There is little reference to gambling in this book beyond some desultory keno playing.

Thompson's book is also of its own kind, chronicling as it does a drug- and alcohol-ridden trip to Las Vegas to cover a story. The narrator says of the assignment, "But what *was* the story? Nobody had bothered to say. So we would have to drum it up on our own. Free Enterprise. The American Dream. Horatio Alger gone mad on drugs in Las Vegas. Do it *now*: pure Gonzo journalism." As it turns out, his assignment is to cover the Mint 400, an off-road race long abandoned in the interests of the fragile desert ecology. Still, he says of the adventure, "our trip was different. It was a classic affirmation of everything right and true and decent in the national character. It was a gross, physical salute to the fantastic *possibilities* of life in this country—but only for those with true grit. And we were chock full of that."

If Dunne's book is a diary of the dark night of the soul worked out in a Las Vegas appropriate to that depressed state of mind, then Thompson's is an account of Gonzo gone wild, of, well, sex, drugs, and rock and roll, in a Las Vegas representative of a country gone to hell in a handbasket.

What does all this add up to, anyway?

Who cares what the popular writing of the day makes of our Valley home?

In answer, I return again to Robert Lacey's *Little Man: Meyer Lansky and the Gangster Life.*

For some years Lansky ran a casino called the Colonial Inn in Hallandale, Florida, just south of Hollywood. When George Raft, the film actor who made a career of portraying gangsters in 1940s B movies, came there to visit "Benny Siegel and his other friends," it was assumed that Raft would study the real-life gangsters to find out how better to play them on the screen. "But the reverse proved the case. It was the gangsters who spent their time studying Raft."

Oscar Wilde said it so clearly decades ago in "The Decay of Lying": "Life imitates Art far more than Art imitates Life. This results not merely from Life's imitative instinct, but from the fact that the self-conscious aim of Life is to find expression, and that Art offers it certain beautiful forms through which it may realize that energy."

Las Vegans may not see Las Vegas the same way many of the writers who write about it see it, but they should not ignore those other versions of it, because those other versions are as responsible, if not more responsible, for the reputation of the place as are those of us who live out our lives here.

What has happened both in and to Las Vegas since World War II truly is one of the most exciting and interesting stories of growth in our time—and *stories* is a key word here. We all know that a version of reality virtually becomes the reality when it is successful.

In other words, since the experience of reality is one thing and the story about that experience is, no matter how accurate, quite another, what is taken as the truth about a thing often gets to *be* the truth simply because enough people agree it is the truth. That is, the story overpowers the facts, swallows them and then regurgitates something else, which even if similar, is not the same.

It was ever thus.

And so, as Las Vegas spreads not only its culture of gaming but its wider culture as well, and as the rest of the country becomes more and more like Las Vegas, we wait watchfully to see what comes next to this jewel in the desert, as Kevin Starr called it. Will the fourth *C* alliterate? And if so, what will it be: Clowns? Curmudgeons? Or, in spirit of "Ozymandias," will it be Cactus?

Or even more devastating, will it not alliterate at all, but rather obliterate? Remember: "The Lizard God remembered when rock flowed like a river, remembered when it would again, the passage between these events no more than the blink of one hooded implacable eye."

The Adult Playground Becomes a Heaven for Families

Dave Palermo

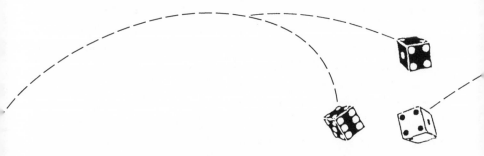

It is still referred to by some Nevada old-timers as "the Mission," a three-week tour of Europe in November 1964 by thirty-four Nevada casino executives, businessmen, and elected officials, ostensibly for the purpose of selling the Silver State to potential foreign investors. Truth be told, it was more a riotous romp through the nightclubs and clip joints of London, Paris, Munich, and Amsterdam by a gang of wealthy, middle-aged good ol' boys set free from the prying eyes of their wives and the local press.

"They were a pretty rambunctious bunch," recalls a tactful Bob Faiss, aide to then-governor Grant Sawyer and the junket's advance man. "I don't think [Philip] Roventini slept once the entire twenty-one days," Jud Allen, then manager of the Reno Chamber of Commerce, said of the late Carson City car salesman. Gaming pioneer Jackie Gaughan said formal gatherings for foreign travel agents and dignitaries were "kind of stuffy." "But we had parties after the parties," he recalled. "It was thought the trip might change opinions of Nevadans; that we didn't all wear green aprons and crawl out from under a crap table," said Sawyer, fondly reflecting on the tour in an interview some thirty years later in his high-rise law office in downtown Las Vegas. Sawyer's frequent trips to promote Nevada earned him the moniker Gallivantin' Grant.

"The image of Nevada nationally and internationally was not good at all," Sawyer said of an era when organized crime was prominent in operating casinos and skimming the profits. "The image was that of general corruption and crime—the Mafia and all that." Sawyer flipped his cigarette at an ashtray and rested his chin in the palm of his hand. "Of course," he said with a mischievous smile, "some of it maybe was true."

Casino executive Burton Cohen, who came to Las Vegas in 1966, glanced out an upper-floor window of the Sheraton Desert Inn one day some twenty-eight years later and gazed down at the rolling, green fairways of the hotel's world-class, PGA-rated golf course. It was about 7 A.M. or so, an ungodly hour even for a twenty-four-hour town, and the rising sun left long shadows on the pristine, manicured greens. "This is how the good Lord would have done it," Cohen thought to himself as he surveyed the picturesque landscape. "If He had the money, of course." Something caught Cohen's eye. It was a man in his thirties in white tennis shorts and knee-socks, trotting on the course. "He was jogging. At 7 A.M. Jogging." Cohen, a cherubic seventy-year-old man, shook his head at the notion. "What happened to the good ol' American male who ate red meat and stayed out all night drinking and gambling and, and . . ." Cohen waved off the need to explain the habits of good ol' American males in the days when he first came to Las Vegas. "Now they're in bed at eleven," he said. "Jogging on the golf course. At seven, mind you. That's how this town has changed."

After all these years dealing blackjack at the since defunct Sands Hotel, Tony Badillo still hears the familiar compliment. "You got soft hands, Tony." Hands of magic, almost, with his thumb resting light as a feather on top of the deck. "If a dealer deals with his thumb," Badillo advises, "watch out, because he's dealing from the bottom of the deck." Badillo goes back forty years with the Sands. He recalls the hotel's glory days in the 1950s, 1960s, and early 1970s, fanning cards across the green felt to celebrities like Nat King Cole and James Garner and Rat Packers Frank Sinatra, Dean Martin, Sammy Davis Jr., Joey Bishop, and Peter Lawford. "I dealt to all those people," Badillo said. "Back in those days we used to let Frank and Sammy and those guys deal the game. Of course, with the Gaming Control Board, you couldn't do that now. Frank was a pretty good gambler. He was a good guy. Of course, sometimes he'd get angry. Like if a woman at the table didn't laugh at his jokes. He'd say, 'Tony, get that broad off my table.' I'd say, 'Frank . . .'" Badillo shrugged his shoulders, palms up. Helpless. "'What can I do?'" Badillo flashed a conspiratorial wink. "But

Former Desert Inn Hotel chief Burton Cohen, 1983. (Courtesy Las Vegas News Bureau)

we got somebody to get the girl off the table. Oh, it was fun back then. You really looked forward to going to work. The casinos would give the customers everything. Food. Drinks. A room. And a girl. In the old days, people were classy. All dressed up. You got dressed up to go to the shows. Today, people come into the casino with jeans. T-shirts. Sandals."

But the real change in Las Vegas, said Badillo, began about two years ago, when he would glance up from his cards and occasionally spot a child toddling through the casino. "The first time I seen it, I could not believe it," he said. "Kids. Walking through the casino licking ice cream cones and eating hot dogs. In the casino. It's mind-boggling. This town should be adults only. I think it's a big mistake what they're doing to this town, and it's not going to work."

Yuppies jogging on the golf course? Well, okay. Maybe. But children? In Las Vegas? Kids in the casino? No notion is more contrary to the perception of Las Vegas as America's crap table—a kind of neon, adult sandbox in the midst of the Mojave Desert—than a child tottering among the blackjack tables at the Sands, licking an ice cream cone, fer crissakes.

Kids in the casinos. And strollers on the Strip, their tiny passengers shaded with hotel room towels from the relentless blast furnace of a Nevada summer. It is becoming a common sight as Las Vegas's gaming industry, facing competition from riverboat and American Indian casinos in other states, tries to sell itself as a resort destination not only for gamblers but for their wives and children as well.

The concept is not entirely new. Gaming pioneer Jay Sarno targeted middle-America gamblers and their families in 1968 when he crammed a casino, trapeze acts, and a carnival midway under a huge, pink, concrete tent on the north end of the Strip and called it Circus Circus. His successor, Bill Bennett, expanded on the idea in 1990 with the Excalibur, a 4,032-room medieval castle with multicolored turrets towering over Las Vegas Boulevard at Tropicana Avenue.

But nothing so dramatically altered the course of Las Vegas's future as the openings, during ten weeks in late 1993, of billionaire Kirk Kerkorian's MGM Grand Hotel and Theme Park, Circus Circus's pyramid-shaped, Egyptian-themed Luxor hotel, and Mirage Resorts' pirate-themed Treasure Island hotel and casino.

The three megaresorts, built at a combined cost of nearly $2 billion, were a massive economic boom to Clark County, generating fifteen thousand jobs and adding some eleven thousand rooms to the valley's inventory of hotel and motel accommodations. But the impact of the three new properties on the image of Las Vegas was far more profound.

MGM Grand's thirty-three-acre theme park and Wizard of Oz entryway, Luxor's indoor Nile River and participatory rides by Douglas Trumbull (whose credits include special effects for *2001: A Space Odyssey*), and Treasure Island's outdoor pirate-ship battles all generated massive international publicity, sending out the message: "Hey, Las Vegas is no longer just a gambling town. It's okay to bring the family."

"When the history books are written on gaming in this state," Nevada Gaming Commission chairman Bill Curran said in casting his vote to license MGM Grand, "they will focus on what happens today forward, rather than what has happened in the past." "These new places will take Las Vegas to the next level," said Robert Maxey, president of MGM Grand Inc. "This will deliver on the promise that we've become a destination resort, not just a gambling curiosity."

The message that Las Vegas was becoming a warm, fuzzy, family-friendly place was carried by the *Wall Street Journal, Time, Newsweek, U.S. News & World Report*, and just about every major newspaper and tabloid television show in the country. *Time* even waxed philosophical, calling Las Vegas the "New All-American City," if for no other reason than "America's collective tolerance for vulgarity has gone way, way up." Whatever, MGM Grand, Luxor, and Treasure Island—with their theme parks, high-tech amusement rides, and pirate-ship battles—opened the floodgates to a massive deluge of new tourists. Clark County's monthly visitor figures in early 1995 were running 24 percent ahead of projections, meaning tourism was likely to jump to 29 million for the year.

Las Vegas was finally out-muscling Orlando as the nation's top tourist destination, eventually more than doubling that city's visitor count. MGM Grand, Luxor, and Treasure Island hiked Clark County's room inventory to 86,000—6,000 more than Orlando's. Occupancy rates in the Las Vegas Valley were running in the 90 percent range, compared to the 70 percent range in Orlando. And average daily room rates in the Florida resort city were $90, compared with $50 in Clark County. Orlando blamed its flat figures on highly publicized violent crimes against international tourists. But travel industry analyst James Cammisa said the new Las Vegas projects, combining theme parks, retail stores, and gambling, "are redefining what travel is all about."

"With the articles in *Time* and *Newsweek*, Las Vegas has become the 'in' place to be," said Billy Vassiliadis, president of R&R Advertising, which handles the Las Vegas Convention and Visitors Authority's annual $33.5-million marketing and advertising budget. "We've got Spago. We've got a Hard Rock. We've got shopping—all the exclusive places at the Forum Shops at Caesars." Vassiliadis dipped a fork into a luncheon salad at the trendy Cafe Nicole restaurant off the Strip. "We're hot," he said. "We've become hip. No question about it." Hip? Las Vegas? Hip as in polyester shorts, fanny packs, knee-socks, and K-mart tennies? Hip as in print dresses and sandals? Hip as in red turtlenecks, double-breasted blazers, and penny loafers? Hip as in blue hair ratted higher than the backstop at Yankee Stadium? Is the new Las Vegas the destination of choice for Marge and Homer Simpson, scurrying through the casinos with their rascal Bart, fast on their heels, sloshing ice cream onto slot patrons?

There may have been a flood of new visitors to Las Vegas, but nobody was suggesting they were hip. Or big spenders, for that matter. In fact, the new breed of tourists generated by the three megaresorts was largely middle-class, with far less disposable income (translation: gambling money) than the town was used to. They came for the rides, cheap rooms, fun packs, free mugs, $2.95 prime rib dinners, and family buffets. And a lot of them were not going near the casinos. Hotel and motel occupancy rates ranged above 90 percent. On the long weekends there was not a room to be had. But the projected average gambling budget for 1994, according to USA Capital Management Group Inc., was $171.79, slightly more than in 1980 but nearly $6 less than in 1993. Six bucks times 29 million visitors is a lot of money. "We're getting the people," said Bob Ostrovsky, director of human resources for Bally's Las Vegas. "They just don't have that jingle." Caesars World Inc. chairman Henry Gluck was analytical about the trend. "The market base is growing. This means you may see less spending per person and more people who are not coming here mostly to gamble," he told a 1994 conference of investment bankers in New Orleans. The industry needed to adjust, he said, meaning it had to increase the prices of the rooms, booze, and food and generate more retail business, which for Caesars meant selling more designer shirts and cologne. "Ultimately, we will get more out of these people," Gluck said. The transition to family destination resort was a bit unnerving. Casino executives stunned by the new generation of tourists began sniping at each other. MGM and Circus Circus executives were delighted at the massive flood of middle-income families to Las Vegas. But those who ran the adult-oriented casinos groused at the low rollers, wringing their hands over what was becoming the industry's "f-word": "families." They eyed with a fair amount of contempt the strollers on the Strip, the joggers on the golf courses, the gawkers and pointers in the casinos, and the gridlock of humanity at the T-shirt counters. "My God," said one veteran casino host, "these people aren't even playing the slots. They're just WATCHING!"

In an interview a week before opening Treasure Island, Steve Wynn expressed skepticism over the approach being used in the development of both MGM Grand and Luxor. MGM Grand's theme park attractions were designed to take up to five hours of a visitor's time, hours otherwise spent in the casino. Luxor's motion-simulator rides were situated on a mezzanine separate from the casino floor. "Instead of developing attractions apart from the gaming," Wynn asked, "why not enhance the gaming? I'll never understand that." "It's one thing for the place to be user-friendly to the whole family because the family travels together," Wynn told *Time*. "It's quite a different thing to sit down and dedicate creative design energy to build for children. I'm not, ain't gonna, not interested. I'm after mom and dad."

Manny Cortez, executive director of the Las Vegas Convention and Visitors Authority, shared Wynn's skepticism. Cortez, who as a teenager parked cars at the Dunes Hotel and Country Club, recalled the late Telly Savalas riding into town in his black Lincoln Continental convertible, his kids in the back seat. "We had to find something to keep the kids occupied," Cortez recalled. "It wasn't easy. You even had to be an adult to see the elephant act in the showroom. There was nothing for kids in this town back then. There's a very real danger in becoming a family destination. Take airline seats, for example. A person under twenty-one taking an airline seat is displacing a seat for a gambler. We are a gaming destination, first and foremost. It's not fair to call this town a family resort destination."

Gaming revenues for the first six months of 1994 reflected the number of nongamblers climbing off the planes at McCarran International Airport. Revenues from the more sophisticated games of blackjack and craps dipped slightly (by 1 percent to 2 percent) according to state Gaming Control Board figures, while revenues from the relatively simple game of roulette jumped more than 20 percent. Play on the dollar slots also fell about 4 percent. "Las Vegas is becoming a nickel and quarter town," said Joe Milanowski, a gaming industry analyst for USA Capital Management Group. Perhaps. But even with the increasing emphasis on families, Las Vegas in the early 1990s remained the world center for high rollers. With the possible exception of Macau, a tiny peninsula in mainland China, few gambling resorts in the world match Las Vegas for high-end play. In the first few months of 1994, while the national media plugged Las Vegas as a family destination resort, baccarat play in Nevada was reaching an all-time high. Casinos in the first ten months of the 1993–1994 fiscal year won $380.7 million at baccarat, compared to $294.5 million for all of fiscal year 1992–1993, according to the state Gaming Control Board.

The Southern California gamblers who flocked to the mob-run Las Vegas casinos in the 1960s and 1970s flashed $100,000 bankrolls. The Latin American, Middle Eastern, and, more recently, Asian high rollers targeted by the larger corporations were capable of betting that much on a single hand at the baccarat tables. Today, virtually all the million-dollar gamblers come from outside the United States. The perception of Las Vegas has changed somewhat over the years but basically has remained the same. The town has always been thought of as what it essentially is: a mass of hotel-casinos in the middle of the desert with inexpensive food and rooms, swimming pools, and lounge acts. Hot, dry, sunny weather and the largest mass of legal casinos in the world. A no-lose formula, for sure. The only marketing necessary was to sweep the floors and open the doors. "The Las Vegas image kind of ran itself," Vassiliadis said. Air conditioning, the increasing popularity of the automobile, Teamsters Union pension money, and the vision of organized-crime chieftains like Benjamin "Bugsy" Siegel and Moe Dalitz transformed post–World War II Las Vegas into a boomtown of resort casinos, a kind of mobster metropolis for well-to-do Southern Californians. "The jet set from L.A. came down for long weekends, before there were jets," Cortez recalls. "It used to be a place where people came to rub shoulders with the mob, like they were movie stars," said Michael Gaughan, managing owner of the Barbary Coast and Gold Coast hotels. "Then it became kind of an adult Disneyland." The adult Disneyland phase began in the mid-1960s, about the time reclusive, eccentric multimillionaire Howard Hughes slipped into a blacked-out room on the ninth floor of the Desert Inn and began buying up hotel casinos like so many wooden airlines. He began with the Desert Inn, which he bought in 1967 from Cleveland gangster Dalitz for $13.25 million. Hughes's move to Las Vegas was partly responsible for running the mob out of the Nevada gaming business and legitimizing the industry. In the late 1960s Nevada enacted a corporate gaming act, allowing large, publicly traded companies like MGM, Holiday Inn, Ramada, Hyatt, Del Webb, and others to get into the gaming business. The mob could not compete. It was not until the late 1970s, when Atlantic City legalized casino gambling, that Las Vegas first began actively promoting an image. "We started calling the hotels resorts," said Vassiliadis. "We began stressing entertainment."

An economic slump in the early 1980s served as a wake-up call. "We became pretty defensive," Vassiliadis recalled. A marketing campaign was designed to stress Las Vegas as a value "power trip," a theme intended to capitalize on the trend of Americans to prefer long weekends to the traditional two-week vacations. "Along with the traditional gambler, who didn't want anything more than a room to shower and shave, we got the sneakers, print dresses, and blue-haired set," Vassiliadis said. "We also got the yuppies, lawyers, accountants, and others with disposable incomes. We pushed the golf, tennis, and swimming pools."

The enigmatic Steve Wynn is credited with being a pioneer in the transformation of Las Vegas from a casino capital to a resort destination that, in many ways, transcended gambling. He did it in 1989 with the opening of the Mirage: a 3,000-room, $630-million hotel with a sixty-foot exploding volcano, a nine-story, orchid-rich atrium, a glass-enclosed white tiger cage, shark tanks, and a huge dolphin habitat. Tourists were becoming increasingly sophisticated, Wynn said, and providing them a crap table and a few slot machines was no longer enough. The industry had to provide more entertainment. More excitement. More thrills. Fantasy, even, like pirate-ship battles, Siegfried and Roy, and Cirque du Soleil. "The Mirage will be perceived as changing Las Vegas," Wynn told the *Las Vegas Review-Journal.* "But in reality, it is just a natural progression for the city. This town has never had a fantasy hotel." "The Mirage is not the beginning of an era," Wynn told the *Las Vegas Sun.* "It is a response."

"The white tigers and the volcanoes are nice. They're an enhancement," said Horseshoe Club president Jack Binion while dining in his hotel's Oriental restaurant. "But it's gambling that made Las Vegas." The Horseshoe is a throwback to the days when Fremont Street in downtown's Glitter Gulch was lined with small gambling dens and the Strip was not yet dotted with neon high-rises courtesy of Summa and Howard Hughes, Hilton Hotels, Harrah's, Caesars World, Mirage Resorts, and the other corporate giants. The Horseshoe is reminiscent of a frontier saloon. Men and women in boots, jeans, and Stetsons crowd the gambling tables. The ceiling is low and the casino dimly lit. The air is filled with smoke and thick with action. Binion's has a reputation for being willing to accept any bet, whether on the roll of the dice, the spin of a roulette wheel, or the flip of a card across the green felt of a poker, blackjack, or baccarat table. "Let's just put it this way," the late Benny Binion said of the emergence in Las Vegas of corporate casinos. "We got a little joint and a big bankroll, and all them others got a big joint and a little bankroll." Son Jack, who in 1946 rode to Las Vegas from Texas in Benny's chauffeur-driven Cadillac limousine—sleeping on two suitcases stuffed with $2 million in cash—glanced around his casino one day in the early 1990s, saw an awful lot of old, wrinkled faces, and wondered aloud who was going to take their place. "I suppose there'll always be a few W. C. Fields types," Binion said. "I'll get the W. C. Fields types." He agreed, though, that there was a new breed of gambler in town: young adults raised with computers and video games who never got lessons in blackjack and craps like their fathers and grandfathers, many of whom picked up the games while serving in the military in World War II.

Statewide revenues from slots and video poker machines overtook table games in 1983 and in 1994 account for some 60 percent of Nevada's gaming revenues. Nevada is no longer the only state in the nation with legal casino gambling. The pool of serious gamblers, which over the years was being spread paper-thin as Las Vegas got bigger, grew even thinner with the nationwide explosion of legalized casino gambling, fueled largely by cash-starved state and municipal governments.

Casinos surfaced on the nation's waterways in the early 1990s, first in Iowa and later in Illinois, Mississippi, Louisiana, Missouri, and Indiana. "There's something about water that sanitizes gambling," said Robert Tynan, who with Marlin Torgeson built casinos in Bay St. Louis and Biloxi, Mississippi. Meanwhile, casinos began springing up on American Indian reservations, particularly in Wisconsin, Minnesota, Michigan, upstate New York, and Connecticut. Twenty-three states had legal casinos in early 1994, whether on Nevada's Strip and downtown Glitter Gulch, on Atlantic City's Boardwalk, cruising the Mississippi River, or housed in some neon-lit, cement building on a rural tribal reservation in Heartland, U.S.A. Americans in 1993 legally gambled $394.3 billion, 17.1 percent more than the preceding year, according to *Gaming & Wagering Business*. About 75 percent was bet in casinos, the magazine said—46 percent in Nevada, 19 percent in Atlantic City, and the rest on riverboats and in American Indian gambling halls. Gambling became the nation's fastest growing industry—the industry of the '90s—generating tens of thousands of new jobs. The press moved in to cover the emerging phenomenon and all its potential social, political, and economic consequences. And where else to report from but the gambling capital of the world? Thousands of reporters descended on Las Vegas. Media giants Sam Donaldson, David Brinkley, and Walter Cronkite set up remotes from the Strip and Fremont Street.

"The Las Vegas dateline alone took on a kind of intrinsic news value," said advertising executive Rob Powers. The cameras took aim at what was perceived as a seamy sin city being bulldozed beneath the desert by glistening glass hotels and theme parks. Mothers pushing strollers on the Strip crushed pornographic pamphlets on the side-walk. For every casino video arcade there was a taxicab decorated with a big-chested dancer from the Girls of Glitter Gulch strip club.

A young woman balancing two toddlers on her lap while playing a slot machine at the MGM Grand was told by a security guard that the children were not allowed near the machines. She placed them on the casino floor near a picket fence bordering the Emerald City, about fifty feet away, then returned to her machine, leaving the children gawking at the feet of passing strangers. A hotel executive strolling through his casino grimaced when he spotted a young girl standing by her mother near a video poker machine. "The girl was holding a bucket of coins for her mother, who was playing the machine," the executive said.

A young father struggled to play a video poker machine in the Mirage as his two young girls tugged at his arm. "Mommy wants you," one of the girls pleaded. The man laughed. "But honey," he said, "daddy's winning. Go tell mommy daddy's winning."

It is a misdemeanor violation of Nevada law for persons under twenty-one to gamble or loiter near slot machines or gaming tables. State Gaming Control Board chairman Bill Bible grew alarmed at the number of complaints of underaged gambling and children wandering through the casinos. "Although the casinos have placed a positive emphasis on Nevada as a family destination," Bible said in letters to casino operators dated August 15, 1994, "it is imperative that each licensee police and strictly enforce" the law. His agency began cracking down on casinos allowing underage gambling, beginning with Bally's, which in September 1994 was slapped with a $20,000 fine for allowing a nineteen-year-old to lose $6,300 at a blackjack table. "Nobody likes to be [made] an example, but we're it," Bally's attorney Preston Howard told the *Las Vegas Review-Journal.* "This is a problem we're going to see more of as hotels market their business to families. It's an issue for the whole industry."

William R. Eadington, director of the Institute for Gambling and Commercial Gaming at the University of Nevada, Reno, warned casino operators of the danger in mixing gambling and family attractions. "There is an ideological split within the industry on this issue," Eadington said. Some gaming companies are embracing the move to make Las Vegas a family resort destination, he said, while others oppose the concept. "This is an oil-and-water situation," Eadington said of casinos with attractions for children. "The two are just absolutely inconsistent with each other. It may create a backlash of public opinion against the industry."

The venerable places, synonymous with Las Vegas's past, have taken the hit—places like the Sahara, Sands, Riviera, and the Aladdin. Business has suffered since the opening of themed hotels like the Mirage, Excalibur, MGM Grand, Luxor, and Treasure Island. The big-credit players have moved their action to the south end of the Strip, and table game play is down. Older places have become largely grind joints, surviving on the slot machines. The carpets are bare and the elevators musty. The venerated old entertainers have been stripped off the marquees, replaced by slot promotions and buffet prices. "That's when this town really changed," said one longtime casino executive. "When they took down Frank's name and replaced it with an advertisement for a buck-and-a-half prime rib dinner." The north end of the Strip from the Sahara to Circus Circus—just north of the Stratosphere Tower and a stretch of Las Vegas Boulevard referred to as the Naked City for its low-rent hotels, liquor stores, junk souvenir shops, and topless joints—became seedy with aggressive beggars and homeless drunks sprawled on bus-stop benches and along the sidewalk. Business downtown also dropped off, with the possible exception of the Horseshoe, Golden Nugget, and the Boyd family hotels. A lot of old-timers curse the corporations. From the cab drivers to the showroom and lounge musicians to the dealers to the waitresses and bartenders, the refrain is the same: "This town was better when the mob ran the joints."

But Las Vegas was smaller then; and when it came to casino gambling in the United States, Las Vegas was, indeed, the only game in town. Marty DiPetta, fortyish and the single father of a teenage daughter, has been dealing craps at the Riviera for sixteen years. A normally easygoing and charismatic guy with a loud, generous laugh, DiPetta is apt to get a bit introspective about the old days, when "the Riv" was still a hangout for a good number of the town's high rollers. "I enjoyed my time off, but ya know, it was fun to go to work," DiPetta said. "There was a lot of action, the tips were good, the hotel took care of the gamblers, and the people had a lot of class. Maybe they didn't wear a tie, but at least they had a jacket. Now, well ...," DiPetta shrugged. "Things have changed. And they ain't never gonna be the same."

Contributors

A. D. Hopkins is a former editor of *The Nevadan* and a longtime investigative reporter for the *Las Vegas Review-Journal*.

John H. Irsfeld is a novelist and English professor at the University of Nevada, Las Vegas. He has published three novels: *Little Kingdoms*, *Coming Through*, and *Rat's Alley*.

Sergio Lalli is a veteran Las Vegas free-lance writer who has covered the world of legalized gambling for a variety of magazines.

Bill Moody is a Las Vegas English instructor, jazz musician, and author. His book *The Jazz Exiles: American Musicians Abroad* was published by the University of Nevada Press.

Dave Palermo is a former reporter for the *Los Angeles Times* and the *Las Vegas Review-Journal*.

Mark Seal is a Dallas-based writer who has written for the *New York Times*, *Texas Monthly*, *Rolling Stone*, and *Esquire*.

Jack Sheehan is a Las Vegas–based writer who has sold two screenplays to Hollywood and published four books, including *Buried Lies*, *Las Vegas Stories*, and *Above Las Vegas*.

John L. Smith is a longtime columnist for the *Las Vegas Review-Journal*. He has published two nonfiction books on the world of gambling.

Index

Hacienda, 33
Halley, Rudolph, 5
Hannifin, Phil, 20
Hantges, Tom, 169
Harlow, Jean, 136
Harold's Club (Reno), 133, 149, 192
Harrah, William, 145, 149
Harrah's, 208
Harrah's Lake Tahoe, 150
Harrington, Dan, 62
Harris, Jo, 95–96
Hayworth, Rita, 136
Hecht, Chic, 132
Helldorado Days, 26, 185
Helmsley, Harry, 147
Henderson, 112
Hepburn, Katharine, 136
Hess, Alan (*Viva Las Vegas: After-Hours Architecture*), 95
Hicks, Marion, 7, 8, 28, 30, 31, 32, 34, 109
Hill, Virginia, xi, 81, 82, *84*, 85, 89
Hilton Hotels Corporation, 144, 165, 172, 208
Hoffa, Jimmy, 15, 18, 44; and Moe Dalitz, 36; and Jay Sarno, 93; and Desert Inn, 146. *See also* Teamsters Central States Pension Fund
Holiday Inn, 144, 172, 207
Holliday, Raymond, 147, 153
Hood, Jeanne, *123*
Hoover Dam, 26, 183
Hopkins, A. D., xii
Horseshoe Club, 12, 48, 49, 59, 60, 61–62, 102, 107, 127, 184, 186, 211; gambling limits in, 55–57, 58–59; earnings of, 60; comping in, 62–63; alleged cheating in, 64; clientele of, 208
Hotel Apache, 23, 26
Hotel Nevada, 114
Houssels, J. Kell, Sr., 23, 55, 69, 126, 127, 130
Houssels, J. K., Jr., 113, 127, 131
Houssels, Nancy, 129
Houskey, Frank, 26
Hovnanian, Hirair, 162
Howard, Preston, 210
Hughes, Howard, xi, xii, 31, 65, *135*, 136, *138*, 154–55, 156, 157, 208; impact of, on Las Vegas, 18–21, 157, 192–93, 207;

licensing of, 19; Nevada real estate purchases of, 39–40, 133, 141, 149, 150, 175, 176, 192; arrival of, in Las Vegas, 133, 140; health problems of, 133–34, 154–55; description of, 134; management style of, 136–37, 143–44, 154; broadcasting interests of, 137, 155; marriage of, 138, 140; as movie producer, 141; objectives of, in Las Vegas, 141–42; and Nevada politics, 141, 149; financial losses of, in Nevada, 153–54, 156; mining claim purchases of, 156; and Kirk Kerkorian, 160, 164
Hughes Nevada Operations, 152–53
Hughes Tool Company, 147, 153; sale of, 155
Hull, Tom, 28, 29, 85
Humphrey, Hubert: and Howard Hughes, 149, 152
Humphreys, Murray "the Camel," 85
Hyatt Hotels and Resorts, 207

Iacocca, Lee, 167
Indian reservations: gambling on, 181, 203, 209
Institute for Gambling and Commercial Gaming (University of Nevada, Reno), 210
Internal Revenue Service (IRS): and federal efforts to combat crime in casinos, 12
International Hotel, xiii, 159–60, 164, 165
Interviews: as source of information for book, xii–xiii
Irving, Clifford, 157
ITT Corporation, 21

Jackie Gaughan's Plaza. *See* Union Plaza
Jackpot Club, 107
Jacobs, Louis, 41
Japanese: as clientele of Mirage, 179
Jerde, John, 179
Johnson, Lyndon, 152
Johnson, Marianne Boyd, 119
Jones, Cliff, xii, 6, 13, 25, 27–28, 32–33; and Kefauver hearings, 5; and Thunderbird, 7, 8, 30; legal career of, 23, 33; description of, 25–26; political career of, 26, 27, 29, 30, 32; military